THE FINANCIAL ADVISOR'S ANALYTICAL TOOLBOX

Using Technology to Optimize Client Solutions

THE FINANCIAL ADVISOR'S ANALYTICAL TOOLBOX

Using Technology to Optimize Client Solutions

ED McCARTHY

The Irwin/IAFP Series in Financial Planning

INTERNATIONAL ASSOCIATION
FOR FINANCIAL PLANNING

McGraw-Hill

New York   San Francisco   Washington, D.C.   Auckland   Bogotá
Caracas   Lisbon   London   Madrid   Mexico City   Milan
Montreal   New Delhi   San Juan   Singapore
Sydney   Tokyo   Toronto

332.6
M11f

THE FINANCIAL ADVISOR'S ANALYTICAL TOOLBOX: Using Technology to Optimize Client Solutions

Copyright © 1997 by The McGraw-Hill Companies, Inc. All rights reserved. Printed in the United States of America. Except as permitted under the United States Copyright Act of 1976, no part of this publication may be reproduced or distributed in any form or by any means, or stored in a data base or retrieval system, without the prior written permission of the publisher.

A list of trademarks/credits appears on pages 363–64, and on this page by reference.

This book was printed on acid-free paper.

1 2 3 4 5 6 7 8 9 0 DOC/DOC 9 0 9 8 7

ISBN 0-7863-1052-9

This book was set in Times Roman by Hendrickson Creative Communications. R.R. Donnelley & Sons Company was printer and binder.

This publication is designed to provide accurate and authoritative information in regard to the subject matter covered. It is sold with the understanding that neither the author nor the publisher is engaged in rendering legal, accounting, or other professional service. If legal advice or other expert assistance is required, the services of a competent professional person should be sought.
> —*From a Declaration of Principles jointly adopted by a committee of the American Bar Association and a Committee of Publishers*

McGraw-Hill books are available at special quantity discounts to use as premiums and sales promotions, or for use in corporate training programs. For more information, please write to the Director of Special Sales, McGraw-Hill, 11 West 19th Street, New York, NY 10011. Or contact your local bookstore.

Library of Congress Cataloging-in-Publication Data
McCarthy, Ed (Edward), (date).
    The financial advisor's analytical toolbox: using technology to optimize client solutions / Ed McCarthy.
        p. cm.
    Includes index.
    ISBN 0-7863-1052-9
    1. Financial planners. 2. Finance, Personal—Data processing.
3. Investment analysis—Data processing. I. Title.
HG179.5.M38 1997
332.6—dc21   96–50180

http://www.mhcollege.com

To my wife, Diane, for her unwavering
support and encouragement of this book
and all my other projects; and to Professor
William R. Folks at the University of
South Carolina, for sparking my interest
in quantitative analysis.

University Libraries
Carnegie Mellon University
Pittsburgh PA 15213-3890

In the July 1994 issue of the *Journal of Financial Planning* I published an article, "Using Spreadsheet Simulations in Financial Planning." The journal's editor, Mr. Lynn Hopewell, wrote the following comments about the article in his "From the Editor" column.

> Even if the tools were not simple, but comprehensive, financial planning seems to have missed the revolution in analysis caused by the easy availability of simulation techniques made possible by the PC. Retirement- and insurance-needs analyses are, in essence, probabilistic problems with uncertainty as a central element of the analysis. When will someone die? How much inflation will there be? What investment returns can be expected? Analyses using single points for these variables were compromises, excusable when probabilistic calculations were not feasible. But as Ed McCarthy shows in his article, "Using Spreadsheet Simulations in Financial Planning," these types of calculations are now very feasible. Yet hardly any planners use them. Worse, hardly any academics use them. We get no papers for this journal that use them.
>
> Hello, everyone—step into the modern world, please. There is no excuse now for financial planning to be analytically backward. We say financial planning is a profession. It would help our claim if we acted like one and used state-of-the-art tools.

I agree with Mr. Hopewell: It is time for financial advisors to start using more advanced analytical tools, and I believe this book represents a step forward in that direction. The tools and techniques that the book covers are not new—analysts have used most of them for years. Until recently, though, only computer users with access to large systems could use the techniques because the programs' computational requirements exceeded the capacity of desktop PCs. With today's powerful processor chips and increased memory, PC users now have convenient access to these tools. Analytical software has migrated to the PC, and this book demonstrates its potential value to the financial advisor.

As a financial advisor, you need the ability to analyze the client's situation and make recommendations based on the analysis. Part of this competency is knowledge based: an understanding of the tax laws, for example. Because it is difficult to keep all your accumulated knowledge available in your memory, this skill also involves knowing where to find information when you need it. That could mean using a physical reference source such as a book in your library, or it could mean working with another professional who specializes in a subject like taxes.

There is another aspect to analytical skill besides the ability to give factual answers, though. It is the ability to answer clients' open-ended questions. For instance, a client might ask, How much do I need to save to retire comfortably in 10 years? There is no quick answer for that question—you can't look it up in any database or reference book. You must provide an answer based on assumptions about rates of return, life expectancies, and so on. Your analytical skills, and the tools at your disposal to use those skills, influence the quality of your responses to this type of open-ended question. In the retirement-funding example, if you aren't comfortable working with time value of money calculations, you will find it difficult to answer the client's question.

This book will expand your computational skills. It focuses on practical, PC-based analytical tools for use in your work with clients. The material is not intended for the reader who wants theoretical discussions; instead, it is designed for the financial advisor who deals with real-world problems. Depending on your background, some of the book's material and techniques might be familiar, especially if you had any quantitative methods courses in college. Other material will be new, but I hope that does not diminish your interest. Financial advisors have always impressed me with their eagerness to expand their knowledge and skills. If you are willing to consider new analytical tools, I believe this book will be a valuable addition to your professional library.

You might ask, Why should I want to improve my analytical skills? I believe the effort is justified for several reasons. The first is to ensure your survival in a competitive environment. Improving your analytical skills helps you do better work for your existing clients. That keeps them satisfied, leading to more referrals, which is often the most effective way to get new clients.

The second reason to expand your skills is to protect yourself. A faulty analysis of a client's situation can cause serious problems. You have a disgruntled client, and if the financial consequences of your error are large, you might be facing a lawsuit. Solid analytical skills reduce the odds of this happening, letting you focus your efforts on client service instead of legal self-defense.

The third reason for making the effort is to improve your efficiency. If you are a "veteran" advisor, you remember the days before electronic spreadsheets and word processors. Those were the days of yellow-pad planning, when the only tools available were present and future value tables and perhaps a financial calculator. Even if you weren't working as an advisor then, you still can recognize the incredible leap in productivity the PC has fostered. Can you imagine trying to calculate an efficient frontier for a client's investment portfolio with a hand-held calculator? You could do the calculation for a very small portfolio, but it is a time-consuming procedure. Despite some critics' dire warnings, PCs didn't weaken planners' skills by letting them forget the analytical basics. Instead, the PC freed up planners' time and improved the quality and quantity of the work they did for clients. The tools discussed in this book can have the same impact. They will help you do better work in less time, allowing you to spend more time on other client-oriented activities.

A final reason why the tools in this book should interest you is that they can expand your business activities into new areas. For example, if you advise business owners on their personal finances, you have a ready-made opportunity to consult with them on business decisions, as well. Many of the techniques described here are ideal for small business consulting, allowing you to further diversify your own firm's revenue sources.

As an active financial advisor and computer user during the 1980s, I started thinking about applying these analytical techniques to financial planning and business consulting cases. There seemed to be a natural fit between them, but I couldn't find anyone using these tools in these business markets. Investment managers used simulations and optimizations in their portfolio analyses but that appeared to be the extent of it. When I discussed the potential applications of these techniques with other advisors, they usually responded that the techniques were too high powered for the problems and too difficult to master. To some extent, those comments were true. The programs were often difficult to use without a strong background in the particular technique, and the programs' documentation was rarely very helpful.

With the new graphical operating systems, and Windows in particular, that situation has changed. The new versions of these analytical programs are much easier to use, and the quality of the documentation has also improved. With some of these programs, the software documentation alone allows you to become competent quickly with not only the program but also its underlying theory.

In spite of the increasing ease of using these techniques, I did not see any personal finance applications being discussed in the industry magazines or professional journals. In an attempt to remedy that, in the early

1990s I published two articles in *Financial Planning* magazine. One article discussed the use of decision trees, and the other gave a nontechnical overview of simulation analysis. Based on the positive responses I received from readers, I suspected that planners were interested in these analytical tools. I followed these stories with a more detailed applied-simulation article in the July 1994 issue of the *Journal of Financial Planning*. Once again, the editorial comments and reader response were supportive, strengthening my belief that readers wanted to see this material. The work behind those articles, and the positive feedback they received, eventually led to the material in this book.

As I mentioned earlier, the emphasis in this book is on real-world financial applications of PC-based analytical techniques. Some of my experience with these tools came from my experience as an advisor, when I constantly searched for tools that would increase my productivity. My other source of experience has been my technology review column for *CFP Today* (now the *Journal of Financial Planning*) magazine. I always looked for innovative technologies to review in the column, and you will see some of that search reflected here. Of course, I don't assume that the techniques listed here will give you all the answers to your analytical needs—there certainly are other techniques and programs that I could have included but did not. If you have a suggestion along those lines, drop me a note and share your insight. Life is a learning process, and it would be a pleasure to hear from you.

                                            Ed McCarthy
                                            E-mail: e_mccarthy@ids.net

ACKNOWLEDGMENTS

Many people helped me with this book. They include Mike Snell of the Snell Literary Agency, and Amy Ost and Kevin Thornton at Irwin. I also received technical support from contacts at the firms that produce the software used in the book. They include the following:

Advanced Decision Analysis Inc.: Julia Langel

Attar Software USA: E. Robert Keller 2nd

Business Forecast Systems, Inc.: Eric Stellwagen

California Scientific Software: David Uimari

Expert Choice, Inc.: Ming Mimidis, Dr. Thomas Saaty

FuziWare, Inc.: Karl E. Thorndike

LINDO Systems, Inc.: Mark Wiley, Dr. Linus Schrage

MathSoft, Inc.: David Leschinsky, Dr. Frank Prucell

Palisade Corporation: Vera Gilliland, Christina Kimelberg

Tech Hackers, Inc.: K. Darcey Matthews

The MathWorks, Inc.: Namoi Bullock, Catherine DeYoung, Dave Eiler

Wolfram Research, Inc.: Jean Buck, Rolf Carlson, Leszek Sczaniecki

Wordtech Systems, Inc.: Tyra Wright

CONTENTS

Chapter 3

Simulation

Chapter 4

Fuzzy Numbers

Chapter 5

Forecasting

Chapter 6

Artificial Neural Networks

Chapter 7

Optimization

Chapter 8

Spreadsheet Tools

CHAPTER 1

Expert Systems

INTRODUCTION

Imagine that you have been suffering from an abdominal pain for several days. The pain is not going away so you visit your doctor. The doctor probably would ask you a series of questions as he attempts to diagnose the cause of your symptoms. These questions might include

Where does it hurt?

Is it a constant or intermittent pain?

Is it a throbbing or stabbing pain?

Does it hurt when I touch you here?

The doctor's questions are an example of an expert system in action. He asks you a question, and your answer determines the next line of inquiry. Each response eliminates one or more potential causes as the doctor progressively narrows the list of candidate problems. The questions follow a logical sequence, and the end result of the dialogue is a diagnosis.

Physicians are not the only professional "expert systems," of course. Your work with clients might follow a similar pattern, and this type of interaction probably takes place within your business. For example, think about the flow of information in your own organization. As staff members develop expertise in a subject, other employees naturally gravitate toward the in-house expert for answers to their questions. You might have a resident computer guru whom other employees approach to solve PC problems. Frequently, this in-house expert's status is not official, but in some firms, for example, law or accounting offices, the expertise might be recognized formally with a title: tax partner, audit manager, and so on.

From a business perspective, two potential problems derive from having one employee as the only source of expertise in a subject. First, other employees might utilize too much of the expert's time, reducing his availability for clients and other revenue-generating activities. Excessive utilization can happen even when the information that the employees require is readily available from other sources. The second problem is the difficulty of replacing the key employee's expertise if he should leave. Specialized knowledge often has significant value in the market, and an employee with that knowledge can attract competing job offers. If that employee leaves, his employer may be left with a large gap in its knowledge base.

A PC-based expert system offers a solution to both problems. By transferring the expert's knowledge to a PC program, other employees can access that knowledge base without tying up the expert's time. If the expert leaves the employer, the part of his knowledge that was placed in the expert program stays with the firm.

Before we get into the details of building an expert system, a brief example will help demonstrate the key principles. In this scenario the firm provides personal financial advice. Senior staff members have extensive experience as investment advisors, but newer associates generally lack this experience. To ensure that the firm's investment recommendations are uniform, the senior staff develops a mutual fund recommendation matrix. This matrix incorporates the client's investment goals and risk tolerance levels as the key factors in selecting a fund category. There are three generic investment goals (growth, income, growth and income) and three risk tolerances (conservative, moderate, and aggressive). Combining the investment goals and risk tolerances leads to the matrix in Table 1–1, in which the investment goal is listed by row with risk tolerances by column.

TABLE 1–1

Recommended Fund Categories

	Conservative	Moderate	Aggressive
Growth	Large cap stocks	Mid cap stocks	Small cap stocks
Income	Treasuries	Corporate bonds	High yield bonds
Growth & Income	Balanced	Equity income	Growth income

By cross-referencing the two attributes, the new associates can quickly find the firm's suggested fund type for a particular investor.

Although the sequence is not explicitly listed, the associate using the matrix will follow a logical series of steps in selecting a fund category. The unspoken process will be something like this: If the investor's goal is income and the investor will accept moderate risk, then the recommendation is a corporate bond fund. The if-then sequence acts as a set of rules that is similar to the process a doctor follows in diagnosing patients' ailments. Each response to an if condition leads to a new line of inquiry, with the ultimate goal being a then statement.

This sequential process can be replicated with expert system software. These programs allow the user to engage in a dialogue with the PC, with the questions and resulting recommendations based on the developer's (and the expert's) knowledge of the problem. The following mutual fund selection dialogue was generated by the DOS-based VP-Expert program from Wordtech Systems, Inc. Prompts and statements from the program are in italic, while user responses to the program's prompts are underlined. We discuss the mechanics of constructing the dialogue later in the chapter.

Prompt 1:   *What is the investment Goal?*

Response 1:   Growth   Income   Gro_Inc

Prompt 2:   *What is the investor's Risk_Profile?*

Response 2:   Conservative   Moderate   Aggressive

Statement: *The recommended Fund_Type is Small Cap*

Obviously, a simple two-dimensional problem like this one does not require an expert system, even though the total development time for the application was less than 15 minutes. But we believe it is a useful introduction to the if-then structure of expert systems, and we will use this example again shortly to illustrate the dialogue's underlying code.

BACKGROUND

Expert systems have been used since the early 1960s. They are one of the two forms of artificial intelligence we discuss in this text—artificial neural networks are the other, and we review them later. Today expert systems are used in medical diagnosis, financial management, tax research, and other problems that are based on sequential decisions. Financial users have been active adopters of expert systems. Liebowitz (1990) provides articles describing applications in taxpayer assistance, auditing, financial analysis, and insurance underwriting, among others. Trippi and Lee (1996) discuss the role of expert systems in portfolio selection and management, and Freedman, Klein, and Lederman (1995) provide articles describing capital market applications. We discuss current applications of applied systems in more detail later in the chapter.

Expert systems are useful for standardizing procedures within an organization and teaching others how to think like the expert. Assuming the system is developed properly, it can capture part of the expert's knowledge, reducing dependency on the expert. An expert system can also be expanded and modified over time, allowing its knowledge base to keep up with developments in a field.

There are several ways to build an expert system. The first, which we do not cover, is to create the program using a language like C or LISP. Because this approach requires considerable programming expertise and time, we assume that most readers will not pursue this method. The second approach is to use a shell program, which allows the user to focus on the system's content, not the underlying computer code. We use two shell programs in this chapter to demonstrate the material.

At a minimum an expert system requires a developer and an expert, who may be the same person, depending on a firm's resources. The expert provides the input and logic patterns needed to build the rules and statements. The developer works with the expert system shell to program the expert's rules and statements that will form the program's knowledge base. The expert's role is to validate the knowledge base's content so the program's logic sequence and output match his own. Obviously, an expert system that provides inexpert advice would not be worth much.

The mutual fund selection problem we developed is an example of a rule-based system. The system developer matches a series of rules with outputs that represent an expert's knowledge. The system uses if-then logic to prompt the user for inputs that eventually lead the program to a final goal, usually in the form of a recommendation.

Before starting the development process, the developer and expert should decide if an expert system is the correct tool for their needs. As Lawrence (1993) notes:

> Expert systems are good at procedural types of problem such as strategy, scheduling, and teaching. They are better than manuals because they ask the user for only relevant information, they incorporate past experience into solving the problem, and they answer questions about the reasoning process.
>
> A major weakness of expert systems is that they rely entirely on precise up-to-date rules. An expert system cannot generalize or extrapolate. If

the incoming data is noisy or outside the set of defined rules, you can get unreliable results."[1]

EXPERT SYSTEM SOFTWARE: VP-EXPERT

In this section we revisit the mutual fund selection example to demonstrate the development of a consultation system built with the VP-Expert software. We begin by describing the key terms used in expert system development. The source for this material is the VP-Expert manual.

An expert system's knowledge is stored in the form of if-then rules. The person seeking advice from the system provides information in response to the prompts he receives. The system's intelligence, which combines the knowledge and information to make decisions, is called the inference engine.

We have used the term *knowledge base* loosely so far to signify the expert system's contents. To be more precise, a knowledge base file has three elements:

- The ACTIONS block
- Rules
- Statements

A fourth element, clauses, is contained within the ACTIONS block and rules of the knowledge base.

The ACTIONS Block

The ACTIONS block defines the problems of the consultation and the sequence followed to reach their solution. It tells the inference engine what it needs to find out and in what order. It does this by using FIND clauses that tell the program to find the values of one or more goal variables.

Rules

The system's expertise is contained in its if-then rules. In its proper format, our mutual fund example structures its rules as follows:

RULE 0

IF   Goal = Growth AND

         Risk_Profile = Conservative

THEN   Fund_Type = Large Cap;

---

1. J. Lawrence, *Introduction to Neural Networks,* 5th ed. (Nevada City, CA: California Scientific Software Press, 1993), p. 36.

Rules have four elements:

- Rule name
- Rule premise
- Rule conclusion
- A terminating semicolon

In VP-Expert, the rule's name must begin with the keyword RULE (RULE 0) and meet certain character restrictions. The premise begins with the keyword IF and can contain up to 20 conditions. Conditions are used to compare the contents of a variable to a value (IF Goal = Growth). The user is not restricted to the *a* equals *b* relationship. We list other relational operators in Table 1–2.

The rule's conclusion follows the keyword THEN (THEN Fund_Type = Large Cap;). The equation following the THEN keyword assigns the value (Large Cap) to the variable (Fund_Type) if the premise of the rule is true.

VP-Expert offers a useful feature called the *induction table* that speeds the creation of the knowledge base. For the mutual fund example, we created the induction table (see Table 1–3) using a text editor.

The top row of Table 1–3 contains column headings that define a set of variables. The variable in the right-hand column, Fund_Type, contains the goal variable, which is the type of fund recommended for a client. The value of the item in the last column is determined by its predecessors in the row.

The reader will note that the information in Table 1–3 closely resembles the matrix in Table 1–1. This is by design because the induction table is a representation of the if-then questions behind the system. You can

TABLE 1–2

Relational Operators

Relation	Symbol
Or	|
Greater than	>
Greater than or equal to	>=
Less than	<
Less than or equal to	<=
Not equal to	<>

TABLE 1-3

Induction Table

Goal	Risk_Profile	Fund_Type
Growth	Conservative	Large_Cap
Growth	Moderate	Mid_Cap
Growth	Aggressive	Small_Cap
Income	Conservative	Treasuries
Income	Moderate	Corporates
Income	Aggressive	High_Yield
Growth_Income	Conservative	Balanced
Growth_Income	Moderate	Equity_Income
Growth_Income	Aggressive	Growth_Income

translate each row in Table 1–3 into its equivalent if-then statement, as shown in the following text:

IF Goal is Growth and Risk_Profile is Conservative,
THEN Fund_Type is Large_Cap.

IF Goal is Growth and Risk_Profile is Moderate,
THEN Fund_Type is Mid_Cap.

IF Goal is Growth_Income and Risk_Profile is Aggressive,
THEN Fund_Type is Growth_Income.

VP-Expert takes the information in the induction table and creates a knowledge base that is available for user consultation. Here is the mutual fund knowledge base file created from the induction table in Table 1–3.

Example: Mutual Fund Knowledge Base

ACTIONS
    FIND Fund_Type
    DISPLAY "The recommended Fund_Type is {Fund_Type}~";

RULE 0
IF   Goal = Growth AND
    Risk_Profile = Conservative
THEN Fund_Type = Large_Cap;

RULE 1
IF   Goal = Growth AND
      Risk_Profile = Moderate
THEN Fund_Type = Mid_Cap;

RULE 2
IF   Goal = Growth AND
      Risk_Profile = Aggressive
THEN Fund_Type = Small_Cap;

RULE 3
IF   Goal = Income AND
      Risk_Profile = Conservative
THEN Fund_Type = Treasuries;

RULE 4
IF   Goal = Income AND
      Risk_Profile = Moderate
THEN Fund_Type = Corporates;

RULE 5
IF   Goal = Income AND
      Risk_Profile = Aggressive
THEN Fund_Type = High_Yield;

RULE 6
IF   Goal = Gro_Inc AND
      Risk_Profile = Conservative
THEN Fund_Type = Balanced;

RULE 7
IF   Goal = Gro_Inc AND
      Risk_Profile = Moderate
THEN Fund_Type = Equity_Income;

RULE 8
IF   Goal = Gro_Inc AND
      Risk_Profile = Aggressive
THEN Fund_Type = Growth_Income;

ASK Goal: "What is the investment Goal?";

CHOICES Goal: Growth,Income,Gro_Inc;

ASK Risk_Profile: "What is the investor's Risk_Profile?";

CHOICES Risk_Profile: Conservative,Moderate,Aggressive;

We now walk through the steps the inference engine takes in using a knowledge base such as this one. The code starts with the ACTIONS block.

ACTIONS

FIND Fund_Type

DISPLAY "The recommended Fund_Type is {Fund_Type}~";

The FIND clause instructs the engine to find a goal variable, which in this case is Fund_Type. The DISPLAY clause is used to display messages to the user. When the clause is executed, the message within the double quotes is displayed. In this instance, we use the clause to display the conclusion message that tells us what type of fund to use.

We have identified Fund_Type as the goal variable, and the inference engine begins searching the knowledge base for the first rule that has Fund_Type in its conclusion. Rule 0 satisfies that condition.

RULE 0

IF   Goal = Growth AND

       Risk_Profile = Conservative

THEN Fund_Type = Large_Cap;

After finding the rule with the goal variable, the engine looks at the first variable named in the rule's premise (Goal). Because it does not know the value of the variable, it looks for the first rule containing that variable in its conclusion. There is no such rule in the knowledge base, so the engine scans through the remaining rules. After scanning the last rule, rule 8, the program looks for an ASK statement that prompts the user to select a value for the variable goal.

ASK Goal: "What is the investment Goal?";

CHOICES Goal: Growth, Income, Gro_Inc;

When the inference engine cannot find a variable in the conclusion of a rule, it looks for that variable in an ASK statement. These statements prompt the user for information that has not been entered in the knowledge base. The prompts take the form of choices on the PC's screen that the user can highlight to indicate a selection. The CHOICES statement that immediately follows the ASK statement creates a menu of options to accompany the question during the consultation. As we showed earlier, this combination produced the following screen display:

Prompt 1:   *What is the investment Goal?*

Response 1:   <u>Growth</u>   Income   Gro_Inc

When we choose the Growth response, the engine assigns a value of Growth to the goal variable. Now that it has a value for that variable, the engine returns to rule 0. Goal equals growth in rule 0, so the engine moves to the next variable in the premise, Risk_Profile, and begins searching for the first rule containing Risk_Profile in its conclusion. It does not find one, so it looks for an ASK statement that includes the variable Risk_Profile. It finds one in the next to last line, accompanied by a CHOICES statement:

ASK Risk_Profile: "What is the investor's Risk_Profile?";

CHOICES Risk_Profile: Conservative, Moderate, Aggressive;

These lines generate the following input request on the screen (user response underlined):

Prompt 2:   *What is the investor's Risk_Profile?*

Response 2:   Conservative   Moderate   <u>Aggressive</u>

Once again, the search engine returns to rule 0, but this time the user's response to the Risk_Profile prompt, Aggressive, does not match the rule's value of Conservative. The engine moves to rule 1 and then to rule 2 before it finds a match for Risk_Profile = Aggressive. At that point rule 2 passes, and the value Small_Cap is assigned to the variable Fund_Type. The engine returns to the DISPLAY clause and we see the final output:

Statement: *The recommended Fund_Type is Small Cap.*

To summarize, the inference engine searches the knowledge base to satisfy certain conditions. If the knowledge base has been constructed properly with no contradictions, the final result will be the only conclusion that simultaneously satisfies the problem's premises. In this example, the program cannot recommend a high yield bond fund to a conservative growth investor because the investor's Goal must equal Income and the Risk_Profile must be Aggressive. Failure to fulfill either of those requirements will prevent the high yield bond fund recommendation from appearing.

Modifications: Adding a Variable

We decide to add another variable relating to tax bracket for the conservative and moderate risk income investor. For investors in the high tax bracket, we will suggest municipal bonds: insured municipal for the conservative investors and "regular" municipals for the moderate risk investors. There are no changes in the recommendations for low-tax-bracket income investors.

To include this change we must modify the knowledge base file. First we change the rule numbers so they start with one instead of zero. (This change is unrelated to the tax-bracket issue.) Next we add the following lines at the end of the file:

ASK Tax_Bracket: "Which tax bracket is the investor in?";

CHOICES Tax_Bracket: Low, High;

These lines will prompt the user for information on the investor's tax bracket. The user will have a choice of Low or High for responses. But we want this new prompt to appear only for conservative and moderate income investors. To implement this modification, we change rules 4 and 5 (formerly rules 3 and 4, respectively), and we add new versions of those rules:

RULE 4
IF   Goal = Income AND
        Risk_Profile = Conservative AND
        Tax_Bracket = Low
THEN Fund_Type = Treasuries;

RULE 4a
IF   Goal = Income AND
        Risk_Profile = Conservative AND
        Tax_Bracket = High
THEN Fund_Type = Insured_Municipals;

RULE 5
IF   Goal = Income AND
        Risk_Profile = Moderate AND
        Tax_Bracket = Low
THEN Fund_Type = Corporates;

RULE 5a

IF   Goal = Income AND
      Risk_Profile = Moderate AND
      Tax_Bracket = High
THEN Fund_Type = Municipals;

These new rules will add a third prompt for conservative and moderate risk income investors. Here is a sample of the expanded dialogue (user responses underlined):

Prompt 1: *What is the investment Goal?*
Response 1: Growth   <u>Income</u>   Gro_Inc

Prompt 2: *What is the investor's Risk_Profile?*
Response 2: <u>Conservative</u>   Moderate   Aggressive

Prompt 3: *Which tax bracket is the investor in?*
Response 3: Low   <u>High</u>

Statement: *The recommended Fund_Type is Insured Municipals.*

Providing User Guidance

When learning something new, it is natural to ask occasionally, Why am I doing this particular step? VP-Expert allows users to ask this type of question when they are running a consultation. The user can ask Why? by hitting the Why? key, and if the developer has provided explanatory material, it will appear on the screen. This feature helps users develop a deeper understanding of the task they are performing. To include this type of explanation, we add the BECAUSE text to the rules. In this example, if users want to know why the program prompts them for an investor's goals and risk tolerance, they will receive the response contained in the BECAUSE text's quotation marks. Here is a revised rule 1 to demonstrate the syntax:

RULE 1

IF   Goal = Growth AND
      Risk_Profile = Conservative
THEN Fund_Type = Large_Cap
            BECAUSE "We need to know the client's goals and risk tolerance level before making a fund category selection.";

We add this text to the remaining rules, giving our mutual fund knowledge base program its final form.

VP-Expert Mutual Fund Knowledge Base

ACTIONS
   FIND Fund_Type
   DISPLAY "The recommended Fund_Type is {Fund_Type}~";

RULE 1
IF   Goal = Growth AND
      Risk_Profile = Conservative
THEN Fund_Type = Large_Cap
         BECAUSE "We need to know the client's goals and risk
tolerance level before making a fund category selection.";

RULE 2
IF   Goal = Growth AND
      Risk_Profile = Moderate
THEN Fund_Type = Mid_Cap
         BECAUSE "We need to know the client's goals and risk
tolerance level before making a fund category selection.";

RULE 3
IF   Goal = Growth AND
      Risk_Profile = Aggressive
THEN Fund_Type = Small_Cap
         BECAUSE "We need to know the client's goals and risk
tolerance level before making a fund category selection.";

RULE 4
IF   Goal = Income AND
      Risk_Profile = Conservative AND
      Tax_Bracket = Low
THEN Fund_Type = Treasuries
         BECAUSE "We need to know the client's goals and risk
tolerance level before making a fund category selection.";

RULE 4a
IF   Goal = Income AND
      Risk_Profile = Conservative AND
      Tax_Bracket = High

THEN Fund_Type = Insured_Municipals
     BECAUSE "We need to know the client's goals and risk tolerance level before making a fund category selection.";

RULE 5
IF   Goal = Income AND
    Risk_Profile = Moderate AND
    Tax_Bracket = Low
THEN Fund_Type = Corporates
     BECAUSE "We need to know the client's goals and risk tolerance level before making a fund category selection.";

RULE 5a
IF   Goal = Income AND
    Risk_Profile = Moderate AND
    Tax_Bracket = High
THEN Fund_Type = Municipals
     BECAUSE "We need to know the client's goals and risk tolerance level before making a fund category selection.";

RULE 6
IF   Goal = Income AND
    Risk_Profile = Aggressive
THEN Fund_Type = High_Yield
     BECAUSE "We need to know the client's goals and risk tolerance level before making a fund category selection.";

RULE 7
IF   Goal = Gro_Inc AND
    Risk_Profile = Conservative
THEN Fund_Type = Balanced
     BECAUSE "We need to know the client's goals and risk tolerance level before making a fund category selection.";

RULE 8
IF   Goal = Gro_Inc AND
    Risk_Profile = Moderate
THEN Fund_Type = Equity_Income

BECAUSE "We need to know the client's goals and risk tolerance level before making a fund category selection.";

RULE 9
IF   Goal = Gro_Inc AND
        Risk_Profile = Aggressive
THEN Fund_Type = Growth_Income
            BECAUSE "We need to know the client's goals and risk tolerance level before making a fund category selection.";

ASK Goal: "What is the investment Goal?";
CHOICES Goal: Growth, Income, Gro_Inc;

ASK Risk_Profile: "What is the investor's Risk_Profile?";
CHOICES Risk_Profile: Conservative, Moderate, Aggressive;

ASK Tax_Bracket: "What is the investor's tax bracket?";
CHOICES Tax_Bracket: Low, High;

Linking to a Database

The mutual fund example was very simple, but it showed how making rule changes and maintaining a knowledge base can be time-consuming. A more efficient approach, which we demonstrate here, is to store most of the varying information in a database or worksheet file. This approach allows the developer to keep the rules, which do not change very frequently, in a separate rule base. VP-Expert allows the user to link the rule file and the data file, and data can be transferred in both directions.

To avoid confusion, we use different terms to distinguish the knowledge base's components. We will refer to the file that holds the varying data as an *information base,* while the file that holds the rules will be the *rule base.* Previously, we used only one term—knowledge base—because one file contained both rules and data. We now expand the term *knowledge base* to include both components, and this section uses the two terms to prevent misidentification.

The following example allows the user to access an information base of real estate listings. The file was created in a dBASE format and has 22 records. Table 1–4 shows the file's format and a sample of the data.

Next we examine the VP-Expert rules base that we use to access the data records in the dBASE file.

TABLE 1-4

Real Estate Data File

Development	Price	Bedrooms
Oakridge	87,500	3
Oakridge	79,900	2
Oakridge	95,500	4
Linsdale	160,000	3
Linsdale	149,000	2

ACTIONS

    MENU the_development, ALL, houses, development

    FIND the_development

    WHILEKNOWN development

    GET the_development = development, houses, ALL

    DISPLAY "Our listing shows a {bedrooms} bedroom house in the {development} development.

The asking price for this house is {price}.~"

    CLS

END

DISPLAY "~";

ASK the_development: "Our listing includes houses in these developments. Which development are you interested in?";

Parts of the rule base should look familiar from the mutual fund example, but several new elements appear here. One immediately noticeable feature is the rule base's size—it is much smaller than the mutual fund file. As we did with the mutual fund example, we work through the file to understand its operation.

The first clause in the ACTIONS block at the top of the file is a MENU clause:

ACTIONS

    MENU the_development, ALL, houses, development

The MENU clause creates a menu of selection options from which the user can indicate a choice. The selection takes its values from a field of a database file.

The FIND clause instructs the inference engine to find a value for a variable. In this case the variable is the_development:

ACTIONS
      MENU the_development, ALL, houses, development
      FIND the_development

The FIND clause causes the execution of the ASK statement, which is located at the end of the rules base:

ASK the_development: "Our listing includes houses in these developments. Which development are you interested in?";

This statement leads to the following screen display, shown here with the program's prompts in italics:

Prompt 1: *Our listing includes houses in these developments. Which development are you interested in?*

Oakridge   Linsdale   Crestview
Bishop_Park   Turtle_Cove   Skyview
Lakeview   Bishop_Shore   Elm_Glen
Elmwood

The execution of the ASK statement displays the menu that was created by the MENU clause. The list of developments come from the first column in the information base file.

The WHILEKNOWN clause creates a loop in the consultation.

ACTIONS
      MENU the_development, ALL, houses, development
      FIND the_development
      WHILEKNOWN development

The ACTIONS block causes all the clauses between the WHILEKNOWN keyword and the END keyword to execute repeatedly until the variable in the WHILEKNOWN clause becomes unknown. Therefore, as long as *development* has a known value, the clauses between WHILEKNOWN and END keep executing.

The next clause, GET, transfers values from a database to the rule base by assigning the values in fields from a selected record to variables with the same names as the fields from which the values are taken.

ACTIONS
      MENU the_development, ALL, houses, development

FIND the_development

WHILEKNOWN development

GET the_development = development, houses, ALL

The GET clause has several key features:

- It retrieves values from a database one record at a time.
- After a GET is issued, the record accessed by the GET becomes the current record of the database; that is, the record pointer is positioned at that record.
- A GET always moves forward from the record pointer to the next record matching the selection criterion.

In this example, the GET clause selects the next record whose DEVELOPMENT field matches the value of the variable, the_development, which the user has selected from the menu.

The DISPLAY clause produces the message enclosed within the quotation marks. The field names in the curly brackets will be replaced by individual property records, based on the user's menu selection.

ACTIONS

MENU the_development, ALL, houses, development

FIND the_development

WHILEKNOWN development

GET the_development = development, houses, ALL

DISPLAY "Our listing shows a {bedrooms} bedroom house in the {development} development.

The asking price for this house is {price}.~"

This ACTIONS block produces the following screen display after Oakridge is selected from the menu:

Our listing shows a 3 bedroom house in the Oakridge development. The asking price for this house is 87,500.

The final clause, CLS, is simply a clear-screen instruction.

Interpreting the Example

When users consult with the real estate knowledge base, they are first asked to select a menu (created by the MENU clause) from the available housing developments. The selection is assigned to the the_development variable. The GET clause then uses the menu selection to select a record from the dBASE file. The GET clause also instructs VP-Expert to assign all the field values in the record to variables having the same names as the fields from which they are taken. These variables' values are displayed in one or more messages by a DISPLAY cause. GET and DISPLAY are part of a WHILEKNOWN loop, so a message is displayed for each record that conforms to the database rule used by the GET clause to select records from the database.

This section concludes our development of examples with the VP-Expert software. Readers who wish to see additional applications will find two additional knowledge bases in the appendix. One deals with income tax issues, and the other generates an insurance underwriting consultation.

EXPERT SYSTEM SOFTWARE: XPERTRULE

The second program we work with to demonstrate expert systems is XpertRule, which is a Windows program produced by Attar Software. In the first part of this section we replicate the previous mutual fund selection example to introduce the program.

In XpertRule, the basic unit of knowledge is a decision-making "task" that is represented by a decision tree or as set of pattern rules. The decision-making task normally consists of an outcome, such as a decision or conclusion, and attributes (factors) that affect the outcome. The decision tree represents the relationship between the outcome and the attributes. The program allows the user to view a problem from several perspectives. We start building the mutual fund knowledge base by using the Attributes view. This view is not used for decision making—we use it to begin structuring the problem.

Example: Mutual Fund Advisor

The first information we enter will be the outcomes of the task. The firm recommends nine categories of mutual funds to clients: large cap, mid cap, small cap, treasuries, corporates, high yield, balanced, equity income, and growth income. (We introduce tax-exempt bonds later.) Next, we add the client's risk-tolerance level as a new attribute and assign it one of three values: conservative, moderate, or aggressive. Finally, we add the attribute and its three values that describe the client's investment goal: growth, income, or growth and income. Figure 1–1 shows the information we entered. The outcomes are listed in the last column, Fund Advisor,

FIGURE 1–1

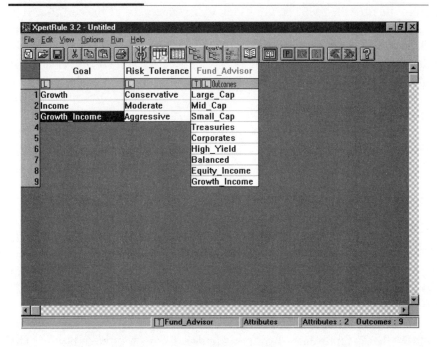

with the attributes of Risk_Tolerance and Goal in the second and first columns, respectively.

The order of the first two columns in Figure 1–1 is not critical and we can rearrange them if needed. It is a requirement, though, that the outcome column is placed last on the right. By creating the layout in Figure 1–1, we have now defined the outcomes, the initial attributes, or factors, and values that can be used in arriving at the outcomes.

We move now from Attributes view to Examples view. (The user accesses the program's views through the View pull-down menu.) Using the Options pull-down menu, we select Truth Table. The truth table method creates a complete set of examples that covers every possible combination of the attributes and values we entered. Some of the entries in the program's original table, which we do not show here, do not match attributes and outcomes correctly. We correct the entries with a point-and-click method until we have the correct mix of examples shown in Figure 1–2. Readers will note that Figure 1–2 contains the same information as Table 1–3, the induction table for the VP-Expert program.

We can use the examples in Figure 1–2 to create a decision tree, which is the main knowledge representation method used in XpertRule.

FIGURE 1–2

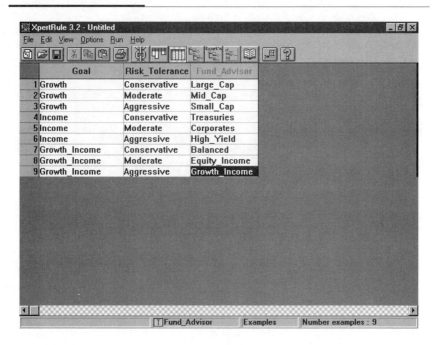

To create the tree, we change to Decision Tree view and select "Induce from Examples" on the Options pull-down menu. Figure 1–3 shows the resulting screen.

Figure 1–3 illustrates an advantage of using the Windows graphical environment. Because this problem is small, the user can grasp the problem's structure in a single glance. The decision tree's logic is easy to follow by starting on the far left of the diagram. The quasi-diamond-shaped objects represent decisions. The first decision is investment goal: Does the client want to invest for growth, income, or growth and income? That decision takes the user to the appropriate second node in the chain, which is also a decision. At this point the user must specify the client's risk tolerance: conservative, moderate, or aggressive. The response to that decision will take the user to an outcome (oval-shaped nodes), which is based on the previous two decisions.

We can also describe the decision tree as an if-then logic chain where the decision nodes are if statements and the outcomes are then results. For example, IF the client's goal is income AND the risk profile is moderate, THEN we recommend corporate bonds. Once again, there is a direct correspondence with the chapter's earlier material, where the if-then statements are listed explicitly in the rules base.

FIGURE 1–3

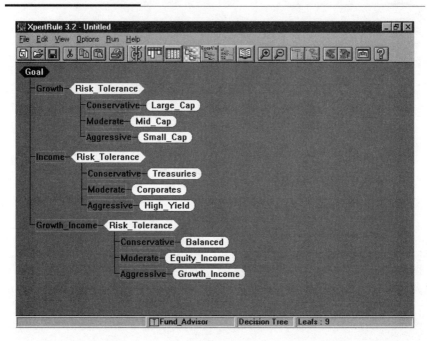

We are now ready to use the decision tree in a consultation. We switch to Map view, click on the Run icon, and the dialogue box in Figure 1–4 appears.

The dialogue box in Figure 1–4 functions like any Windows application dialogue box. We click on our selection (Growth) to highlight it and press OK to enter the selection. The consultation moves to the next level and asks for input on the client's risk tolerance as shown in Figure 1–5.

We select Moderate from the menu in Figure 1–5, enter it, and the receive the outcome screen in Figure 1–6, which recommends a mid cap fund.

In the previous work with this example, we added a question on the client's tax bracket for income investors. For conservative income investors in the high tax bracket, we added a recommendation for insured municipal bonds. The corresponding recommendation for moderate risk, high tax bracket, income investors was standard (not insured) municipal bonds. To include these new investment options, we add the new outcomes Insured_Munis and Municipals to our list of outcomes. We also add the tax-bracket attribute and its values (High, Low) to the table in Figure 1–7.

FIGURE 1-4

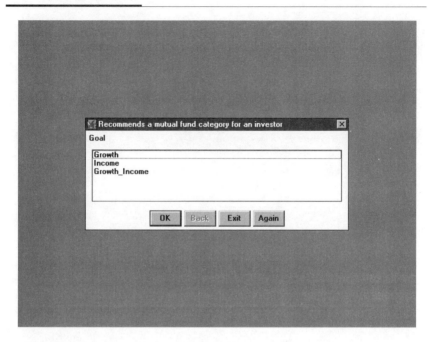

FIGURE 1-5

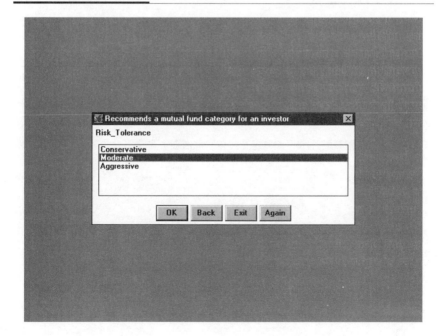

FIGURE 1–6

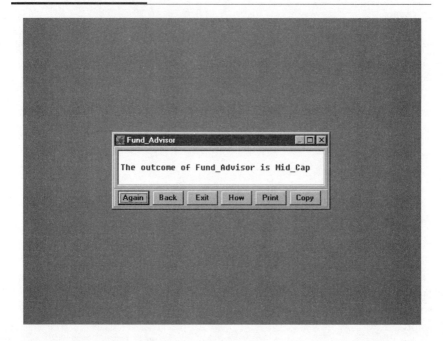

FIGURE 1–7

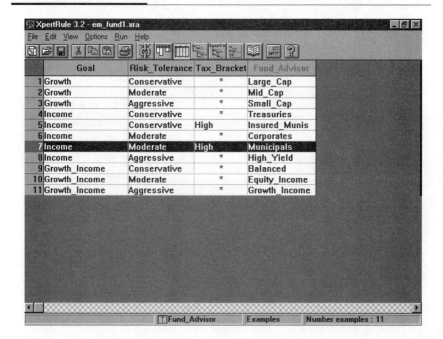

We change views to Example mode and revise our truth table. We do not want the tax-bracket prompt to appear in every case—we want to use it only with conservative and moderate income investors. We signify that in the truth table by placing asterisks in the truth table for rows in which we do not want to apply the tax-bracket attribute. Figure 1–8 shows these asterisks in the attribute column labeled Tax_Bracket.

The asterisks mean "don't care." In other words, they indicate that any value for the Tax_Bracket attribute can apply, and the outcome will still be the one listed in the Fund_Advisor column.

We use the revised table in Figure 1–8 to regenerate our decision tree. Figure 1–9 shows that part of the tree that was revised to include the tax-bracket attribute. If we run the consultation now and select a conservative or moderate income investor, we will receive an additional prompt requesting tax-bracket information.

Example: A Cost Control Application

XpertRule provides four primary methods for building a task, which we list in Table 1–5. This choice of methods gives the user flexibility in approaching a problem. The first three methods lead to decision-tree infer-

FIGURE 1–8

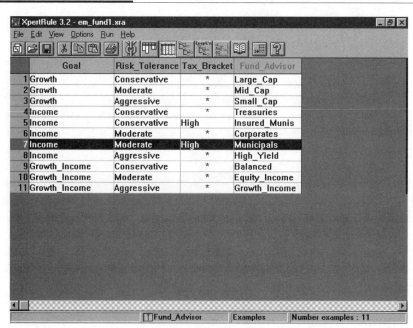

FIGURE 1-9

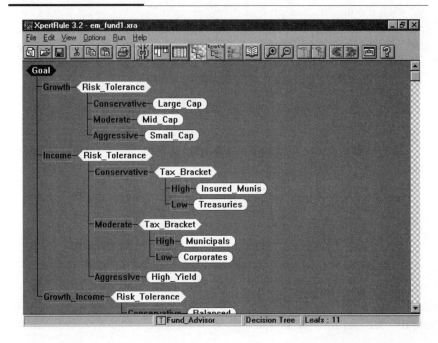

TABLE 1-5

XpertRule's Task-Building Methods

Method	Description
1	Define attributes, enter examples, induce decision tree
2	Define attributes, enter exception tree, induce decision tree
3	Define attributes, enter decision tree
4	Define attributes, enter pattern rules

ence, as we saw in the previous example, while the fourth method leads to pattern-rule inference. We use the next scenario, which is provided as an XpertRule tutorial, to examine these methods and the program's features in more detail.

In this scenario your client is concerned about the time required to process his employee's business-travel expense claims. He would like to develop an expert system that can quickly determine if the expenses meet the firm's requirement for reimbursement. Two outcomes are possible for any claim:

Accept: claim complies with company policy and is paid.
Reject: claim does not comply and is not paid.

The factors that the system must consider are

Rank: the employee's position within the company.
Department: employee's department.
Hotel: the standard of the hotel where the employee stayed.

Using the information that the client provides, we use method 1 to create the table of attributes and outcomes in Figure 1–10.

Figure 1–10 shows three attributes (rank, department, and hotel) and one outcome (accept or reject). There are three levels of personnel: managing director, vice president, and staff, and the system will be used for two departments: service and sales. Each hotel that the firm uses is assigned a letter grade for its cost, ranging from A (highest) to C (lowest). The firm's travel reimbursement policy allows managing directors from both departments to stay in any category of hotel. Vice presidents and sales-staff members may stay in B and C grade hotels, but service-staff members will be reimbursed for C hotels only. Figure 1–11 shows the truth table for those conditions. We use the asterisk (*) or don't-care entry for the managing directors' expenses because those always will be paid.

FIGURE 1–10

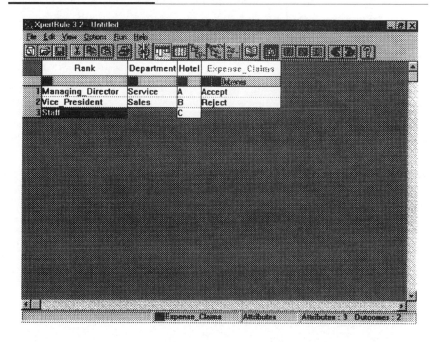

FIGURE 1–11

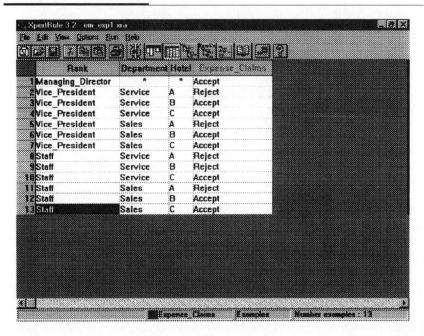

Following the same procedure as the mutual fund example, we have the program induce a decision tree (not shown) directly from the truth table. However, a potential problem appears with the application as we have structured it here. The example assigns each hotel a grade of A, B, or C. But what happens if an employee stays at a hotel that has not been classified? To prevent that problem, we add a subtask that determines which classification a hotel should receive. The subtask will examine two factors: hotel location and room cost. If the employee stays in a major city, such as New York or Los Angeles, we allow higher expenses for each hotel class. To add this subtask, we use method 3, editing the decision tree directly from the hotel node. Table 1–6 provides the price and class categories we want to use.

Working directly with the decision tree, we produce the decision diagram in Figure 1–12. (Remember that this does not complete the decision diagram—it is only one part of the original decision tree.)

Because we created this tree as a subtask, XpertRule can run the tree in Figure 1–2 alone or as part of the full decision diagram shown in Figure 1–13. The sequence of prompts for the full task shown in Figure 1–13 will be

- Cost of room (in dollars)
- Major city (yes/no)

TABLE 1–6

Hotel Classifications

	Major City	Other Cities
Class A	> $200	> $150
Class B	$125–$200	$75–$150
Class C	<$125	<$75

FIGURE 1–12

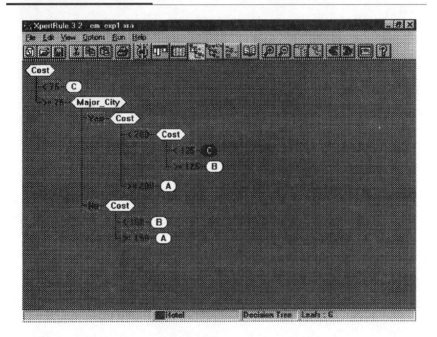

- Employee rank (managing director, vice president, staff)
- Employee department (service or sales)
- Outcome (accept/reject)

Making an Exception

We have used methods 1 and 3 to structure our employee-travel expense application. In this section we use method 2, the exception tree. As you might suspect, the exception-tree method lets the user first specify a single default outcome and then enter the exceptions to the default in a treelike format.

FIGURE   1–13

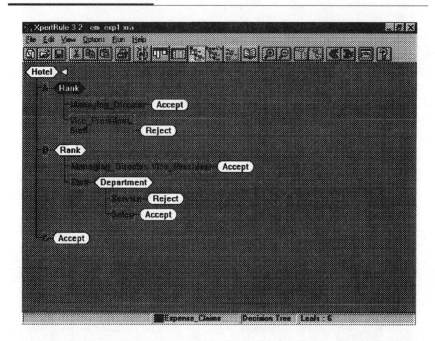

Most of our cases in this example led to Accept decisions, so it is very easy to handle the exceptions. We use XpertRule's exceptions input screen (not shown) to produce the exception tree shown in Figure 1–14.

We can interpret the exceptions in Figure 1–14 as follows: Vice presidents and staff will not be reimbursed for A-level hotels; in addition, service staff will not be reimbursed for B-level hotels. This exception tree is unusually simple, but it illustrates the ease of structuring the task with this view when appropriate.

Because XpertRule's fourth method of structuring an application, pattern rules, is similar to the examples in the first part of the chapter, we do not discuss it here. Although we used only a small part of XpertRule's features in the text, we hope that the examples have conveyed the program's versatility. Allowing the user to choose the view that is most appropriate to structuring the problem can reduce substantially development time.

CURRENT APPLICATIONS OF EXPERT SYSTEMS

We mentioned earlier that a wide range of financial institutions have adopted expert systems. Table 1–7 lists some of the applications that have been described in the literature.

FIGURE 1-14

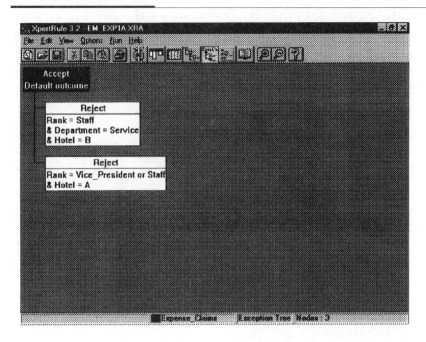

TABLE 1-7

Articles on Expert System Applications

Author(s)	Application	Source
Beckman	IRS: Taxpayer Service Assistant	1
O'Leary and Watkins	Auditing	1
Blocher	Financial analysis	1
Mui, Hassel, and Curtis	Financial statement analysis	1
Loofbourrow and Loofbourrow	Trading and portfolio management	2
Freedman and Stahl	Assessing credit quality of municipal bonds	2
Mikel and Ryan	Mortgage underwriting	2
Okeneski	Commercial real estate lending	2
Beshinske and McCarthy	Credit evaluation	2
Gers et al.	Credit evaluation	2
Curet and Killin	Auditing	2

Source: Liebowitz (1990); Freedman, Klein, and Trippi (1995).

SOURCES AND
RECOMMENDED READING

1. Freedman, R. S.; R. A. Klein; and J. Lederman, eds. *Artificial Intelligence in the Capital Markets*. Burr Ridge, IL: Irwin Professional Publishing, 1995.

2. Lawrence, J. *Introduction to Neural Networks*. 5th ed. Nevada City, CA: California Scientific Software Press, 1993.

3. Liebowitz, J., ed. *Expert Systems for Business and Management*. Englewood Cliffs, NJ: Yourdon Press, 1990.

4. Trippi, R. R. and J., K. Lee. *Artificial Intelligence in Finance and Investing*. Burr Ridge, IL: Irwin Professional Publishing, 1996.

5. *VP-Expert Users Manual*. Concord, CA: Wordtech Systems, Inc., 1995.

SOFTWARE RESOURCES

VP-Expert
Wordtech Systems, Inc.
1590 Solano Way, Unit C
Concord, CA 94520-5300
Tel. 510-689-1200
Fax 510-689-1263
Suggested retail price: $349

XpertRule
Attar Software USA
2 Deerfoot Trail on Partridge Hill
Harvard, MA 01451
Tel. 508-456-3946
Fax 508-456-8383
Web: http://www.attar.com
Suggested retail price: Contact Attar Software USA

CHAPTER 2

Decision Analysis

INTRODUCTION

Have you ever faced a difficult decision? That is a rhetorical question, of course—you probably classify most of the decisions you make for your own business or on which you advise clients as difficult. It also is likely that some of these decisions deal with critical issues, in which poor judgment would have major financial consequences. But have you ever thought about the method you use to make decisions? Do you use an analytical approach, compiling reams of data to create multiple scenarios? Perhaps you favor "gut level" decisions, following the path that your instincts tell you is best. Or do you combine the two approaches with the goal of getting input from each method?

In this chapter we look at several widely used decision-analysis tools, including influence diagrams, decision trees, and the analytical hierarchy process. These tools are not intended to replace your judgment. Instead, they serve as aids that can organize your approach to making decisions and complement your experience and skills. By using these tools, you will make more consistent and better-informed decisions. Of course, even these tools cannot guarantee that you will make the right decision every time—no one has figured out how to program infallibility yet! But you will have more confidence in your decisions, and you will be in a better position to explain those decisions to clients.

Before getting into specific decision analysis (DA) methods we review the key elements of the decision process. For instance, why are some decisions so difficult, while others are easy? What external factors should you consider in approaching decisions? How do you design an efficient DA process? We discuss those questions in the following sections.

DECISION FACTORS

Why are some decisions so difficult? These tough decisions consume valuable time, they cause us stress, and in general, they can make life very unpleasant. In contrast, some decisions are easy. We make them quickly, and we don't worry too much about their consequences before or after we make them.

Clemen (1991) identifies four sources that influence the difficulty of a decision. The first is complexity: some decisions are much more multifaceted than others. Deciding between tea or coffee for a breakfast beverage is easy—you have only two alternatives and your preferences that morning will determine your selection. Contrast that choice with a decision you might face later that same morning. Your client wants to establish a 401(k) plan for her company, and she has asked you to evaluate proposals from six plan vendors. You must rate each proposal in several areas, and it is possible that no single plan will have an obvious advantage in every area. This decision is complex and potentially difficult.

The second factor influencing a decision's difficulty is the situation's uncertainty. Consider the decision to launch a new product or offer a new service to the market. Before you make your decision, you do not know with certainty the outcomes of many critical elements such as costs, market demand, and competitors' reactions. This uncertainty makes the decision more difficult than it would be if you had "hard" data on the key variables.

A third element is the potential presence of trade-offs in the available choices. A classic example of this is the trade-off between increasing market share versus increasing profitability. An increase in market share often means a more aggressive pricing policy that accepts a lower unit profit to allow a lower selling price. These lower prices can attract new customers, but there is no guarantee the higher volume will offset the lower unit profits. Another example can be seen in the investment selection process. The ideal investment would offer both price stability and high returns. Because this combination is usually unattainable in most investment markets, the investor must choose between price stability and investment return. Here is the trade-off: Investments that offer price stability usually produce lower returns, so the client must decide between conflicting goals.

The final reason a decision may be difficult is that different perspectives can lead to different decisions. A firm's marketing department might want customized products that can create a unique image for the firm, while the manufacturing department prefers a simpler design that is easier to produce. The two departments' different perspectives on the product's desired attributes can lead to very dissimilar decisions, even when they are working with the same set of facts.

A final factor worth mentioning is the decision maker's attitude toward risk, which economists have classified through utility functions. Based on their risk tolerance, some decision makers are classified as *risk averse,* while others are *risk neutral* or *risk seekers.* Although we cannot directly perceive an individual's risk tolerance, we can use measures like questionnaires to estimate her profile. Even if we have a reasonably accurate profile of the decision maker, though, we still must allow for irrational actions. History has shown human nature to be frequently unpredictable, and no decision-making model can account for every action, especially those that defy logic.

THE DECISION-ANALYSIS PROCESS

Clemen (1991) has identified several key steps in the decision-analysis process. The first step is to identify the problem correctly. While some problems are obvious, in other cases we might confuse a symptom with the problem that is its underlying cause. To avoid this situation, the parties who have a role in making the decision should agree on the problem before taking further steps.

The second step is to identify the most important objectives that the DA process should achieve. The objectives should be stated clearly and ranked by priority: We want to maximize profit, reduce income taxes, and so on. This step is particularly important if the problem causes conflicting objectives. If the conflicts are left unresolved at this stage, reconciling competing solutions later in the process will be difficult or impossible.

Step three in the process is to decompose and model the problem. Decomposing a problem involves breaking it down into smaller elements. As a simple example, we assume your client's objective is to maximize her firm's profits. We know that the profit equation has two elements: revenue and expenses. We can break each of these into smaller, more manageable pieces: Unit sales price, manufacturing costs, and so on. By decomposing the problem, we can distinguish between the critical areas that we can influence and those that are beyond our control.

The second part of this step is to model the problem properly. At best, a model will match up reasonably well with the problem being considered. It is not necessary, and it is certainly impractical, for the model to capture every aspect of a problem. If the model incorporates the problem's key features, though, we can work with it successfully. In practical terms, the model must capture the problem's structure (time sequences of decisions, events, and outcomes), uncertainty, and the user's preferences. The remaining material in this chapter focuses on PC-assisted methods for modeling and analyzing decision problems.

After modeling and analyzing the problem, the next step is to choose the best alternative from those available. Another worthwhile activity is to conduct a sensitivity analysis before implementing the decision. If the sensitivity analysis shows that one decision variable is significantly more influential than the others, we should reexamine that variable to measure the impact of changes in its value. As an example, we assume a particular level of interest rates to estimate a project's net present value (NPV). If the sensitivity analysis shows that interest rates are a critical factor in the analysis, we should examine the impact on NPV of unexpected changes in rates.

If the sensitivity analysis reveals potential weaknesses in the model, the decision maker should work through the DA process again to identify the source of the problem. Once the model is acceptable, it is time to implement the selected course of action.

Because this book emphasizes PC-based analytical tools, we move directly to the problem decomposition and modeling stage of the DA process. This leap is not meant to downplay the importance of properly identifying the problem and stating the objectives. We proceed on the assumption that the reader will complete those steps successfully before moving to the decomposition and modeling stage.

INFLUENCE DIAGRAM SOFTWARE: DPL

One of the most difficult steps in decision making is keeping track of the problem's elements. This is especially true with complicated decisions in which you may need to consider a wide range of influences and possible outcomes. The influence diagram graphically represents the components of a decision problem—decisions, uncertainties, and values—and the relationships between them. Figure 2–1 is a simple influence diagram that is developed from Clemen (1991), using the DPL Decision Analysis Software for Microsoft Windows from ADA Decision Systems.

Figure 2–1 represents an investment decision, and it contains the basic components used to develop influence diagrams. Squares represent deci-

FIGURE 2–1

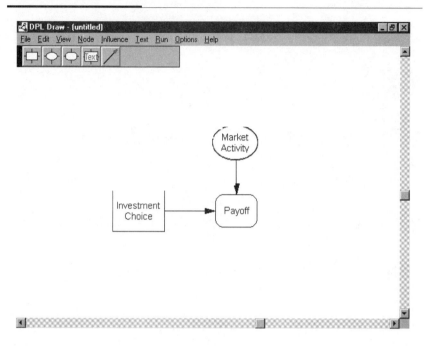

sions, circles represent chance events, and rectangles with rounded corners stand for values. These three elements are called nodes, and we link the nodes with arrows, or arcs. A node at the beginning of an arc is a predecessor node, while the node at the end of the arc is a successor node.[1]

In this example, we have one decision node that represents the decision to invest. We assume the decision is to invest in a risky asset like stocks versus a guaranteed-return bank account. Naturally, this decision precedes the payoff. The chance node also precedes the payoff, and it represents the investment market's potential returns. Although we do not show the input screen, we assume three possible states for the market's return: low, average, and high. In the payoff node, we assign each state a return: minus 5 percent for low, 10 percent for average, and 25 percent for high. Because the bank account's return is guaranteed, it pays a 5 percent return regardless of the market's activity. The payoffs are shown as the endpoints in Figure 2–2.

The example in Figure 2–2 represents the simplest type of decision problem. It has a single decision (select a risky or safe investment), one

---

1. The illustrations here are shown here in black and white. The original DPL program diagrams used colored nodes and arrows to make visual interpretation easier.

FIGURE 2-2

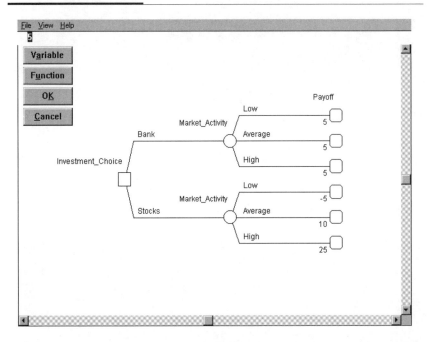

uncertain event (the investment's return), and an outcome that is influenced by both the decision and the uncertain event. At this level the diagram does not tell us much, but it does serve one useful purpose: It forces us to clearly identify any decisions we must make, the uncertain events that influence the outcome, and the possible outcomes to the decision. As we discussed previously, these steps are critical in developing an effective DA model. We will return to this example later as we show how influence diagrams and decision trees present different views of the problem.

Before developing a more complex example, we should mention a common error that can arise in interpreting influence diagrams. An influence diagram is a snapshot of the decision maker's knowledge of a decision's elements. It represents the decision maker's attempt to account for all the critical elements at a particular point in time. You should not see the diagram as a sequential flow chart. Although a sequence (or set of sequences) of decisions, uncertain events, and outcomes behind the decision probably exist, the influence diagram does not necessarily illustrate that sequence. We will demonstrate this shortcoming more clearly when we use decision trees.

Example: Capital Investment

Most businesses face periodic capital investment decisions: Should we buy new equipment, expand our manufacturing capacity, and so on? In this next example, we demonstrate the use of an influence diagram in a capital investment decision.

Your client is always looking for ways to improve her product, and her company has an active research and development (R&D) program to assist in that improvement. She needs advice on two decisions: the amount she should invest in R&D and whether she should increase her plant's capacity. In this case, there is a sequence to the decision process. Her first decision is to decide on the R&D budget, and she will have the R&D results before she makes the plant investment decision. She outlines the decision process in this way (amounts are in thousands):

Step 1. Decide level of R&D investment amount: none ($0), moderate ($10), or high ($20).

Step 2. Get R&D research results: bad, nominal, or good.

Step 3. Make plant investment decision: none (cost $0), yes (cost $100).

Your client's experience has shown a positive relationship between the amount spent on R&D and the research results. In other words, as the firm spends more on R&D, the probability of getting good results increases. Table 2–1 shows her estimate of the relationship.

TABLE 2–1

R&D Budget and Research Results

R&D Budget	Outcome	Probability of Outcome
None	Bad	1.0
	Nominal	0
	Good	0
Moderate	Bad	0.4
	Nominal	0.5
	Good	0.1
High	Bad	0.2
	Nominal	0.5
	Good	0.3

If the firm spends nothing (R&D budget: none) on product improve-ment R&D, the company obviously has no chance of improving the prod-uct. This decision leads to a "bad" result with certainty, which we express as a probability of 1.0. With a moderate R&D budget, the odds of creat-ing product improvements increase: 50 percent (0.5) for a nominal improvement and 10 percent (0.1) for a good result. Finally, spending a large amount on R&D creates the highest likelihood of getting nominal (0.5) or good (0.3) results. We enter these values in the influence diagram, although we do not show the input screen.

The R&D results also will influence demand for the product, because customers will respond to product improvements by increasing their orders. It's uncertain, though, how strongly the customers will respond. Based on her judgment, your client classifies the demand response to product improvements as low, nominal, or high. She combines the possible sales impact of product improvements and customer response in Table 2–2.

The ideal outcome would be a good response to the R&D efforts com-bined with a high customer response to the product improvement, resulting in a sales increase of 40,000 units. There is one catch, though: If the firm does not invest in expanded plant capacity, it will not be able to meet the increased demand. Because of the interrelated nature of the issues, you sketch an influence diagram for your client, shown in Figure 2–3.

One benefit of the influence diagram technique is immediately apparent from Figure 2–3. It lets the decision maker step back from the

TABLE 2–2

R&D Result and Customer Response

R&D Result (Product Improvement)	Customer Response	Sales Increase (000 units)
Bad	Low	0
	Normal	0
	High	0
Nominal	Low	5
	Normal	10
	High	20
Good	Low	10
	Normal	20
	High	40

FIGURE 2–3

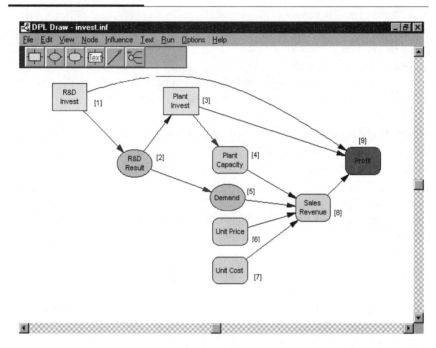

detail level to see the big picture and the relationships between the decision elements. Let's walk through the diagram to clarify its structure. We use bracketed item numbers [] in the text to refer to corresponding diagram elements.

Element [1], R&D Invest, represents the first of two decisions your client must make: Should she spend funds on the R&D for product improvement research? As discussed previously, she is considering spending nothing, $10,000 (moderate), or $20,000 (high). Note the arc going from the R&D Invest decision node to the Profit [9] value node. This arc shows that the R&D investment decision precedes the profit node and it has a direct influence on profit. Specifically, if the firm invests in R&D, it will incur a cost, which reduces profit, regardless of the research results.

We represent the uncertainty in the R&D Result node [2] by drawing it as a circle. As discussed previously (see Table 2–1), we assign probability levels to the node's three possible outcomes (bad, nominal, good) that are a function of the amount spent on R&D.

Because R&D Result influences both the Demand node [5] and the Plant Invest decision node [3], we draw arcs from R&D Result to those nodes.

The Plant Invest [3] decision will influence both Plant Capacity [4] and Profit [9]. We structure the plant investment node as a simple yes or no decision. A no decision will not cost anything and will not increase plant capacity. A yes decision will require a $100,000 expenditure and an increase in plant capacity by 45,000 units.

The Unit Price [6] and Unit Cost [7] nodes hold per unit values of 10 and 6, respectively. These nodes, combined with Plant Capacity [4] and Demand [5], precede the Sales Revenue [8] node. In contrast to the previous nodes, which held dollar and probability values, we enter a formula in this cell: Sales Revenue = (Unit_Price – Unit_Cost) * min(Demand, Plant_Capacity). This formula multiplies the per unit net margin by the lesser of the Demand value or the Plant_Capacity value. In a sense, the formula acts as an if programming statement: If Demand is greater than Plant_Capacity, use the Plant_Capacity value; if Demand is less than Plant_Capacity, use the Demand value.

The final node is the Profit value [9]. As Figure 2–3 shows, it is the final successor value, influenced directly or indirectly by all the preceding decisions and uncertain outcomes. Please note that profit is not an uncertain value in this diagram. By the time we reach the Profit node, we know the values for all the preceding nodes. We have already made the investment decisions on R&D and plant capacity, and the uncertain sales demand has been resolved. Knowing these outcomes removes the uncertainty from the Profit node, making it a deterministic (certain) value.

Figure 2–3 is a useful overview of the decision elements, but you probably could replicate it manually with your PC's word processor or drawing program. The DPL program allows the user to analyze the information embedded in the influence diagram. Before we get into the details of those analyses, though, we introduce our next decision-analysis tool: the decision tree.

DECISION TREE SOFTWARE: DPL

Like influence diagrams, decision trees are an attempt to graphically portray the decisions, uncertain events, and potential payoffs in the decision-making process. Unlike influence diagrams, though, decision trees explicitly show a sequence (or multiple sequences) of events, and the tree's structure depends on the chronology of events. The graphics for decision trees are similar to those of the influence diagram: squares represent decision nodes, circles represent uncertain outcomes, and potential payoffs are shown as amounts at the end of tree's individual branches. Figure 2–4 shows a decision tree created in DPL illustrating a choice between two alternatives, one of which has two uncertain outcomes.

Several features in Figure 2–4 are worth noting. First, there must be at least two alternative branches at a decision node, even if one of those branches represents the decision to do nothing. Second, the possible outcomes of an event node are mutually exclusive: either one or the other outcome is possible, but not both simultaneously. Finally, the decision tree follows a chronological sequence: Time moves forward as we move from left to right on the diagram. The decision maker must make a decision to follow the "risky" branch before the uncertain event can take place.

We used the example of an investment decision earlier in the chapter to illustrate a basic influence diagram. Figure 2–5 illustrates the same decision problem in decision tree form.

In Figure 2–5, the decision maker has two choices: Invest in a bank account with guaranteed 5 percent return or invest in the uncertain stock market. The market investment has three potential payoffs as shown in Table 2–3.

Each outcome is one branch of the tree that follows the uncertain outcome node (the circle). The top branch represents the high return, which has a .30 probability of occurring and a 25 percent (one-year return) payoff. The center branch, the normal return, has a .40 probability of occurring, and it would provide a 10 percent payoff. The bottom branch

FIGURE 2–4

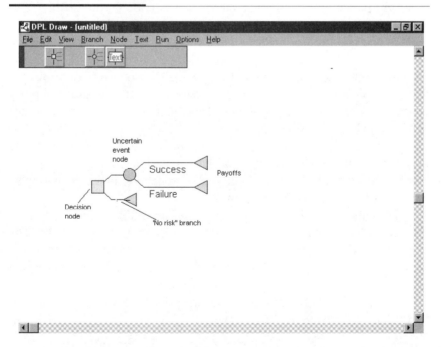

FIGURE 2–5

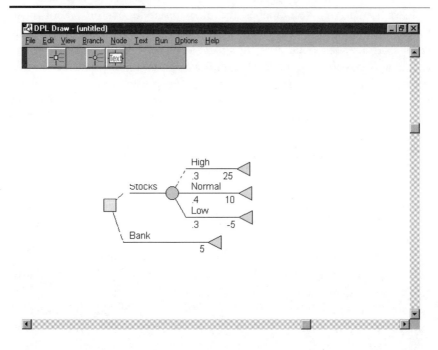

from this node is the low return, which has a .30 probability and a minus 5 percent payoff (loss). Because the market payoffs are mutually exclusive, the probabilities stemming from the uncertain event node sum to one. In this case, the probability values in an event node are subjective estimates, based on the decision maker's (or her advisor's) experience. As we show in Chapter 3, on simulation, in some cases we may be able to develop probability estimates based on historical data. Because each problem tends to be unique, though, most decision trees require user estimates of the probability distribution.

The other branch from the decision node, Bank, is riskless: If the investor puts her money in the bank she will earn a guaranteed 5 percent on her funds. That return will occur with a probability of 1.0 if chosen, so we do not show a probability estimate here.

Decision trees give the decision maker an informative overview of the alternatives and the possible outcomes of any uncertain events. The diagram's usefulness as a decision-making aid comes from the next step in the process, though, which involves "rolling back" the branches to select the best alternative. Before examining that technique, we briefly review the concepts of expected value and the time value of money as they relate to decision tree cash flows.

TABLE 2-3

Investment Payoffs

Investment Result	Probability	Payoff
High	.3	25
Normal	.4	10
Low	.3	−5

Handling Future Cash Flows

Because the decision tree involves future payments and receipts, some of which are uncertain, we need a method for estimating and comparing the payoffs that can result from each decision. We use two standard calculations to do this: expected value and net present value.

In a decision tree, an expected value is a probability-weighted cash flow. Using the stock market payoffs in Figure 2–5 as an example, we have the following payoffs (corresponding probability in parentheses): 25 (.3), 10 (.4), and -5 (.3). To find the expected value, we multiply each payoff by its probability and sum the results.

$$(25 * .3) + (10 * .4) + (−5 * .3) = 10$$

We can express the expected value of X more generally in the following formula where x_i represents cash flow in period i:

$$X = \sum_{i=1}^{n} x_i P(X = x_i)$$

$P(X = x_i)$ is the probability that X will take on a specific value x_i. We calculate the expected value of each uncertain event node in the tree using this method.

In a problem like this one, which has a short horizon of one year, the time value of money is not critical. In longer-horizon problems, though, it becomes an important issue that we must consider. To reflect the time value of money, we will calculate a cash flow stream's net present value using the following formula:

$$NPV = \sum_{i=0}^{n} \frac{c_i}{(1+r)^i}$$

where c_i represents the cash flow (paid or received) in year i and r equals the appropriate rate used for discounting period i's cash flow. We assume the reader is familiar with NPV calculations, so we do not elaborate on the calculation here.

Rolling Back the Tree

The key to using a decision tree is as to select the path with the highest expected payoff. Finding this payoff involves two steps. First we calculate the expected value at each event node. Next we select the branch from the decision node with the highest expected value. Let's look at the investment decision tree in Figure 2–5 to demonstrate the method.

Step 1. Calculate the expected value at each event node. We did this earlier, and the result for the stock return's node was 10.

Step 2. Compare the expected values of the branches from the decision tree. The lower branch, which represents the decision to put the money in the bank, has an expected value of 5 (probability of 1.0 times the payoff of 5). The upper branch, Stocks, has an expected value of 10. The result: Take the branch with the greater expected value of 10 and invest the funds in stocks.

With a simple example like this one, you can calculate the necessary values manually. For more complicated examples, you can use DPL's automated analysis functions, which will select the highest expected value path for you. As Figure 2–6 shows, the program produces a graph with the highest expected value path highlighted in bold and the expected values shown in brackets.

To illustrate a more complicated decision, we return to the dual-decision (R&D and plant investment) problem. As shown in Figure 2–3 and described in Tables 2–1 and 2–2, that problem involved two decisions (R&D Investment and Plant Investment) and two sources of uncertainty (R&D Results and Customer Demand). Instead of creating the decision tree manually, as we did in the investment example, we allow DPL to use the information in the influence diagram to create the tree automatically. We then run the analysis, and the program generates the diagram in Figure 2–7.

We have reduced the level of detail from the final tree structure slightly, so the terminal nodes do not appear in Figure 2–7. Also, we do not describe the calculations behind the values because the process is the same as that described above. We focus instead on the interpretation of the diagram and its implication for the decision maker. The analysis shows that the company should invest in a new plant only if the R&D shows good results. This result comes from rolling back the diagram's terminal points (not shown) and calculating each node's expected value. We show six final event nodes here, each of which has two values: one above the branch and one

FIGURE 2-6

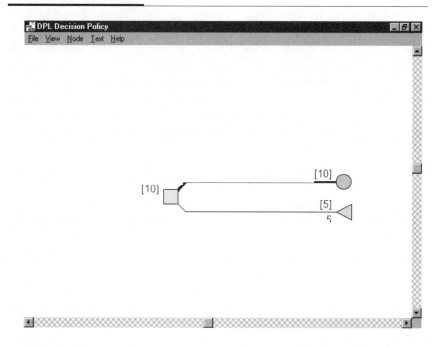

FIGURE 2-7

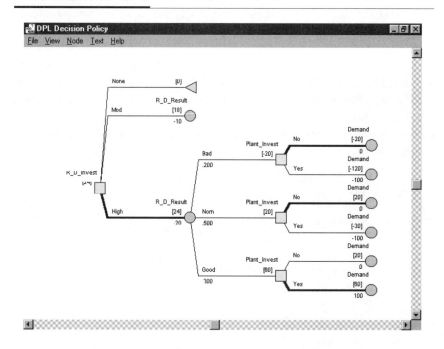

below. The value above the branch shows the net expected value (sales revenue minus costs) for each event node. (These final event nodes represent customer demand.) The value below the branch shows the costs (or revenue) incurred at that point in the tree. At each decision point, the program selects the branch with the highest expected value

Starting at the far left of the diagram, we see the first decision, which is the level of R&D investment. The analysis shows that we should choose a high investment level and then make the plant investment decision after seeing the R&D results. We summarize these results in Table 2–4.

Sensitivity Analysis

After completing the decision tree analysis, your client might have questions on the sensitivity of the key variables. For example, what are the odds of losing money on the project even if the firm spends the high amount on R&D? To answer that question, the program can provide a cumulative distribution chart, shown in Figure 2–8.

Figure 2–8 shows the potential profit outcomes, which range from a loss of about $40,000 to a profit slightly over $200,000. The break-even point (0 on the x-axis) intersects the y-axis at the .30 level, which means that there is still a significant risk of losing money in the project, even after making the high investment in R&D.

Another useful graph is the rainbow diagram, which we have produced in Figure 2–9 for the Unit_Price variable.

Figure 2–9 shows how the expected profit varies from $0 to over $40,000 as the unit price changes. The breaks that distinguish the different shaded sections on the graph indicate the point where a change in unit price affects the expected value of the profit figure. In this example, we interpret the graph to mean that if unit price can possibly drop below $9, we should model price with a probability distribution to gauge the results' sensitivity.

TABLE 2–4

Recommendations

R&D Result	Invest in Plant?
Bad	No
Nominal	No
Good	Yes

FIGURE 2–8

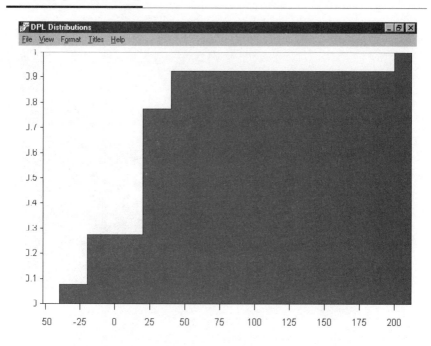

The DPL program has other sensitivity analyses that we have not discussed. The primary motivation for using these analyses is to avoid unpleasant surprises. Any decision that involves uncertainty requires the decision maker to take a risk. Performing sensitivity analyses can point to the areas most susceptible to changes in any uncertain elements. If you highlight and explain these potential problem areas to your clients in advance, they will have a better understanding of the risks involved with any decision.

THE ANALYTICAL HIERARCHY PROCESS

Try to recall the last time you bought or leased a car. Your objective was to find the car that best suited your needs. As you began evaluating various models, you probably used a checklist to compare different vehicle features: safety, cost, comfort, and so on. Depending on your personal preferences, you might have ranked these features from most to least important. Whether you wrote down the list of features or kept it in your head, your method was an attempt to evaluate multiple selection criteria in some form of ranking system.

FIGURE 2–9

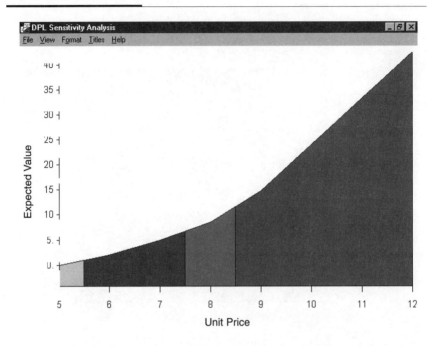

This intuitive approach of breaking down decisions into components and arranging the components in a hierarchy forms the basis for the analytical hierarchy process (AHP), which is the next decision-making tool we discuss. The AHP was developed by Thomas L. Saaty, a mathematician at the University of Pennsylvania's Wharton School. Dr. Saaty describes the AHP as "a method of breaking down a complex, unstructured situation into its component parts; arranging these parts, or variables, into a hierarchic order; assigning numerical values to subjective judgments on the relative importance of each variable; and synthesizing the judgments to determine which variables have the highest priority and should be acted upon to influence the outcome of the situation."[2]

As a decision-making aid, the AHP allows the user to include both tangible and intangible factors. This flexibility can be particularly valuable in your work with clients who tend to favor intuitive decisions in which they rank intangible factors highly. The AHP lets the decision maker organize her thoughts in a logical, hierarchical structure. The process uses pairwise comparisons to rank preferences, and it allows the

2. T. L. Saaty, *Decision Making for Leaders* (Pittsburgh, PA: RWS Publications, 1995), p. 5.

decision maker to see the inconsistencies in her rankings. This ability to recognize inconsistencies is useful, since most of us are not perfectly logical in every decision we make. The AHP has been incorporated in the Expert Choice software program, which we use in the following sections to demonstrate applications of the process. Before working with the software, though, we examine the AHP theoretical foundation and examine its approach to making decisions.

The easiest way to grasp the AHP approach to decision making is to visualize how the process structures a problem. In its most basic format, the decision maker will use a chart like that in Figure 2–10.

The Goal in Figure 2–10 is the overall objective of the decision making process: find the best car, select the best investment, and so on. The Criteria are the factors that the decision maker will use in forming her judgment (car safety, resale value), and the Alternatives are the choices available to the decision maker (car 1, car 2).

The Principles of Analytic Thinking

Saaty also distinguishes three principles that underlie the process of solving problems by explicit logical analysis: constructing hierarchies, establishing priorities, and logical consistency. As an example of constructing hierarchies, think of how we view the material that makes up the universe: subatomic particles, atoms, molecules, and so on. We do the same with other entities such as businesses: employee, unit, department, up to the company level. This method of forming hierarchies helps us deal with complex systems. As Saaty notes, "By breaking down reality into

FIGURE 2–10

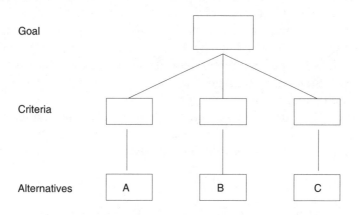

homogenous clusters and subdividing these clusters into smaller ones, we can integrate large amounts of information into the structure of a problem and form a more complete picture of the whole system."[3]

We also can establish relationships and preferences among the things we perceive: Object A is larger than object B, or I prefer a sweet taste to a sour taste. We use these relationships and preferences when we make decisions. For example, when you compare automobiles, you might prefer a certain body design over others. Your preference might be intense (I only buy four-door sedans) or weak (I prefer a four-door sedan, but I'm willing to compromise). The AHP measures the strength of these preferences and uses their rankings in making decisions.

The third principle underlying analytic thought is *logical consistency*. We use the term here as it is defined by Saaty, who gives it two meanings. The first is the ability to group objects or ideas according to relevance or homogeneity. As an example, a grape and a marble belong to the same set if shape (roundness) is the criterion, but we would not put them in the same set if we used flavor as the criterion. The second meaning is that we can establish rankings among ideas or objects. If we like vanilla ice cream twice as much as we like strawberry, and chocolate twice as much as we like vanilla, we should like chocolate four times as much as strawberry. We know from experience that most people are not perfectly consistent in their judgments, but that does not prevent us from establishing reasonably consistent rankings. Reality itself is not always consistent: Team A beats team B, team B beats team C, but team C beats team A. The AHP allows the user to model reality's inconsistencies.

Measurement Scales

One problem that arises frequently in multiple-criteria decisions is the need to compare objects or ideas that are measured on different scales. We measure some things by units such as length and temperature, while others use scales like time and money. The AHP handles the problem of combining values from different scales by first expressing all values on a priority scale. Preferences pose another problem: How do you combine one person's preferences with another person's?

The AHP is designed to handle both tangible and intangible factors, and it can be used in cases where direct comparisons seem unachievable. According to Saaty, it is possible to compare objects that initially do not appear to be similar.

---

3. Ibid., p. 23.

The old adage that one cannot compare apples and oranges is false. Apples and oranges have many properties in common: size, shape, taste, aroma, color, seediness, juiciness, and so on. We may prefer an orange for some properties and an apple for others; moreover, the strength of our preferences may vary. We may be indifferent to size and color, but have a strong preference for taste, which again may change with the time of day. It is my thesis that this sort of complicated comparison occurs in real life over and over again, and some kind of mathematical approach is required to help us determine priorities and make tradeoffs. The analytic hierarchy process is such an approach.[4]

Specifically, with the AHP users first compare an apple to an orange using one property at a time and then compares the properties themselves for preference. Next they synthesize the results to determine whether the apple or orange is most preferred.

An Overview of the AHP Steps

AHP users follow a series of steps as they begin the analytical process. These steps are as follows:[5]

1. Define the problem and specify the solution desired.
2. Structure the hierarchy from the overall managerial (or decision maker's) viewpoint. (Figure 2–10 is an example of a basic hierarchy.)
3. Make pairwise comparisons of the relevant contribution or impact of each element on each governing criterion in the next higher level. In comparing two elements most people prefer to give a judgment that indicates the dominance as a whole number. (We show this shortly when we work with Expert Choice.)
4. Use the information from step 3 to obtain priorities and test for consistency.
5. Repeat steps 3 and 4 for all levels and clusters in the hierarchy.
6. Evaluate the results and check for consistency. If inconsistencies are large, revise the problem area(s).

Before moving to applications of the AHP using Expert Choice, we digress briefly to examine the technique used for measuring inconsistency. In some cases it is easy to recognize inconsistency in the decision-making process. As an example, if I prefer A to B, and I also prefer B to

---

4. Ibid., p. 23.
5. Ibid., p. 94.

C, I should prefer A to C. But if I rate A and C as equally preferred, there is an inconsistency in my preferences. Recognizing the inconsistency is an important first step, but we need to move beyond it by quantifying the degree of inconsistency and determining if it is important to the decision. The following example from Saaty shows the AHP method for establishing pairwise comparisons and testing for inconsistency.

Example: Leasing a Car

You are in the market for a new car, and you are comparing the comfort of three models: a Chevrolet (C), a Thunderbird, (T), and a Lincoln (L). You take a test drive of each car and based on your perception of the ride, you rate the Chevrolet as one-half as comfortable as the Thunderbird and one-fourth as comfortable as the Lincoln. Using these relative rankings, you create the matrix in Table 2–5.

The key to creating and reading the matrix is to remember that the element in the left-hand column is always compared with the element in the top row, and the value is given to the element in the column as it compares to the element in the row. If the first element is regarded less favorably than the second, the judgment is a fraction. As an example, work down the C column. The numbers in this column list the relative comfort comparisons described earlier. The first value, listed where the C row and column intersect, is one. Intuitively, that makes sense, because you are comparing the car with itself. Next, you believed the Thunderbird is twice as comfortable as the Chevrolet, so we enter 2 in the box where C column intersects the T row. Finally, we enter the value of 4 at the intersection of the C column and the L row because the Lincoln is four times as comfortable as the Chevrolet. We repeat this process for the remaining two columns.

As you inspect these values, you will notice that each column of the matrix is filled with the inverse values of the corresponding row. For

TABLE 2–5

Comparing Auto Comfort

Comfort	C	T	L
Chevrolet (C)	1	1/2	1/4
Thunderbird (T)	2	1	1/2
Lincoln (L)	4	2	1
Column Total	7	3 1/2	1 3/4

example, the first column (C) has values of 1, 2, and 4, which are the inverse of the first row's values of 1, 1/2, and 1/4. The same holds true for the second and third columns. (You can reverse the logic, and each row will be the inverse of its corresponding column.) Because this example is manufactured, the result is intentional. As we show shortly, this result does not occur when inconsistencies exist in the relative rankings.

The matrix entries are used to rank priorities and to develop a consistency index. Because the Expert Choice program performs the necessary calculations, we describe a method here that is a close approximation. The first step is to add the values in each column. These results are given in the last row of Table 2–5. Next we divide each entry in each column by its respective column total. This creates the normalized matrix shown in Table 2–6.

The next step is to calculate the average value of the elements in each row:

C: $(1/7 + 1/7 + 1/7) \div 3 = 0.14$

T: $(2/7 + 2/7 + 2/7) \div 3 = 0.29$

L: $(4/7 + 4/7 + 4/7) \div 3 = 0.57$

This calculation gives the relative preferences for the three cars: at 29 percent, the Thunderbird is twice as comfortable and the Lincoln is four times as comfortable as the Chevrolet. By extension, the Lincoln is twice as comfortable as the Thunderbird. These results confirm our stated comparisons of the cars' relative comfort.

We can perform a second calculation using the same data. Notice that the column sums from Table 2–5 and the normalized row averages are reciprocals: $1/7 = .14$; $1/3.5 = .29$; and $1/1.75 = .57$. Therefore, the product of each column sum times its corresponding normalized row average equals 1, and for n columns, the sum of the multiplications should equal n. The method works in this example where n equals 3: $[7 * (.14) + 3.5 * .(29) + 1.75 * (.57)] = 3$ (slight rounding). If this value does not equal 3, there must be an inconsistency in the rankings matrix, as Table 2–7 shows.

TABLE 2–6

Normalized Rankings Matrix

Comfort	C	T	L
Chevrolet (C)	1/7	1/7	1/7
Thunderbird (T)	2/7	2/7	2/7
Lincoln (L)	4/7	4/7	4/7

Let's assume you retain the same relative rankings as in Table 2–1 for the Chevrolet versus the Thunderbird and Lincoln, but you do not maintain the same consistency for the Thunderbird–Lincoln pairing. Table 2–7 shows the revised rankings.

You can see the problem in the L row, T column entry. You previously ranked the Lincoln's comfort as twice that of the Thunderbird, but the value here rates it four times higher. This rating causes the column totals to differ from the example in Table 2–5. Next we divide each entry by its appropriate column sum (Table 2–8) and calculate the average normalized row sums.

Average Row Sums

$(1/7 + 1/11 + 1/6) \div 3 = 0.13$

$(2/7 + 2/11 + 1/6) \div 3 = 0.21$

$(4/7 + 8/11 + 4/6) \div 3 = 0.66$

Most of the matrix values, and all the average row sums, are different from the first example where the entries were consistent. Although we do not give the mathematical details here, the next step is to compare the values between the two calculations. If the values are significantly different (more than 5 or 10 percent, depending on the size of n), then the decision maker should revisit the problem to resolve the inconsistency.

TABLE 2–7

Inconsistent Comfort Comparisons

Comfort	C	T	L
Chevrolet (C)	1	1/2	1/4
Thunderbird (T)	2	1	1/4
Lincoln (L)	4	4	1
Column Total	7	5 1/2	1 1/2

TABLE 2–8

Normalized Inconsistent Comfort Comparisons

Comfort	C	T	L
Chevrolet (C)	1/7	1/11	1/6
Thunderbird (T)	2/7	2/11	1/6
Lincoln (L)	4/7	8/11	4/6

This method of evaluating pairwise comparisons in a matrix is used to make comparisons throughout the decision hierarchy. After all comparisons are made, the results are combined to get an overall estimate of the relative rank of the problem's alternatives, which are the cars in this case. In the next section we use the Expert Choice software to demonstrate the process as we analyze several business decisions.

AHP SOFTWARE: EXPERT CHOICE

Example: A Location Problem

In this first example, your client owns and operates ice-cream stores, and she must decide where she should open her next store in a particular town. Her goal is to find the best location for the new store, and the criteria she must consider are rental space cost, potential customer traffic in terms of passersby, visibility of the store, and the number of competing ice cream stores in the area. We use Expert Choice to structure the problem in the following hierarchy, shown in Figure 2–11.

Figure 2–11 shows the initial Expert Choice setup screen. The objective, or goal, which sits at that top of the hierarchy, is stated as "Select the best retail site for the new store." The criteria are listed directly below the

FIGURE 2–11

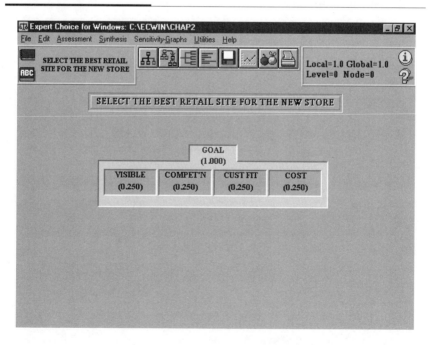

goal: store visibility (VISIBLE), local competition (COMPET'N), number of passersby who could be customers (CUST FIT), and the monthly rental cost per square foot (COST). Because we have not performed any pairwise comparisons yet, each criterion carries the same weight of 0.25.

Your client is considering three alternative sites: a suburban shopping center, a suburban mall, and a Main Street business location. Each location has its unique mix of qualities, which makes the decision complicated. We enter the sites as alternatives in the Expert Choice hierarchy. Although we do not show the details here, the program places the three alternatives below each of the criteria, as shown in Figure 2–12.

Now that we have built the model, the next step is to evaluate the elements by making pairwise comparisons. This process ultimately will lead us to the derivation of priorities for each alternative under each criterion and for each criterion under our goal. The Expert Choice user can choose from three types of pairwise comparisons in the program: importance (comparing criteria), preference (comparing criteria), and likelihood (comparing probability of outcomes). You can make the comparisons in several modes: verbal (English language terms), graphical (charts), and numerical (matrix or questionnaire). We demonstrate several of these features in the following sections.

FIGURE 2–12

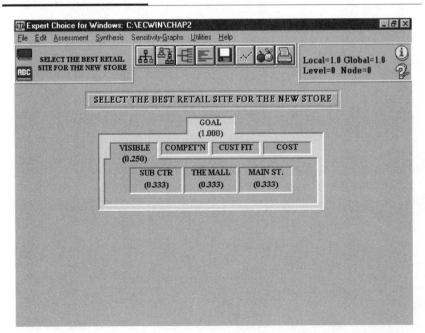

Your client's next step is to begin making the pairwise assessments of the alternatives' features. We start with the VISIBLE node and instruct the program to use the preference comparisons in a verbal mode. This sequence generates the input screen in Figure 2–13.

The screen in Figure 2–13 asks, "With respect to VISIBLE (Visibility), is the SUB CTR (suburban shopping center) more PREFERABLE, equally PREFERABLE, or less PREFERABLE than THE MALL: SUBURBAN MALL LOCATION?"

We are making a pairwise comparison. The program's prompt is asking us to state a preference for the visibility criterion between the suburban shopping center and the mall. Because we believe the SUB CTR is less visible than THE MALL, we click on the Less PREFERABLE button, which brings up the comparison screen shown in Figure 2–14.

Because we selected the verbal mode in Figure 2–14, the program prompts us to compare the two locations on a verbal scale that ranges from equally preferable to extremely preferable. Before we discuss the scale, the reader should note that the program changed the language in the prompt. The previous screen (Figure 2–13) listed the SUB CTR as the first element in the comparison. In response to that prompt, we indicated that the SUB CTR was less preferable than the mall. In Figure 2–14 the ele-

FIGURE 2–13

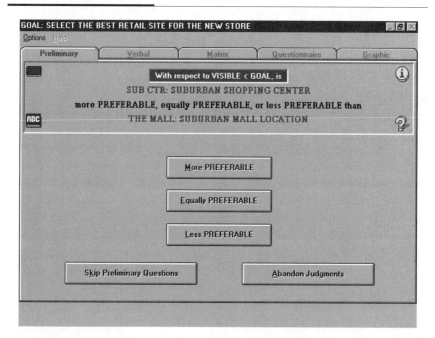

FIGURE 2–14

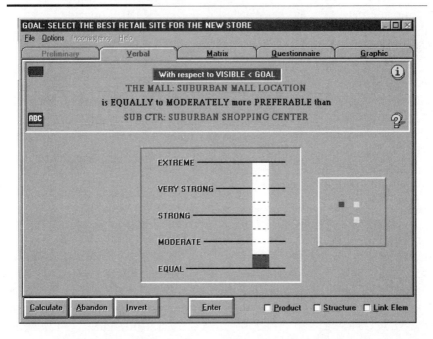

ments are reversed, with THE MALL listed first. Reversing the order in this way makes the comparison scale more consistent and easier to understand by avoiding the need for a negative scale.

The scale in Figure 2–14 uses verbal comparisons, and the user clicks on the graph next to the desired degree of comparison. The program also allows for mixed measures, as shown in the illustration. By positioning the graph marker between Equal and Moderate, the program recognizes this selection as meaning "equally to moderately" more preferable. (The prompt is context sensitive and displays the user's selection.)

The program uses a common scale for pairwise comparisons, which we list in Table 2–9. This is the software's normal scale, which is used to compare elements of the same order of magnitude (within 9.9 times of each other). Other scales are available for comparisons when the elements are not of the same order of magnitude.

After entering our judgment for the mall's visibility versus the suburban shopping center, the program uses the same sequence of prompts for the remaining comparisons under the VISIBLE node. Table 2–10 lists a summary of the responses.

TABLE 2–9

Fundamental Scale for Making Judgments

Numerical Scale	Verbal Scale	Explanation
1	Equal importance of both elements.	Two elements contribute equally to the property.
3	Moderate importance of one element over the other.	Experience and judgment favor one element over the other.
5	Strong importance of one element over the other.	An element is strongly favored.
7	Very strong importance of one element over the other.	An element is very strongly dominant.
9	Extreme importance of one element over the other.	An element is favored by at least an order of magnitude.
2, 4, 6, 8	Intermediate values between the above adjacent values.	Used for compromise between two judgments.
Increments of 0.1	Finer gradations of 0.1 allowed in matrix mode.	Used for finer gradations of judgments.

Source: Expert Choice Tutorial and User Manual, version 9.0. Pittsburgh, PA: Expert Choice, Inc., 1995, p.95.

TABLE 2–10

VISIBLE Node Responses

Site 1	Preference	Site 2
THE MALL	Moderately to strongly preferred to	SUB CTR
SUB CTR	Moderately preferred to	MAIN ST
THE MALL	Strongly to very strongly preferred to	MAIN ST

The reader will note that this process is identical to the automobile-comfort comparison we performed earlier. When the user selects the software's verbal mode, the program automatically creates the underlying comparison matrix and it examines the responses for consistency. After the user completes the entries for each node, the program calculates the inconsistency ratio and displays the resulting priorities graph for that node as shown in Figure 2–15.

FIGURE 2–15

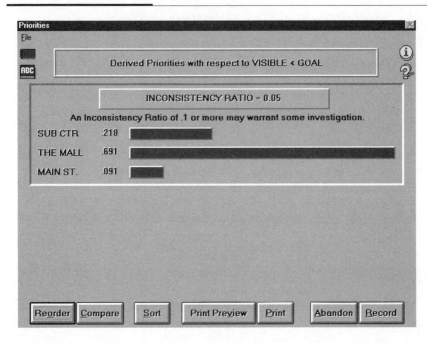

The inconsistency ratio for the visibility node in Figure 2–15 is 0.05, an acceptable level. As expected, the mall location ranks highest for visibility, followed by the suburban shopping center and the Main Street location.

Our next step is to enter pairwise comparisons for the COMPET'N, CUST FIT, and COST criteria. We do not show the input screens, but the process is the same in each case. It is worth repeating, though, that the verbal mode is only one of the input methods available. Depending on personal preferences and the nature of the comparison, the user can select from matrix, questionnaire, and graphic comparison screens. The cost data, for instance, is entered as a dollar cost per square foot for each alternative, not as a set of comparisons. Table 2–11 summarizes the remaining input.

After entering data for the three alternatives (SUB CTR, THE MALL, MAIN ST.), we move up a level to make judgments about the four criteria (VISIBLE, COMPET'N, CUST FIT, COST). The process is the same. We enter pairwise comparisons about each criterion; the program develops a matrix and generates a priority list. Table 2–12 lists the pairwise comparisons we enter in the verbal mode.

After entering these comparisons, the program calculates the following priorities and inconsistency ratio, which we provide in Table 2–13.

TABLE 2-11

Summary of Node Responses

Criterion	Comparison	Mode	Input
COMPET'N	SUB CTR vs. MALL	Graphical	3 to 1
	SUB CTR vs. MAIN ST.	Graphical	2 to 1
	MALL vs. MAIN ST.	Graphical	1 to 2
CUST FIT	SUB CTR vs. MALL	Matrix	4.0
	SUB CTR vs. MAIN ST.	Matrix	3.0
	MALL vs. MAIN ST.	Matrix	2.0
COST	SUB CTR	Data	12
(per square foot)	MALL	Data	17
	MAIN ST.	Data	22

TABLE 2-12

Criteria Pairwise Comparisons

Pairwise Comparisons	Verbal Rating
VISIBLE vs. COMPET'N	VISIBLE strongly more important than COMPET'N
VISIBLE vs. CUST FIT	VISIBLE equally as important as CUST FIT
VISIBLE vs. COST	COST moderately more important than VISIBLE
COMPET'N vs. CUST FIT	COMPET'N equally as important as CUST FIT
COMPET'N vs. COST	COST strongly more important than COMPET'N
CUST FIT vs. COST	COST moderately more important than CUST FIT

Expert Choice determines an alternative's relative priority by using the multiple sets of pairwise comparisons we entered in the steps described above. After we enter all the necessary data and correct any inconsistencies, we are ready to synthesize the input to find the highest ranked alternative. The program offers two methods for synthesizing the data: the ideal mode and the distributive mode. The ideal synthesis mode is recommended when you are (1) concerned only with the highest ranked alternative, and (2) several alternatives have equal weights for most of the objectives. The distributive synthesis mode works best when (1) you are prioritizing alternatives, (2) your alternatives have unique values for most of the objectives, and (3) the problem involves a scarcity of resources. Because we are concerned with selecting the best single site in this prob-

TABLE 2-13

Criteria Priorities

Criteria	Priority
VISIBLE	.243
COMPET'N	.094
CUST FIT	.155
COST	.509
Inconsistency Ratio	0.01

lem, we use the ideal mode. Figures 2–16 and 2–17 show the program's outputs after synthesizing in the ideal mode.

Figure 2–16 shows the relative ranking of the alternatives, based on the input we provided. The mall location receives the highest priority, followed by the suburban shopping center and the Main Street location. The inconsistency index is 0.07, which is below the problem level of 0.10.

Figure 2–17 provides the analytical details. In the first column, Level 1, each criterion's priority is given, with each alternative's relative ranking listed next to the criteria in the column Level 2. In the ideal synthesis mode, the highest ranked alternative for each criterion receives the same priority as the criteria, while the remaining alternatives receive a relative weighting. For example, the Cost criterion has a priority of .509. In the next column, the program assigns SUB CTR a priority of .509 with lower relative priorities given to THE MALL and MAIN ST. This process is repeated for each criterion listed in the first column.

We now have our answer: Given the preferences and information we provided, the mall is the best location for the store. But does that result still hold if we decide to revise the relative importance of the criteria we used? What happens if we decide that the number of nearby competitors deserves more emphasis? Will that change the result, or are the priorities insensitive to changes in the criteria's importance?

To answer these questions, we use the program's sensitivity-analysis features. We can perform these analyses from the GOAL node to judge the alternatives' sensitivity with respect to the criteria listed below the goal. If the model has more than three levels, the user can also examine the sensitivity of lower-level nodes to their underlying criteria.

Figure 2–18 demonstrates the program's dynamic sensitivity-analysis screen. The bars on the left represent the original priorities for the criteria: COST (.509), VISIBLE (.243), CUST FIT (.155), and COMPET'N (.094).

FIGURE 2–16

Alternative Priorities

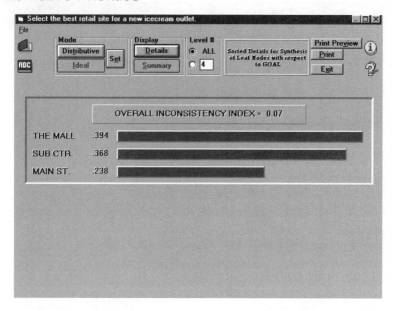

FIGURE 2–17

Details of the Analysis

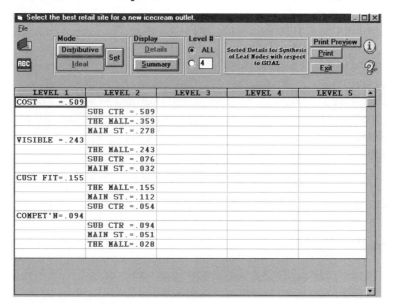

FIGURE 2–18

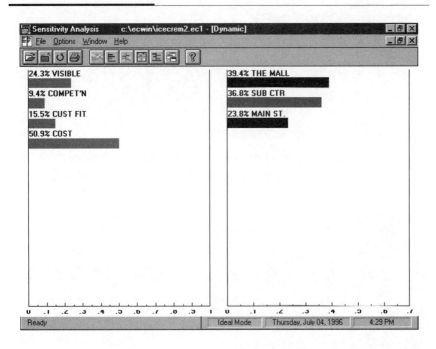

The graph's right side shows the alternatives' rankings: THE MALL (39.4 percent), SUB CTR (36.8 percent), and MAIN ST. (23.8 percent).

The graph in Figure 2–18 is dynamic: By extending or shrinking the criterion bars on the left side, the user can see the impact of changing priorities on the right side's alternatives. For example, in Figure 2–19 we increase the priority on COMPET'N from 9.4 percent to 30.1 percent, and SUB CTR replaces THE MALL as the highest ranked alternative. Similar changes can be made to any of the criteria on the left side, allowing users to get instant feedback to "what if" questions. The program also provides several other sensitivity-analysis tools that we do not discuss here.

Example: An Investment Decision

In this next example, we develop a more complicated hierarchy that involves allocating funds among different investment classes while facing an uncertain economic outlook. Before selecting assets, most investors examine economic conditions. For instance, is the economy growing rapidly or is it slipping into a recession? What is the outlook for inflation and interest rates? The asset's performance under the various economic conditions is also important.

FIGURE 2–19

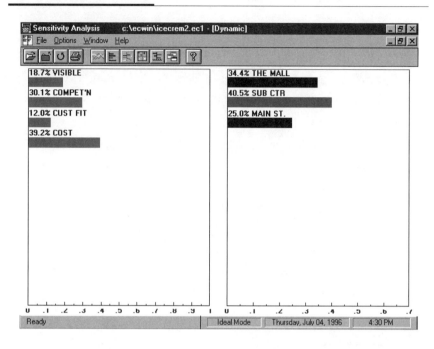

How does the asset perform in a period of low or high inflation? Does the asset do well in a period of strong economic growth? A prudent investor or advisor will examine these issues before committing funds.

Figure 2–20 shows the analytical hierarchy for the allocation decision. The goal is to select the asset allocation that best meets the investor's needs, given the individual's judgments about the investments' features and the economy. We structure the problem with six economic scenarios in the second level of the hierarchy:

STAT QUO (status quo—no changes in inflation and growth from current levels).

STRGRWTH (strong growth—economic activity increases sharply).

MILDRECSN (slight contraction).

SVRRECSN (severe recession).

INFLAT'N (annual rate of inflation increases significantly from current level).

STAGFLTN (stagflation: combination of mild recession and higher inflation).

We list the investment alternatives' characteristics (criteria) in the third level:

SAFETY (safety of principal).

EROSION (sensitivity to loss of purchasing power from inflation).

GROWTH (potential for increase in real (after inflation) value).

EFFORT (effort required to track and manage an investment).

Finally, we consider six alternative investments:

CASH (including cash equivalents like Treasury bills).
US STOCK.
INTLSTCK (international stocks).
BONDS (including other fixed income securities).
REAL EST (real estate and real estate securities).
METALS (precious metals).

We begin the analysis by making pairwise comparisons for the alternatives listed under each criterion. Table 2–14 provides a partial sum-

TABLE 2–14

Pairwise Comparisons with Economy: Status Quo
Criterion: Safety

Asset	Comparison
Cash	Moderately more preferable than U.S. stocks.
	Moderately to strongly more preferable than international stocks.
	Strongly more preferable than bonds.
	Moderately more preferable than real estate.
	Strongly to very strongly more preferable than metals.
U.S. stocks	Moderately more preferable than International stocks.
	Moderately more preferable than bonds.
	Moderately more preferable than metals.
International stocks	Moderately more preferable than bonds.
	Moderately more preferable than metals.
Bonds	Equally as preferable as metals.
Real estate	Strongly more preferable than metals.
	Moderately more preferable than U.S. stocks.
	Moderately to strongly more preferable than international stocks.
	Moderately to strongly more preferable than bonds.

mary of the comparisons. (We list the comparisons for only one criteria under one economic scenario.)

As in the previous example, we enter the pairwise comparisons for each alternative under each of the four criteria (not shown here). Next, we enter the likelihood of the economic conditions, as summarized in Table 2–15.

TABLE 2–15

Pairwise Comparisons of Potential Economic Conditions

Economic Condition	Comparison
Status quo	Strongly to moderately more likely than strong growth.
	Strongly more likely than severe recession.
Strong growth	Equally to moderately more likely than severe recession.
Mild recession	Moderately to strongly more likely than status quo.
	Moderately to strongly more likely than strong growth.
	Strongly more likely than severe recession.
	Equally to moderately more likely than inflation.
	Equally to moderately more likely than stagflation.
Inflation	Equally to moderately more likely than status quo.
	Moderately to strongly more likely than strong growth.
	Moderately to strongly more likely than severe recession.
	Moderately more likely than stagflation.
Stagflation	Moderately to strongly more likely than status quo.
	Moderately to strongly more likely than strong growth.
	Strongly to very strongly more likely than severe recession.

TABLE 2–16

Suggested Asset Allocation

Asset	Percent of Portfolio
Real estate	26.2%
Cash	22.4
Metals	21.2
Bonds	12.3
U.S. stock	10.5
International stock	7.5
Overall inconsistency index	0.08

After entering the comparisons, we have Expert Choice synthesize the input. Because we are looking for an allocation (versus a single-asset decision), we use the distributive mode. Table 2–16 lists the program's suggested allocation.

The AHP and Expert Choice program have a wider range of applications than shown in the material here. In particular, the method is well suited for group decision making.

SUMMARY

Decisions have consequences. Some have a minor impact on the decision maker's financial status, while others are critical. An advisor who can offer clients a disciplined approach to decision making brings an important skill to the relationship. Of course, there is no guarantee that a decision or an advisor's recommendation will be correct—no analytic technique or computer program offers infallibility (yet!). In spite of that shortcoming, combining experience-based judgment with decision analysis offers the best opportunity for reaching a good decision.

SOURCES AND RECOMMENDED READING

Clemen, R. T. *Making Hard Decisions: An Introduction to Decision Analysis.* Belmont, CA: Duxbury Press, 1991.

DPL User Manual. Belmont, CA: Duxbury Press, 1995.

Expert Choice Tutorial and User Manual, version 9.0. Pittsburgh, PA: Expert Choice, Inc., 1995.

Saaty, T. *Decision Making for Leaders.* Pittsburgh, PA: RWS Publications, 1995.

Saaty, T. *Fundamentals of Decision Making and Priority Theory.* Pittsburgh, PA: RWS Publications, 1994.

SOFTWARE RESOURCES

DPL for Windows
Applied Decision Analysis, Inc.
2710 Sand Hill Road
Menlo Park, CA 94025
Tel. 888-926-9251
Fax 415-854-6233
E-mail: dpldept@adainc.com

Suggested retail prices
Standard version: $495
Advanced version: $995
Free demo available

Expert Choice for Windows
Expert Choice, Inc.
5001 Baum Boulevard Suite 650
Pittsburgh, PA 15213
Tel. 412-682-3844
Fax 412-682-7008
Web: http://www.expertchoice.com

Suggested retail prices
Expert Choice Pro for Windows
Single-user version: $595
Five-user network version: $1,995
Demo disk available for $20
Books available on AHP process

CHAPTER 3

Simulation

INTRODUCTION

Are you ready for your first quiz? Please answer the following questions:

1. What will be the inflation rate for the next 10 years?

2. What will be the value of the S&P 500 stock index in three years?

3. What will happen to interest rates for the next five years?

You might react skeptically and reply that you cannot answer these questions accurately. No one can predict the future, you argue, so any answer you might give is just an informed guess. If forced to answer, you might take the recent average for each variable and use that as the basis for your estimate. If you had extensive data, you could develop a sophisticated econometric or time-series model to help with your forecasts. (These forecasting techniques and others are discussed in detail in Chapter 5.)

Ultimately, though, any answer you give is only an estimate of a random variable's future value. In spite of this uncertainty, you probably make frequent predictions about variables like these in your work because your work with clients might not give you an alternative. Clients hire you to help them plan for an unpredictable future—they look to you for solutions that will help them solve their problems and reach their goals. This expectation makes forecasts unavoidable. For example, most personal financial planning clients want to save enough funds to ensure a comfortable retirement. That means they need to project their future expenses and incomes, which in turn depend on inflation and investment results, both of which are unpredictable. Ideally, clients start planning long before they actually retire, but that timing compounds the uncertainty in your forecasts. Should you tell them to come back to see you when they are close to retirement so you can have more confidence in your forecasts? You could, but your business probably would not survive very long.

Businesses also face uncertainty: How much will sales increase over the next three years? What will happen to the cost of inputs like materials and labor? The answers to these questions influence a wide range of decisions about investment in new equipment, staffing levels, marketing expenditures, and so on. External variables such as economic growth, inflation, interest rates, and competitors' actions also affect business results. Like individuals, businesses must make plans today to get them through an uncertain tomorrow.

As an advisor, you can choose from three methods to estimate these uncertain variables. The first technique is a point estimate. Using a five-year inflation forecast as an example, let's assume you believe inflation will average 3 percent over the period. A quick calculation (1.03^5) gives you an inflation factor of 1.159. In other words, an item that costs $100 today will cost roughly $116 at the end of five years. The accuracy of a point estimate such as this one depends on the volatility of the forecasted variable and the length of the forecast period. If inflation has been holding steady at 3 percent, a short-term forecast (less than one year) has a chance at reasonable accuracy. In periods of unstable prices, or with longer forecast periods, you probably won't make a very accurate forecast. (Inaccurate predictions about the economy do not necessarily mean the end of your career as a forecasting guru, however. The key to your long-term survival is to have plausible excuses prepared in advance. Obviously, if we judged economists by the accuracy of their forecasts, very few of them would hold a job for more than one year!)

Another approach is to create multiple scenarios with the hope that the actual value will fall somewhere in the range you specify. Continuing with the earlier example, you could use a worst-case scenario of 6 percent average annual inflation, a best case of 2 percent, and a most likely case of 4 percent. You could assign a weight to each estimate and develop a weighted estimate. Although this method recognizes the uncertainty in the forecast by specifying a range rather than a single value, it does not help you explain that uncertainty to the client. For example, how likely is it that inflation will be under 5 percent or more than 3 percent? To provide a more detailed analysis, we can design these analyses as simulations, which is the subject of this chapter.

In Chapter 2 we discussed decision trees, a technique for identifying and assigning probabilities to a decision's outcomes. You can think of a simulation as a very bushy decision tree—one with so many endpoints that the decision tree approach is impractical. Using the five-year inflation forecast example, you assume that each year's inflation rate will be between 2 percent and 6 percent. If you measure inflation to one decimal point accuracy (3.2 percent, for example), you would need 40 outcome nodes to cover the range from 2.0 to 6.0 percent. Then you would need to match each of those 40 possible outcomes from the first year with the next year's 40 possible values, and so on. As you can see, using this approach with so many outcomes creates an unwieldy analysis.

Simulations solve this problem by using a repeated sampling technique. In this example we tell the simulation program that there are 40 values for each year ranging from 2.0 percent to 6.0 percent. We also assume that any value in the range is as likely to occur as any other value, so each outcome has a probability of 1/40. The program randomly picks a number in that range from each year for the five years. It makes its first pass through the five years and gives these possible results:

Year 1: 2.7 percent

Year 2: 3.4 percent

Year 3: 2.1 percent

Year 4: 4.0 percent

Year 5: 5.0 percent

If you have trouble visualizing the random number selection process, think of each year's results as a prize drawing. You reach into a barrel holding 40 numbers (2.0, 2.1,...6.0), withdraw a ticket, note the number, and replace the ticket. You then move to the next barrel and repeat the process. Each barrel has an identical set of tickets, and we assume that what happens in the first drawing doesn't affect the outcome of the second drawing.

With a computerized simulation you can repeat this type of sampling selection many times very quickly. Each pass through the five years is an iteration, and it is not unusual for a simulation to run hundreds or thousands of iterations for a problem. Once the program completes the simulations, we should have a good idea of the distribution of possible results, which we can analyze and graph. As we show shortly, simulation gives the user a powerful tool for visualizing the uncertainty in a forecast.

BUILDING MODELS

When we hear the term *simulation*, we often think of physical models. You might have seen the television ad for an airline that shows pilots being trained in a flight simulator. The pilot sits in a mock flight deck, and the simulator creates various weather patterns and mechanical problems to challenge the pilot. Other examples of physical simulations include testing automobile models in wind tunnels and outdoor machinery in weather rooms. The idea behind each simulation is the same: It is an attempt to model an important variable to allow analysis in a controlled environment. If the model closely matches its real world counterpart, simulation gives users a valuable tool. Airline pilots can learn how to handle mechanical problems without risking their lives and equipment. Auto and machinery manufacturers can subject their equipment to a variety of harsh climatic conditions in a much shorter time period than normally needed to test their durability.

It is easy to grasp the relationship of a physical model to the object or process being modeled, but financial models are intangible—they exist only on paper or in electronic form. In spite of that potential conceptual difficulty, finance relies heavily on models. For example, look at the traditional business income statement. It summarizes a wide range of business activities into a very simple model: Revenue – Expenses = Profit. Despite its simplicity, this formula accurately captures the business's overall activities and relationships in an easily understood model. The model can become more complex as we add categories of income and expenses, but its essence remains the same.

Personal financial planners use a similar modeling approach to develop projections for clients. The planner develops a cash flow model, often using a spreadsheet, that projects the client's assets, income, and expenses. This approach is used for a variety of situations: planning for a child's education, a client's retirement or estate, and so on. In retirement planning, for example, the retiree's problem resembles the business's: Generate a positive cash flow or at least ensure that enough assets are available to sustain a negative cash flow for an acceptable period.

Part of the advisor's role in building financial models is helping the client identify the key variables. When a business projects its income statements for the next period, it must estimate a variety of expenses. Management can control some of those expenses, while others vary unpredictably. The advisor's role in building the analysis is to help identify and quantify those variable factors. Depending on the details of the problem, these could include economic or demographic variables and competitors' actions, among others.

After identifying the key variables, the advisor must also specify any relationships that exist among those variables. For example, interest rates strongly influence industries such as new home construction. As interest rates move higher, mortgage payments for a given loan amount increase. Higher payments mean fewer prospective customers, leading to a decrease in new home construction. If you work with a client in an interest rate sensitive industry, you must recognize the dependency on interest rates for your models to work properly.

Recognizing the uncertainty in and relationship among the factors influencing your clients' outcomes is the first step in building a financial model. As a second step, you need to quantify that uncertainty, which is the subject of the next section.

STATISTICS REVIEW

Before we start building and running simulations, we need to review some basic statistics. This section's material is not very difficult, and it is important for understanding the concept behind computer simulations. If you have a good statistical background and understand probability distributions, you can jump ahead to the next section.

We start with a straightforward example. Let's assume you teach an introductory finance course at a local college and you just gave the class an exam. You have 28 students, and they earned the grades shown in Table 3–1.

To get a better understanding of the test results, we calculate some descriptive statistics. The first is the average, or mean, score on the exam. This statistic is simply the sum of the individual scores (x) divided by the number of students (N) taking the test. Using standard notation, this formula is expressed as

$$\mu = \frac{\sum x}{N} \qquad (3.1)$$

which results in an average test score of 76.07. (We use the Greek letter μ (pronounced "mu") to signify the mean.) Another useful statistic is the test scores' standard deviation, which tells us the scores' dispersion around the mean. A large standard deviation means the scores fall into a wide range around the mean, while a small standard deviation shows that the scores

TABLE 3-1

Student Grades

Grade	# Students
95	3
85	6
75	12
65	5
55	2

are bunched more tightly. The formula for a population's standard deviation is

$$\sigma = \sqrt{\frac{\sum (x - \mu)}{N}} \qquad (3.2)$$

and we use the symbol σ (Greek letter sigma) to denote it. The standard deviation of the students' grades is 10.47.

A comment on population statistics versus sample statistics might prevent confusion later. When we use an entire population to calculate statistics, we refer to those values as *population statistics*. In this example we used all the students' grades, so we are working with the entire population. If we used only 15 (or any number less than the full 28 grades) of the students' grades in our estimates of mean and standard deviation, we would need to use the sample mean and the sample standard deviation. Equation 3.3 gives the formula for sample mean (denoted by $\bar{x}$), and Equation 3.4 shows how to calculate the sample standard deviation (s).

$$\bar{x} = \frac{\sum x}{n} \qquad (3.3)$$

$$s = \sqrt{\frac{\sum (x - \bar{x})^2}{n - 1}} \qquad (3.4)$$

Another useful technique for examining data is to plot them in a *frequency histogram*, which is a diagram that groups the data by frequency. The data in Table 3–1 are arranged in the proper format so we can create the histogram in Figure 3–1 easily.

You can also view this data in terms of percentages: What percentage of students scored between 60 and 90, for example? To convert the frequency distribution into percentages for a probability distribution,

FIGURE 3-1

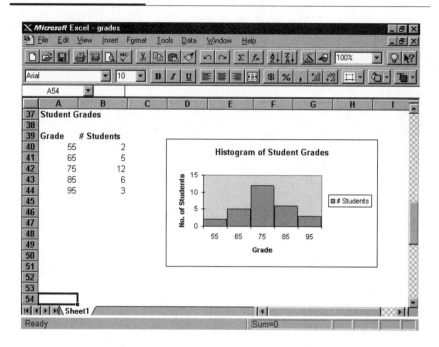

divide the number of students in each group into the total number of students. Since 28 students are in the class, we divide 3 (scores of 95) into 28, 6 (scores of 85) into 28, and so on. We then plot the results again, but this time we use probability percentages for the vertical axis instead of the raw number in Figure 3-2.

Figure 3-2 shows the number of grades in each interval as a percentage of the total class size. It also lets you estimate the probability that a student's grade selected at random will fall within a given interval. For example, 18 percent of the grades are in the 65 (grade) category, and 43 percent are in the 75 (grade) category. Consequently, the probability that a randomly drawn grade will be in either the 65 or 75 category is 61 percent. If you combine the 80–90 and 90–100 intervals, the probability that a randomly selected grade will fall in that range is 32 percent (.21 + 11). We can also view the data in a cumulative fashion by adding the relative frequencies as shown in Figure 3-3.

The format of Figure 3-3 adds the relative frequencies and lets us determine the probability that a result will be less than a specified value. For example, the probability that a score will be less than 95 is 89 percent. (If you check the original data, you will see that only 11 percent of the

FIGURE 3-2

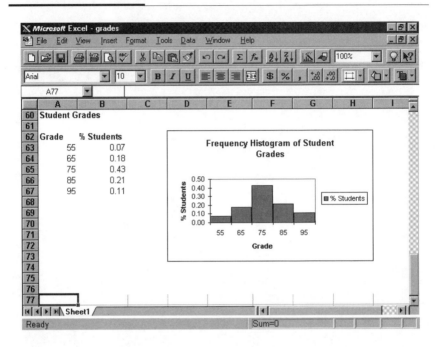

FIGURE 3-3

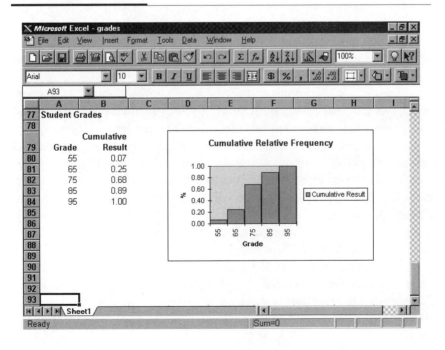

scores were in the 95 category, so this result makes sense.) Continuing to the right across the graph, we see that the probability that a randomly drawn score will be 75 or less is 68 percent. (Once again you can verify this result from the data by adding the relative frequencies for the first three categories: .07 (55) + .18 (65) + .43 (75) = .68.)

This carefully manufactured example introduces the main point of this section. We can use diagrams like Figures 3–2 and 3–3 to study events in the real world. When we do so, we find that different events produce very different distribution graphs. Some distributions are symmetrical, like the students' grades. Others are much flatter or have peaks at one end. Statisticians have identified dozens of distributions, some of which occur frequently and others that are fairly rare. The distribution that most of us recognize immediately is the normal distribution, characterized by the bell-curve graph. Figure 3–4 graphs a normal distribution with a mean value of 0.00 and a standard deviation of 1.00.

Another well-known example is the uniform distribution. In this distribution we know the minimum and maximum values (the endpoints) that the distribution can take. Every value between the endpoints has an equally likely chance of occurring. Figure 3–5 uses the endpoints for the inflation example developed earlier to illustrate a uniform distribution.

F I G U R E   3–4

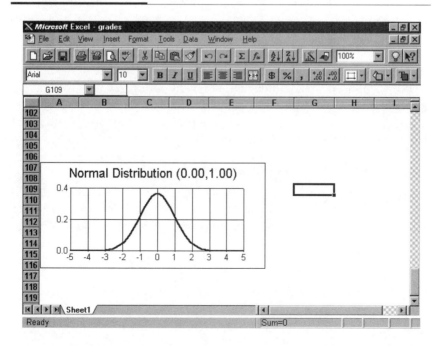

FIGURE 3–5

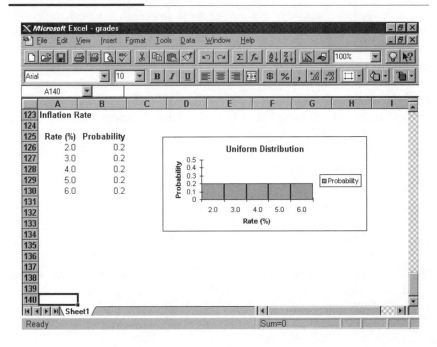

We can now discuss the reason why probability distributions are important to our work with simulations. When we design a simulation model, we need to know the random variables' underlying distributions because each distribution has unique properties. For example, in a standard normal distribution we know that roughly 68 percent of the curve's area lies within ±1 standard deviation. Ninety-five percent of the curve's area falls within 2 standard deviations. That means if we run enough iterations drawing sample values from a normal distribution, the simulated values should have that dispersion pattern around the mean.

Other distributions have their own unique dispersion patterns based on their means and variances. In the inflation example, we assumed each inflation rate had the same probability of occurring as the other rates in the 2.0 percent to 6.0 percent range. Equation 3.5 gives the equation for the uniform distribution's mean and Equation 3.6 shows its standard deviation formula.

$$\bar{x} = (\text{min} + \text{max}) \div 2 \qquad (3.5)$$

$$s = \sqrt{\frac{(\text{min} - \text{max})^2}{12}} \qquad (3.6)$$

In contrast to the normal distribution, we don't expect the uniform distribution's data points to cluster around the mean. As the name suggests, they are uniformly distributed between the minimum and maximum values. If we mistakenly use a normal distribution to characterize data that are from a uniform distribution, our simulation results will reflect the normal distribution's inputs.

To clarify this point, look at the students' grades in Table 3–1 again. By design, these grades have a normal distribution. If they were uniformly distributed, the results would look something like the grades in Table 3–2.

Although we don't calculate the statistics, you can see how the frequency distribution would be much flatter for these grades than for the original set. Also, if you had to estimate cumulative frequencies, the probabilities of the student earning the various grades would also be different. The point is that even if two data sets have the same mean value, they might come from very different underlying distributions. If you use the wrong distribution in your simulation, the dispersion in the simulated results will differ from the true dispersion. Having said that, how do you identify the data's underlying distribution? Identifying distributions is very challenging, but fortunately you don't need a Ph.D. in statistics to do it. Now you can have your PC examine the data, as we see in the next section.

DISTRIBUTION FITTING SOFTWARE: BESTFIT

Even a statistician can find it difficult to "fit" a distribution to a data set. For those of us with limited backgrounds in statistics, it could be a very frustrating effort with no guarantee of success. BestFit, a program from Palisade Corporation, automates the distribution-fitting process. The program compares your data with 37 known distributions to find the distribution that best fits your data. BestFit cannot guarantee that it will fit your

TABLE 3–2

Student Grades (Uniform Distribution)

Grade	# Students
95	6
85	6
75	5
65	6
55	5

data, but it can tell you how closely your data match a known distribution. This information is valuable because you need to tell the simulation program what distribution it should use for your models.

We describe the technical details of the distribution-fitting process in the appendix, but a basic understanding of the concept behind the method is useful. We mentioned earlier that distributions have unique properties. BestFit takes your data and determines how closely it matches the properties of these known distribution by using several tests that generate "goodness of fit" statistics. You probably will not find a perfect match, so the program uses several tests and provides relative rankings of the results. The following example demonstrates how the program works.

Example: Fitting a Distribution

You have a set of 100 sample data points that range in value from –1.994 to +3.999 and you want to identify the underlying distribution. You enter the data into BestFit and generate the histogram in Figure 3–6 and summary statistics in Table 3–3.

Looking at the histogram in Figure 3–6, we get the impression the data have a roughly normal distribution, but that is only an intuitive esti-

FIGURE 3–6

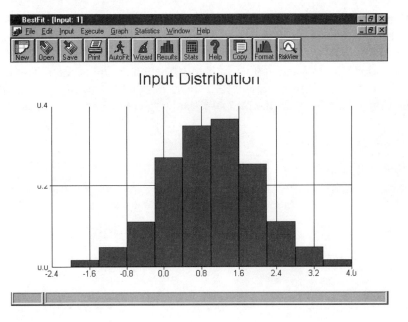

TABLE 3-3

Summary Statistics

Input Distribution	
Minimum	−1.99373
Maximum	3.998875
Mean	0.997206
Mode	1.302203
Median	0.980374
Standard deviation	1.024781
Variance	1.050176
Skewness	−0.023288
Kurtosis	3.219024

mate. We still need to know the underlying distribution for the data, and we run the data through the program. To identify the distribution, BestFit applies three goodness-of-fit tests to the data: chi-square, Kolmogorov-Smirnov, and Anderson-Darling. The results from the data's comparison with each known distribution are ranked, with lower scores indicating a better fit. Table 3–4 shows the numerical results from our sample data.

Don't let the amount of information in the table throw you—we need to focus on only the key findings to interpret the numbers. Table 3–4 shows the results of BestFit's evaluation of the sample data. It compared the distribution of the data to the distributions listed in the first row: normal, logistic, Weibull, and so on. (We list only the three best-fitting distributions here, although the program evaluated 37 of them.) With each comparison, the program calculates the three goodness-of-fit measures. Each test measures the data's goodness-of-fit slightly differently, and they can produce different ranks for different probability functions when comparing the same data. As you can see in Table 3–4, all three tests ranked the normal distribution as the best fit, followed by the logistic distribution. Based on our visual inspection of the histogram and the numerical analysis, our sample data appears to come from a normal distribution with the parameters (mean = 1.00, standard deviation = 1.02).

BestFit ranks the distribution with the lowest chi-square measure as the best-fitting distribution by default. However, you should always accept that ranking without question: You must avoid the "black box" mentality and use your judgment to evaluate the program's results. To do

TABLE 3-4

Sample Data Results

	Input Distribution	Normal	Logistic	Weibull
Parameter 1		0.997	0.997	3.290
Parameter 2		1.025	0.561	3.449
Parameter 3				
Formula		N(1.00,1.02)	Logistic(1.00,0.56)	W(3.29,3.45,1,−2.11)
Minimum	−1.994			
Maximum	3.999			
Mean	0.997	0.997	0.997	0.983
Mode	1.302	0.997	0.997	0.979
Median	0.980	0.997	0.997	0.975
Standard deviation	1.025	1.025	1.018	1.035
Variance	1.050	1.050	1.036	1.071
Skewness	−0.023	0.000	0.000	0.067
Kurtosis	3.219	3.000	4.200	2.625
Results				
Chi-square				
Test value		0.565	1.243	1.757
Confidence		>0.99	>0.99	>0.99
Rank		1.000	2.000	3.000
Kolmogorov-Smirnov				
Test value		0.016	0.029	0.032
Confidence		>0.15	>0.15	>0.1
Rank		1.000	2.000	4.000
Anderson-Darling				
Test value		0.042	0.111	0.189
Confidence		>0.15	>0.15	>0.25
Rank		1.000	2.000	3.000

so, you can use the program's other statistics and graphics to get a better insight into the analysis. Figure 3–7 shows the results of fitting the normal and uniform distributions to the sample data. In this case the uniform distribution is a poor match. You can do this type of side-by-side comparison of the graphs if the analytical results are mixed.

You'll notice that the normal distribution's graph in Figure 3–7 is not a perfect fit, and this result reinforces the program manual's warning: "BestFit does not produce absolute answers; it just identifies the distribu-

FIGURE 3—7

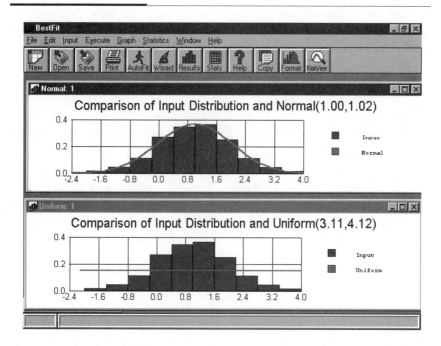

tion that is most likely to have produced your data. . . .You should keep in mind that the results of a best fit calculation are only a 'best estimate,' as it is nearly impossible to find a distribution that exactly fits your data."[1] Although the program provides only an estimate of the underlying distribution, it is still a much more accurate estimate than intuition would provide. In the next section we show how to use this information about the distribution's type and parameters in a simulation.

SIMULATION SOFTWARE: @RISK

You probably use financial simulations in your work now, although you might not think of the work that way. For example, when you develop financial projections for clients, you estimate a future date's financial status. Perhaps you didn't run a formal simulation, but the underlying concept is the same. You developed a model, projected results from the random possible outcomes, and used the results in your analysis. You might

1. *BestFit User's Guide* (Newfield, NY: Palisade Corporation, 1995), pp. 2–3.

have taken it one step further to try a what-if analysis. What if sales increase by only 5 percent, not the projected 12 percent? What if my investment portfolio earns 22 percent instead of 12 percent? These what-if projections are simulations, although they exist only on paper or in your PC and not in a physical sense.

Just like their physical counterparts, financial simulations give users a powerful analytical tool: an inexpensive, risk-free method to examine uncertain outcomes. Even if you do not discuss the simulation's full results with your clients, you can improve the analyses you perform for them. This additional analysis increases the quality of your work and your confidence in your analytical results.

Several methods are available for running simulations on a PC. The first is to write a simulation program in a language such as C. This approach gives the user complete control over the program, but it requires extensive knowledge of a programming language and numerical analysis. Another approach is to use a spreadsheet's built-in capabilities for generating random numbers. This method is fairly easy to implement, and we describe it more fully in Chapter 8, which reviews spreadsheet tools.

For most readers, however, we believe the easiest and most effective way to build and run simulations is by using spreadsheet add-in programs. These programs, such as @RISK from Palisade Corporation, link the simulation's numerical and graphical output, which saves considerable time for the user. The examples in this chapter were developed using @RISK.

Example: Future Value Projections

We begin the simulation demonstration with a straightforward future value problem. Your client owns a building that is worth $300,000, and he wants to project its value one year from now. What do you tell him? Let's assume that local real estate market experts forecast an average appreciation rate of 7 percent for the coming year. If we use that rate as our point estimate, the projected future value is $321,000 ($300,000 × 1.07). A better alternative might be the best-, most likely, worst-case approach, so we can give the client a range of values. We'll use +15 percent for our best-case number, –2 percent for our worst case, and 7 percent for our most likely case, which gives us a wide range of possible results: a $345,000 maximum to a $294,000 minimum. Let's assume the client can live with the range estimate, but he wants to know the likelihood that he will earn less than 4 percent. Now the computations start to get awkward, and you begin to wonder if there isn't an easier way to generate these estimates.

We begin by creating a simple future value model in our spreadsheet.

	A	B
1	Future Value Projection	
2		
3	Current Value	$300,000
4		
5	Growth Factor	7%
6		
7	Projected Future Value	$321,000

Nothing fancy happens here—we enter the portfolio's current value in cell B3, the estimated growth rate in cell B5, and the Excel formula in cell B7 is =B3*(1+B5). If we want to change the growth projection, we change the number in cell B5. To develop multiple scenarios, we would create more Projected Future Value cells with each using a different growth rate.

We now use @RISK to build and run a simulation in the spreadsheet. The first step is to identify the variable cells. In this example we have just one—the property's projected growth factor in cell B5. Next we use the @RISK functions to express the uncertainty in the variable. For some variables, such as the earlier BestFit example, we have data available for analysis. In other cases, such as this one, we do not have historical data. Instead, we must rely on the decision maker's or our own judgment. We will use the earlier estimates for the projected return of 15 percent best case, 7 percent most likely, and –2 percent worst case.

We take that estimate of the variable's uncertainty and modify our spreadsheet's B5 cell value to read "=RiskTriang(–.02, .07, .15)" as shown in the Future Value Projection spreadsheet.

	A	B
1	Future Value Projection	
2		
3	Current Value	300000
4		
5	Growth Factor	=RiskTriang(–0.02,0.07,0.15)
6		
7	Projected Future Value	=B3*(1+B5)

Cell B5 now contains an @RISK formula that tells the spreadsheet that @RISK will use this cell as the random variable in its simulations. The formula identifies the uncertain variable as coming from a triangular distribution, which is a useful way to characterize a best-, most likely, or worst-case scenario. Figure 3–8 shows a graph of the triangular distribution using these parameters.

Next we instruct the program to start the simulation. As it runs each iteration, @RISK draws a sample from a triangular distribution with the (–.02, .07, .15) parameters. It then uses the value it has drawn to recalculate the B7 cell's value. Because it takes a new sample from the distribution with each iteration, the B7 cell's value probably will change each time. To see the simulation in action, we run just one iteration here. Notice how the B5 cell's value changes from 7.0 percent to –1.0 percent, which in turn produces a value of $297,000 in cell B7.

	A	B
1	**Projected Future Value**	
2		
3	Current Value	$300,000
4		
5	Growth Rate	–0.01
6		
7	Projected Future Value	297000

In this first iteration, the property's value grew by significantly less than the most likely estimate of 7 percent. It is an unpleasant result, but certainly not an impossibility. One iteration does not tell us much, though, and from a statistical analysis viewpoint, it is not very useful. To gain insight into the range of possible outcomes, we need multiple iterations. Because this problem is small, we tell @RISK to run 1,000 iterations. After completing the simulation, the program generates statistical and graphical output. We examine the statistics in Table 3–5 first. (Because they are not critical to this analysis, variance, skewness, and kurtosis are reviewed in the appendix.)

The second column, Projected Future Value, lists the key statistics for the simulation's output in cell B7. You can see the range and dispersion that the simulated values took. The information is repeated for the variable cell (B3) in the third column. Figure 3–9 presents the simulation results for cell B7 in a histogram.

FIGURE 3–8

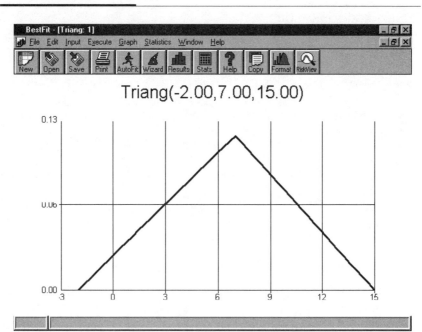

The simulated results' distribution in Figure 3–9 looks good—it has the expected shape for a triangular distribution. You should not read too much into that result, though; it only means that @RISK performed as expected in running the simulations. It does not validate our earlier decision to use a triangular distribution for the growth rate.

The distribution graph and statistics give us a description of the simulation's results. That is useful information, but it has limited value. What if the client wants to know the probability that the property could increase in value by less than 5 percent or by more than 10 percent over the next year? To answer these questions, we use another statistical analysis that is part of @RISK's tool kit: the cumulative probability curve, shown in Figure 3–10.

The key to reading the graph in Figure 3–10 is the vertical axis legend, Prob of Value <= x-axis value. This translates to "How likely is it that the realized value will be less than the value on the x-axis?" As an example, your client wants to know the probability that the value will grow by less than 7 percent. In dollar terms, that works out to a year-end value of $321,000. To answer this question, we estimate the location of $321,000 on

TABLE 3–5

Simulation Results

Name	Projected Future Value	Growth Rate
Description	Output	Triang(–0.02, 0.07, 0.15)
Cell	B7	B5
Minimum	294731.70	–0.0176
Maximum	344240.30	0.1475
Mean	320000.10	0.0667
Standard deviation	10416.30	0.0347
Variance	108499300.00	0.0012
Skewness	–0.0576	–0.0576
Kurtosis	2.4001	2.4001
Errors calculated	0	0
Mode	322191.20	0.0740

the x-axis. With this graph's scale we cannot pinpoint 321 exactly, so we use a point just to the right of 319.50. (The program also gives exact numerical values, as you will see shortly.) We move up the chart until we reach the curve and then read the corresponding value from the left axis, where it looks like .50 is a reasonable estimate. In other words, there is a roughly 50 percent chance the return will be less than 7 percent. At the far right side of the x-axis we see the probabilities approaching 1.0, or certainty. What is the probability the future value will be less than $344,200 (344.20)? Using the same procedure as above, it looks like a 100 percent probability.

Estimating probabilities from the graph is imprecise, but the program gives you an alternative. You input your target numbers into the Target Value boxes, and the program returns exact values based on your cumulative probability curve. We enter the values $300,000, $321,000, and $340,000, as shown in Figure 3–11

The results in Figure 3–11 indicate a 2.70 percent probability that the future value will be less than $300,000, a 53.02 percent probability of a result less than $321,000, and a 97.97 percent probability that the result will be less than $340,000.

You can enter up to 10 target values, which should allow you to answer most client queries about possible outcomes and ranges of outcomes. Of course, the simulation process does not guarantee the predictive power of these numbers. We based the simulation on the assumption that the triangular distribution was appropriate, and if that assumption is wrong, you cannot depend on the results. Let's assume that the triangular

FIGURE 3-9

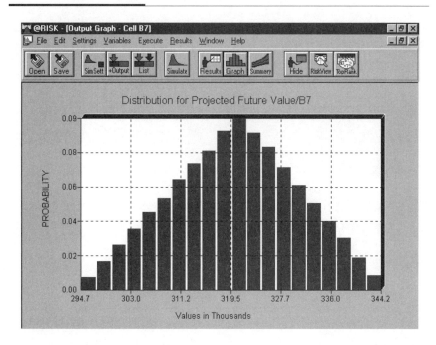

FIGURE 3-10

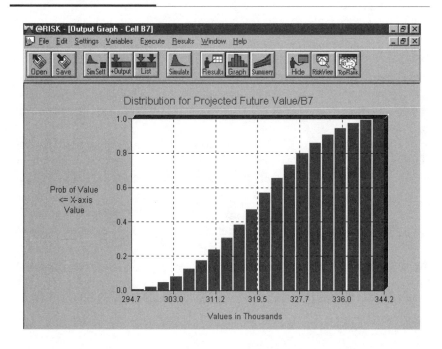

FIGURE 3–11

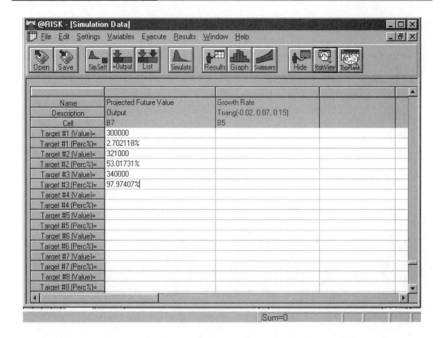

distribution is acceptable so we can examine the simulation's benefits versus point estimates and multiple scenarios. With a point estimate, you know your forecast will be wrong—it's just a question of degree and direction. To minimize your exposure from client disappointment, you might lower your estimates of desired results and increase estimates of undesired outcomes. With multiple scenarios, you hope to bracket the actual outcome, but you cannot quantify and communicate the uncertainty in the results very easily.

Simulation solves these problems. It gives you a tool for understanding the uncertainty in a forecast, and it helps you explain that uncertainty to clients. You can easily demonstrate to your clients that a forecast is only an informed estimate, and you can show them a graphical display of that uncertainty. Of course, you would tailor the presentation to the client's ability to grasp the material, especially for clients who do not understand statistics. Even for these clients, though, you can summarize the simulation's results in an acceptable manner. Also, by keeping the analytical results in the client's file, you have documentation that you reviewed the uncertainty of the scenarios you had discussed.

The illustrative example we developed in this section was straightforward, with one variable and a one-year time frame. There are obviously much wider potential applications of the simulation technology to finance and personal financial planning. You can model any variable that has an uncertain outcome: inflation and interest rates, investment results, and life expectancy are obvious examples. As the model builder, your creativity in developing client analyses imposes the only limit. If you plan to use a particular model frequently, you can build and save it as a template that you can retrieve for future use. That step will save you from recreating the analysis for each new client application.

Simulation offers financial advisors a powerful analytical tool, but it has not gained widespread acceptance apart from investment management and business consulting applications. Business consultants use simulation frequently, and the next section provides an example of the technique being used in this setting.

Example: Launching a New Product

Your client owns a manufacturing company and is thinking of developing a new product. He estimates that design costs would run about $50,000. If the design is feasible, capital investment in new equipment next year would be roughly $200,000. There is a catch, though—the client suspects that a competitor might launch a very similar product. If that happens, your client must lower his product's price to stay competitive. Also, he probably would sell fewer units of the product because the competitor's presence would reduce his sales.

You recognize that the uncertainty in the projections is ideally suited for a simulation analysis. Working with the client, you develop the worksheets in Figures 3–12 and 3–13 using @RISK.

Figures 3–12 and 3–13 show the analysis worksheet in standard Excel format (Figure 3–12) and with the underlying @RISK formulas displayed for the first three years (Figure 3–13). The worksheet is a standard net present value analysis to help your client decide whether to launch the new product, given the uncertainty of the competitor's actions. Let's work through the key elements of the model.

The first part of the worksheet, rows 7 to 10, lists the estimated price and sales volume for the product under the competitor's entry/no entry scenarios. Without entry, your client will set his sales price at $69.25 per unit as listed in cell E7, and he plans to increase that price by 5 percent each year. If the competitor enters, your client must wait and see the competitor's price

FIGURE 3-12

	A	B	C	D	E	F	G	H	I	J	K	L
1		Product Launch Risk Analysis										
2												
3												
4												
5			Year 1	Year 2	Year 3	Year 4	Year 5	Year 6	Year 7	Year 8	Year 9	Year 10
6			======	======	======	======	======	======	======	======	======	======
7		Price No Entry			69	87	118	111	98	93	91	89
8		Price With Entry			53	68	80	64	61	56	55	52
9		Volume No Entry			3500	4340	6580	5565	5180	5180	4970	4935
10		Volume With Entry			3300	4158	3564	3399	3300	3300	3432	3696
11		Competitor Entry:	0									
12												
13		Design Costs	50000									
14		Capital Investment		200000								
15		Operating Expense Factor										
16												
17		Sales Price			69	87	118	111	98	93	91	89
18		Sales Volume			3500	4340	6580	5565	5180	5180	4970	4935
19		Sales Revenue			242358	378659	774575	620411	509339	484230	450833	440824
20		Unit Production Cost			23	24	25	26	27	28	30	31
21		Overhead			5600	6944	10528	8904	8288	8288	7952	7896
22		Cost of Goods Sold			87267	112261	176590	154968	149685	155341	154687	159426
23		Gross Margin			155091	266398	597985	465443	359654	328890	296147	281399
24		Operating Expense			12799	16465	25900	22729	21954	22784	22688	23383
25		Net Before Tax	-50000	0	142292	249933	572085	442715	337700	306106	273459	258016
26		Depreciation		40000	40000	40000	40000	40000				
27		Tax	-23000	-18400	47054	96569	244759	185249	155342	140809	125791	118687
28		Taxes Owed	0	0	5654	96569	244759	185249	155342	140809	125791	118687
29		Net After Tax	-50000	0	136637	153364	327326	257466	182358	165297	147668	139329
30			======	======	======	======	======	======	======	======	======	======
31		Net Cash Flow	-50000	-200000	136637	153364	327326	257466	182358	165297	147668	139329
32		NPV 10%	632273									
33												
34												

FIGURE 3-13

	B	C	D	E
1	**Product Launch Risk Analysis**			
5		Year 1	Year 2	Year 3
7	Price No Entry			=RiskHistogrm(50,90,{10.2,30,40,20,10})
8	Price With Entry			=RiskTriang(30,50,80)
9	Volume No Entry			=RiskNormal(3500,300)
10	Volume With Entry			=3300
11	Competitor Entry:	=RiskDiscrete({0,1},{50,50})		
13	Design Costs	=RiskNormal(50000,10000)		
14	Capital Investment		=RiskNormal(200000,30000)	
15	Operating Expense Factor			=RiskTexpon(1,0.05,0.25)
17	Sales Price			=IF($C$11=0,E7,E8)
18	Sales Volume			=IF($C$11=0,E9,E10)
19	Sales Revenue			=E17*E18
20	Unit Production Cost			=RiskTriang(10,20,40)
21	Overhead			=(0.6*E18)+RiskUniform(0.8*E18,1.2*E18)
22	Cost of Goods Sold			=(E18*E20)+E21
23	Gross Margin			=E19-E22
24	Operating Expense			=E22*E15
25	Net Before Tax	=(C23-C24-C13)	=(D23-D24-D13)	=(E23-E24-E13)
26	Depreciation		=SLN($D$14,0,1,5)	=SLN($D$14,0,1,5)
27	Tax	=0.46*(C25-C26)	=0.46*(D25-D26)	=0.46*(E25-E26)
28	Taxes Owed	=MAX(0,C27)	=MAX(0,SUM($C$27:D27)-C28)	=MAX(0,SUM($C$27:E27)-SUM($C$28:D28))
29	Net After Tax	=(C25-C28)	=(D25-D28)	=(E25-E28)
31	Net Cash Flow	=(C29-C14)	=(D29-D14)	=(E29-E14)
32	NPV 10%	=NPV(0.1,C31:M31)		

and quality before setting his own price. With competition, he estimates setting a worst-case price of $50, a best-case price of $70, and a most likely
price of $60. To model that estimate, you use the triangular distribution
found in cell E8. If he has the only product on the market, your client
believes the demand in Year 3 will be about 3,500 units. Because that is an
estimate, you model it as a normal distribution with a standard deviation of
300 units in cell E9. Finally, if the competitor comes in, your client's volume will be lower, with a flat estimate of 3,300 units in Year 3 (cell E10).

Cell C11 models the risk of the competitor entering the market. We
can think of that risk in terms of a coin toss. If it comes up heads, he
enters; if it is tails, he stays out. @RISK lets you model discrete outcomes
like these with its Discrete distribution. This distribution has the form,
Discrete($\{x_1, x_2, ... x_n\}, \{p_1, p_2, ... p_n\}$). The x values signify the possible
outcomes—in this case we use the values $\{0,1\}$. Zero means the competitor does not enter the market, while 1 means he does. Your client estimates
the odds of the competitor's entry at 50 percent, so we set the Discrete distribution's p values at $\{50,50\}$, as seen in cell C11. You will see shortly
how cell C11 influences other cells in the worksheet.

The client estimates first year design and capital equipment costs will
be $50,000 (standard deviation of $10,000) and $200,000 (standard devia-
tion of $30,000), respectively. You model these with the normal distribu-
tions in cells C13 and D14. Based on his manufacturing experience, your
client believes his operating expense factor will range from 14 percent to 16
percent. Any outcome between these two values is equally likely, so you
model this uncertainty as a uniform distribution in cell E15. The worksheet
uses this value for the Operating Expenses calculation in row 24.

We begin to see the analytical potential of using spreadsheet simulations in rows 17 to 29. Let's examine the unusual cell entries in column E
first, starting with cell E17. This cell entry looks more like computer programming code than a typical spreadsheet cell: =IF($C$11=0,E7,E8).
This cell has a variable value, although it is not an @RISK distribution
cell. You can read IF cells like this: If the condition is true ($C$11=0),
take the value from the first statement (E7) in the list. If the condition
($C$11=0) is false, go to the second item in the list (cell E8). In this
instance, when the spreadsheet program goes to assign a value to this cell,
it looks at cell C11 first. If C11 has a 0 value, then the competitor did not
enter the business. Based on this 0 value, cell E17 takes the value of cell
E7 ($69.25), which is the Year 3 price of your client's product when the
competitor stays out. If cell C11 has a value of 1, the competitor has
entered the business. The spreadsheet then gives cell E17 the value from
the @RISK distribution in cell E8.

The Year 3 Overhead entry in cell E21 demonstrates the use of an @RISK variable as part of a cell's formula. This cell multiplies the value in cell E18 by 0.6 to calculate an overhead expense based on the number of units sold. It then adds a variable charge based on that same volume and totals the two values.

Cells D26 and E26 include the standard Excel formula for straight-line depreciation. In this case your client uses five-year depreciation on his $200,000 capital investment in cell D14. Although this variable is uncertain, its value does not change as the spreadsheet moves from year to year in each iteration. It will change from one iteration to the next, though.

Cells C28, D28, and E28 are decision cells. The spreadsheet compares two values, selects the greater of the two, and places that number in the cell. In this instance we use it to calculate taxes owed in the current year versus any carry-forwards available. If the taxes are greater than the carry-forwards, the program calculates Taxes Owed.

You can lose sight of the spreadsheet's original purpose when you focus on the model's details. For the purpose of evaluating this investment, though, cell C32 is the final and most important calculation in the worksheet. Here we calculate each iteration's net present value (NPV) from cells C31 to L31 using a 10 percent discount rate. As in traditional analysis, a positive NPV signals an acceptable project.

You want the client to focus on two of the simulation's results. The first is the NPV value in cell C32. This cell provides the "bottom line" summary on the project's acceptability, based on the spreadsheet's assumptions. The second set of results you should examine is the annual net cash flows in cells C31 to L31. Those cell values generate the NPV result, and they can give you further insight into the project's possible outcomes. Figures 3–14 and 3–15 show the @RISK graphs for the NPV cell (C32).

Even after 1,000 iterations, we do not get a smooth distribution, in contrast to our earlier simulations. This result isn't too surprising when you consider the large number of variable cells in the worksheet. The cumulative distribution does give us good news, though—the probaility the project will lose money is only 3 percent.

@RISK also produces useful information about the annual net cash flow cells (C31 to L31). You can graph the results in those cells in a time-line fashion to visualize how the uncertainty behaves over time, as shown in Figure 3–16.

Figure 3–16 gives us several pieces of information. First, the project should become profitable beginning in the third year. Second, those profits range from a projected minimum of roughly $45,000 to a maximum of

FIGURE 3-14

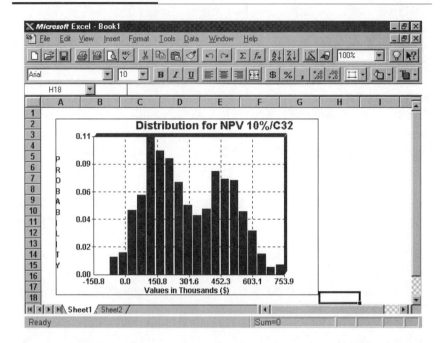

FIGURE 3-15

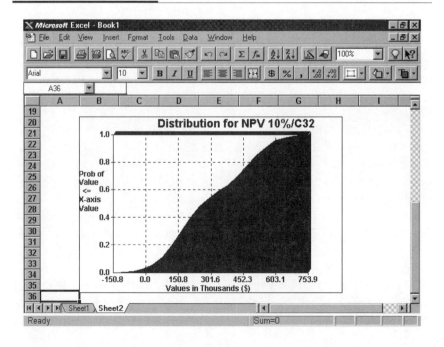

FIGURE 3-16

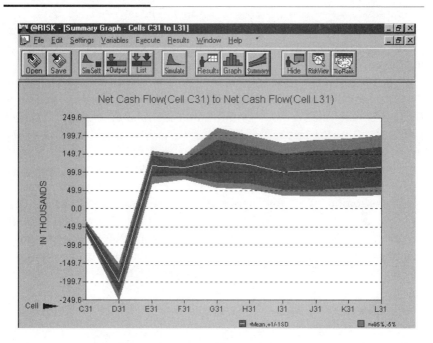

just under $200,000 without much change in the size of that range. The conclusion: Based on the simulation's assumptions, it looks like a good idea to launch the new project.

Example: Simulating Stock Prices

The examples we have shown so far used the @RISK formulas as stand-alone cells. But you can also use them as part of cell formulas to model the uncertainty in the formula. For example, financial analysts frequently use the following formula to model changes in stock prices:

$$P_0 \times \exp\left[(\mu - .5\sigma^2)t + \sigma Z \sqrt{t}\right] \qquad (3.7)$$

where

P_t = Future stock price at time t (unknown now).
P_0 = Stock's price now.
μ = Expected annual growth of stock's price.
σ = Standard deviation of stock's annual growth.
t = Future date (expressed in years).
Z = Random variable with a standard normal distribution (mean = 0, standard deviation = 1).

We can calculate reasonable values from historical data for most of the variables, so we can set those in advance. The only one we can't set is the Z value, which introduces the uncertainty or randomness into the formula. The @RISK spreadsheet in Figure 3–17 will clarify the impact of the random variable, Z.

In Figure 3–17, cells B3, B4, and B5 hold the inputs for P_0, μ, and σ, respectively. These values will not change during the simulation. Cells B9:B13 contain the formula for P_t *without* the random element. In other words, $Z = 0$, so the last part of Equation 3.7 drops out. Table 3–6 lists the formulas for cells B9 and B10 to demonstrate the formula.

In cells C9:C13, the model includes the random variable Z, as shown in the range of results for those cells. (These cell values resulted from one @RISK iteration.) Table 3–7 shows the formulas for cells C9 and C10.

As you see from the results in cells C9:C13 in Figure 3.17, including the random variable Z changes the results dramatically. It also allows you to use @RISK's analytical statistics and graphics to illustrate the simulated one-year portfolio's results, as shown in Figure 3–18.

FIGURE 3–17

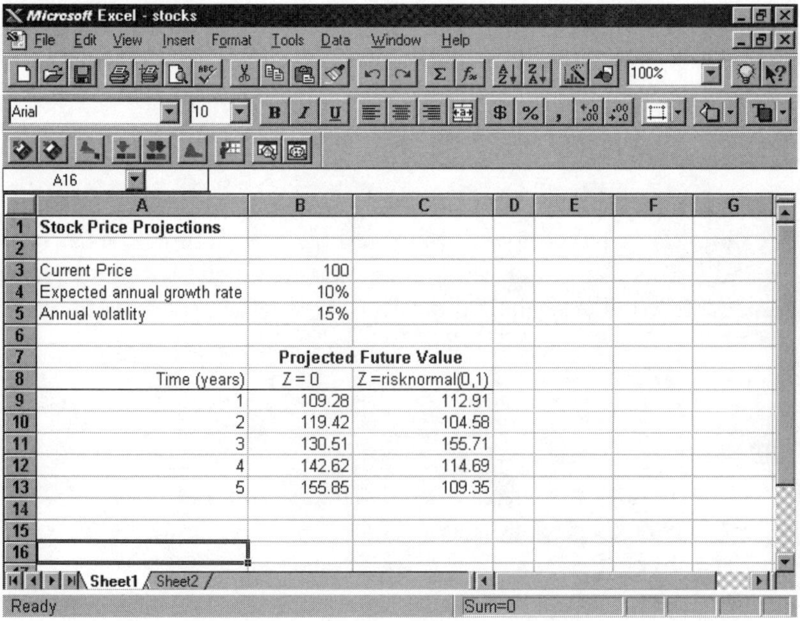

TABLE 3-6

Cell Formulas

Cell	Formula
B9	=$B$3 * EXP(($B$4 − 0.5 * $B$5^2) * $A9)
B10	=$B$3 * EXP(($B$4 − 0.5 * $B$5^2) * $A10)

TABLE 3-7

Cell Formulas

Cell	Formula
C9	=$B$3 * EXP(($B$4 − 0.5 * $B$5^2) * $A9 + $B$5 * RiskNormal(0,1) * SQRT($A9))
C10	=$B$3 * EXP(($B$4 − 0.5 * $B$5^2) * $A10 + $B$5 * RiskNormal(0,1) * SQRT($A10))

FIGURE 3-18

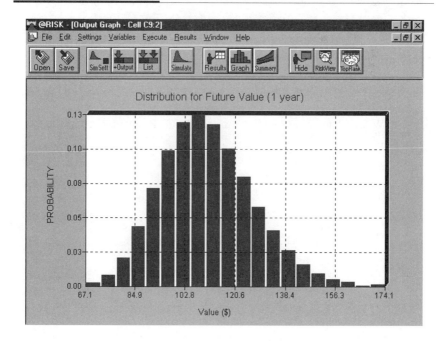

As we mentioned earlier, the simulation's results are a powerful communication tool. Even clients who do not understand statistics can grasp the wide range of potential future stock values by examining the graph.

Basic models like this one can also serve as the foundation for more complex analyses. Prices for derivative securities such as options and futures are based on the value of some underlying asset or index. By modeling the uncertainty in the asset's price, you can study the variability in the derivative's price as well.

You can use simulations to analyze a wide variety of problems. If you can design a reliable model and quantify the uncertain variables, you have a candidate for simulation. It is important to realize, though, that models and simulations are tools to aid decision makers—they are not black box solutions to every problem. You need to use your skills in designing and interpreting the simulation because judgment is still your best decision-making tool.

SOURCES AND SUGGESTED READING

@RISK User's Guide. Newfield, NY: Palisade Corporation, 1996.

BestFit User's Guide. Newfield, NY: Palisade Corporation, 1996.

Clemen, R. T. *Making Hard Decisions: An Introduction to Decision Analysis.* Belmont, CA: Duxbury Press, 1991.

Ragsdale, C. T. *Spreadsheet Modeling and Decision Analysis: A Practical Introduction to Management Science.* Cambridge, MA: Course Technology, Inc., 1995.

Winston, W. L. *Simulation Modeling Using @RISK.* Belmont, CA: Duxbury Press, 1996.

SOFTWARE RESOURCES

BestFit 2.0 and **@RISK 3.5**
Palisade Corporation
31 Decker Road
Newfield, NY 14867-9987
Tel. 800-432-7475 or 607-277-8000
Fax 607-277-8001
E-mail: sales@palisade.com
Web: http://www.palisade.com
Suggested retail prices*
BestFit 2.0: $299
@RISK 3.5: $305

* Call for information on upgrade, site license, and academic pricing.

Microsoft Excel
Microsoft Corporation
One Microsoft Way
Redmond, WA 98052-6399

CHAPTER 4

Fuzzy Numbers

INTRODUCTION

Given a choice between certainty and uncertainty, most people would rather avoid the unknown. We dislike unpleasant surprises—we prefer order and we like neat solutions to our problems. Unfortunately, reality rarely cooperates and uncertainty remains a fact of life. When we must make decisions, accounting for that uncertainty can be difficult. As we discussed in earlier chapters, methods are available for recognizing that uncertainty: decision trees, multiple scenarios, and so on. In this chapter we explore another method: the use of fuzzy numbers. *Fuzzy numbers* are uncertain numbers that represent a range of possible values. They differ from the usual "crisp" or nonfuzzy numbers that represent single values. A fuzzy number is more than just a range, though. As we show shortly, each possible value in the fuzzy number's range has a possibility level or belief attached to it that tells you how possible each value in the range is.

The software we use to examine fuzzy numbers in this chapter is FuziCalc, which is produced by FuziWare, Inc. According to the *FuziCalc User's Guide* (version 1.51j): "Fuzzy numbers are unclear or imprecise because they represent things that are not well known; projections, forecasts, and estimates all contain fuzzy numbers. The numbers may be fuzzy because the events they represent haven't happened yet or they have happened but are hard to measure or quantify."[1]

---

1. *FuziCalc User's Guide,* version 1.5 (Knoxville, TN: FuziWare, Inc., 1994), p. 10.

Fuzzy numbers are based on the fuzzy set theory developed by Dr. Lofti Zadeh at the University of California, Berkeley. Before examining the mathematical foundation of fuzzy numbers, we use an example from the FuziCalc tutorial to demonstrate an application of the technology.

FUZZY NUMBER SOFTWARE: FUZICALC

Example: Fuzzy Cost Projections

In this example we assume your client owns an advertising agency. He has asked for your help in developing cost projections for one of the agency's production jobs because he is frustrated with the inflexibility of traditional spreadsheets. Four cost centers are involved with the project: strategy, creative, design, and production. Each department submits an estimate of the time it will spend on the project, and your client uses these time estimates to figure the project's cost. The departments' hourly rates are fixed, but the time estimates frequently have been imprecise. You want to include that imprecision in the estimate so your client can work with a more reliable cost range instead of a single-point estimate. Using FuziCalc, you develop the spreadsheet model shown in Figure 4–1.

FIGURE 4–1

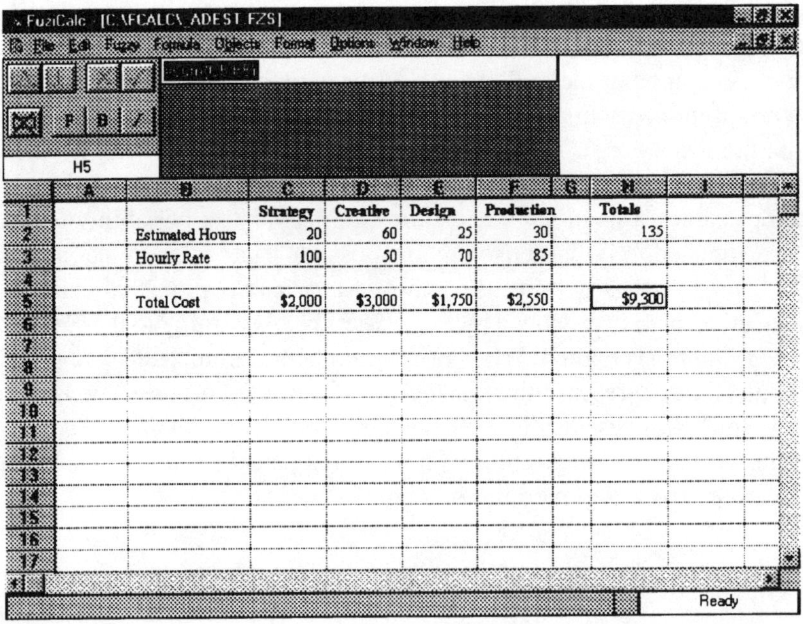

Figure 4–1 introduces the main FuziCalc screen. The program uses the traditional spreadsheet format of assigning numbers to rows and letters to columns for cell identification. FuziCalc is not an add-in to other spreadsheets, though—it is a stand-alone program. It provides many of the traditional spreadsheet functions as well as those used with fuzzy numbers. The palette in the upper-left corner of Figure 4–1 is a toolbar that allows point-and-click access to several of the fuzzy number operations.

The worksheet layout in Figure 4–1 is straightforward. Cells C2:F2 hold each department's initial estimate of the time required for the project, with the total hours calculated in cell H2 (=Sum(C2:F2)). The departments' hourly rates are stored in cells C3:F3, and cells C5:F5 hold the products of the estimated hours times the hourly rates: C5 = C2*C3, D5 = D2*D3, and so on. Cell H5 sums the cells in row 5: =Sum(C5:F5).

We now begin modifying the estimated hours in cells C2:F2 to reflect the estimates' uncertainty. To do this, we "fuzzify" the numbers by using FuziCalc's operations. We start by double-clicking on cell C2, the strategy department's time estimate. This brings up the dialogue box in Figure 4–2, Form a Fuzzy Number.

FuziCalc does three things when the user fuzzifies a number:

FIGURE 4-2

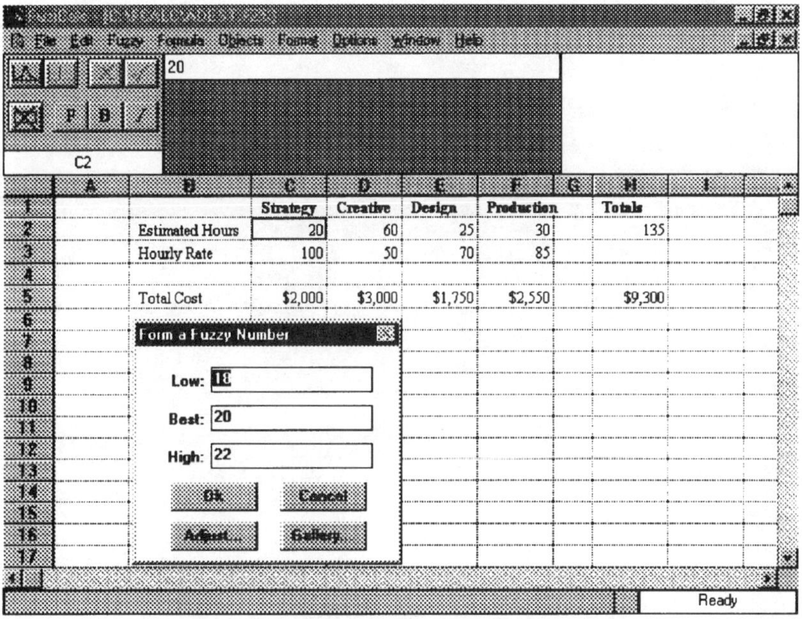

1. It takes the crisp value in the cell and turns it into the peak or most possible value in the fuzzy number. We see that here where the original crisp estimate of 20 is listed as the best value.

2. It subtracts 10 percent from the crisp value to produce the low value (Low = 18).

3. It adds 10 percent to the crisp value to produce the high value (High = 22).

The ±10 percent range is the default, but the user can modify this range. We do so by entering a value of 12 in the Low box and 30 in the High box (not shown here). These changes produce the screen in Figure 4–3.

Figure 4–3 introduces several changes to the worksheet. First, the change to cell C2 has caused the values for cells C2, C5, H2, and H5 to change. The small triangle on the left side of those cells indicates that they are now fuzzy numbers. This worksheet also demonstrates that the user can perform mathematical operations such as multiplication and addition on fuzzy numbers, even when those operations involve nonfuzzy numbers. The other change is the appearance of the diagram in the upper-right corner of the screen. This diagram is the "belief graph" for cell C2. Because belief graphs are an important part of FuziCalc, we discuss them in the following section.

FIGURE 4–3

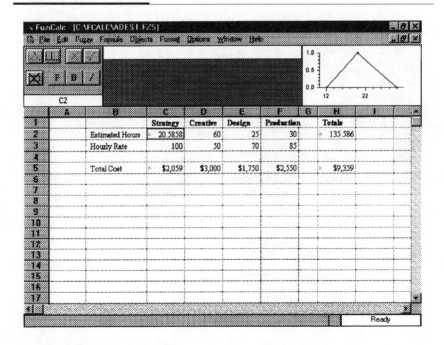

Belief Graphs

The belief graph is FuziCalc's method for showing all the possible values of a number in a concise picture. If you read the material on simulation in Chapter 3, your first impression might be that the graph in Figure 4–3 looks like a frequency distribution. A belief graph is not the same as a statistical distribution, though. It is a distribution of the belief or the degree to which neighboring values belong to the defined fuzzy number. The key distinction is that statistical distributions represent uncertainty as a probability problem. In contrast, "fuzziness portrays uncertainties of a more general, less tightly defined nature—uncertainty that is not necessarily random. This is often called possibility theory. It is a more general theory, looser in its constraints, and more suited to real world problems, which tend to be fuzzy. Nonetheless the mathematics behind the theory and our implementation of it is robust."[2]

The values on the x-axis of the belief graph in Figure 4–3 are the numerical values that the fuzzy number represents. We entered values of 12 for low and 30 for high, and these are the left and right endpoints of the triangle. This particular fuzzy number has three points, which is the minimum, but a number can have more than three points if a greater number is required to describe the problem. The y-axis represents the degree of belief in the number on the x-axis. A higher belief number (up to the maximum of 1.0) represents a higher level of belief in the corresponding x-axis value. The peak value on the graph (1.0 on the y-axis) represents the user's best guess about the variable's value. As we show shortly, the variables' y-scale values do not necessarily sum to 1, because they are not equivalent to mutually exclusive probabilities.

FuziCalc provides five predefined belief-graph shapes for the user's convenience. You can see these shapes in the dialogue box in Figure 4–4. In that box we are defining a fuzzy number for cell F2, the estimated hours for production.

In Figure 4–4, the original crisp value for cell F2 was 30, and we are redefining a range for the cell as a fuzzy number. The dialogue box offers five shapes, which we describe moving from left to right in the Shape box.

1. Triangle: FuziCalc finds the peak value by locating the midpoint of the segment from the low value to the high value.
2. Trapezoid (flat top): Used to reflect a high belief in a range of values.

2. Ibid., p. 11.

FIGURE 4-4

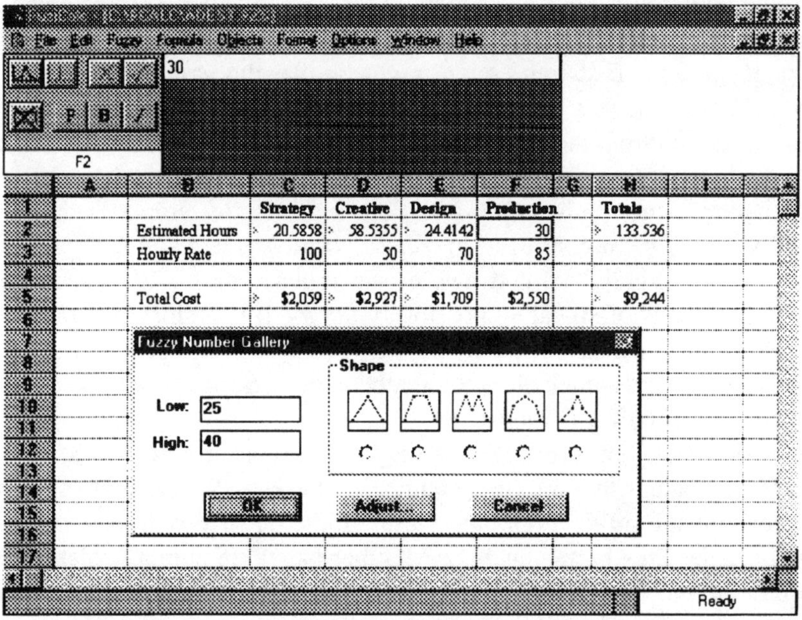

3. Double hump: Confidence is not uniform for values between peaks.

4. Tent shape: Reflects a number that is fairly fuzzy and that you are thinking of in "about" terms ("It's about 20.").

5. Steeple shape: Adds more crispness to the peak number. Use this shape when you are slightly more certain of the peak value.

We stress that a fuzzy number can take any shape, not just these five. The program provides these commonly used shapes for the user's convenience.

Figure 4–5 shows the results of selecting the tent-shaped graph for cell F2, and Figure 4–6 shows the modification of cell C2 from a triangular to a trapezoidal shape. The program allows the user to modify the belief graph's input values graphically or numerically if changes are needed.

After entering the final values, we have a variety of belief graph shapes in cells C2:F2. Table 4–1 lists the inputs.

At this point, you might be wondering how a worksheet can produce a result when the input variables have three distinct shapes. We review fuzzy mathematics in the next section, but fortunately, FuziCalc handles the calcu-

FIGURE 4-5

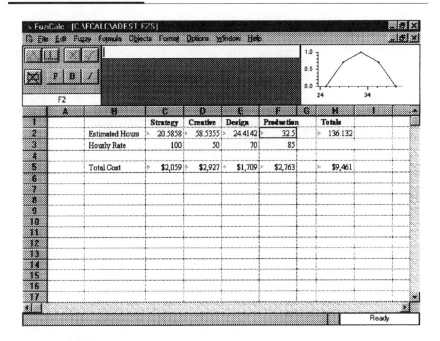

FIGURE 4-6

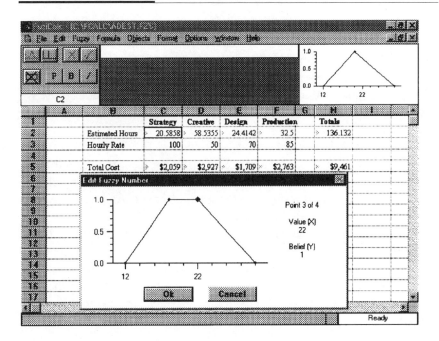

TABLE 4-1

Input Cell Descriptions

Cell	Parameters	Shape
C2	Low: 12, Best: 20, High: 30; Values of 18 and 22 assigned 1.0 Belief	Trapezoid
D2	Low: 45, Best: 60, High: 70	Triangular
E2	Low: 18, High: 20, High: 30	Triangular
F2	Low: 25, Best: 30, High: 40	Tent

lations automatically. The result of the worksheet's calculations appears in cell H5, which sums the total estimated costs. As Figure 4–7 shows, the fuzzy number in cell H5 has a double-hump shape. The graph has two peak values: $9,153 and $9,871. Although you have the highest belief in these numbers (y-values = 1.0), you are less confident about the values in the middle, where the midpoint has a y-value of .7071. In other words, the results indicate that you believe more strongly in the possibility of obtaining the peak results than you do about the values between those peaks.

Fuzzy Arithmetic

In this section we provide a brief introduction to fuzzy arithmetic with triangular and trapezoidal numbers. Readers who want to move beyond this basic level of information should see Kaufmann and Gupta (1991), which we use as a reference here. FuziCalc uses slightly modified algorithms, so the results in this section will not match the program's output exactly. We start by referring the reader to Figure 4–8, which shows two triangular fuzzy numbers.

In Figure 4–8, we label the first triangular fuzzy number T1; it is defined by the points t1, t2, and t3. Similarly, we label the second triangular fuzzy number T2, and it is defined by t4, t5, and t6. The graph's y-axis is labeled b, and it represents the level of belief. As in the previous examples, the belief level ranges from 0 to 1.0.

To perform a mathematical operation on fuzzy numbers like these, we work with values that have corresponding b levels. For example, to add T1 and T2, we would first add the values for the left-hand points, t1 and t4. Next we would add the values for t3 and t6. Finally, for the new peak point, we would add t2 and t5. Table 4–2 shows the calculations with sample values.

FIGURE 4-7

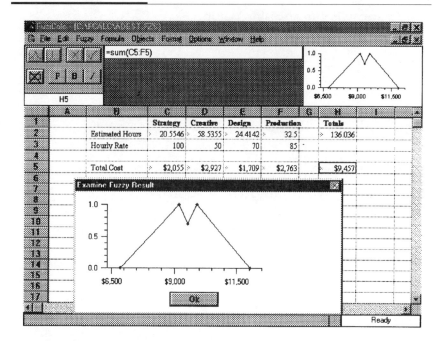

FIGURE 4-8

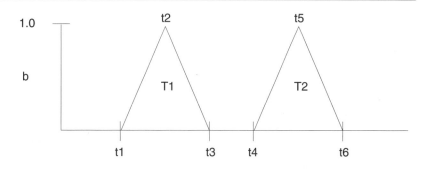

Subtraction works slightly differently. To subtract T2 from T1, our left point on the new number becomes (t1 – t6) and the right point is (t3 – t4). Table 4–3 uses the same numbers as Table 4–2 to demonstrate subtraction.

As the advertising budget demonstrated, it is possible to multiple a fuzzy number by a nonfuzzy number. If we multiply T1 by 2, we get the values in Table 4–4.

Next, we multiply two fuzzy numbers. For T1 and T2, we multiply t1 * t4, t2 * t5, and t3 * t6. Table 4–5 lists the results.

TABLE 4-2
Addition with Triangular Values

	T1	T2	T1 + T2
Left	5	10	15
Peak	6	12	18
Right	7	14	21

TABLE 4-3
Subtraction with Triangular Values

	T1	T2	T1 − T2
Left	5	10	−9
Peak	6	12	−6
Right	7	14	−3

TABLE 4-4
Multiplication by Nonfuzzy Numbers

	T1	T1 * 2
Left	5	10
Peak	6	12
Right	7	14

TABLE 4-5
Fuzzy Multiplication of Fuzzy Numbers

	T1	T2	T1 − T2
Left	5	10	50
Peak	6	12	72
Right	7	14	98

The last operation we examine for T1 and T2 is division. To divide T1 by T2, our left point on the new number becomes (t1 / t6) and the right point is (t3 / t4), as shown in Table 4–6.

Trapezoidal Fuzzy Numbers

In the advertising example we modified cell C2 from a triangular to a trapezoidal (flat top) number (refer to Figure 4–6). Figure 4–9 shows two trapezoidal fuzzy numbers that we label R1 (defined by r1, r2, r3, r4) and R2 (defined by r5, r6, r7, and r8). We assign these numbers the values shown in Table 4–7.

Addition of two trapezoidal numbers is straightforward, as we add points with corresponding values of *b*: (r1 + r5), (r2 + r6), (r3 + r7), and (r4 + r8). Table 4–8 shows the results of adding the two numbers.

Division of trapezoidal numbers is slightly more complicated than addition, but similar to triangular subtraction. In this example the resulting values are (r1 – r8), (r2 – r7), (r3 – r6), and (r4 – r5). Table 4–9 shows the results of subtracting R2 from R1.

TABLE 4–6

Division of Fuzzy Numbers

	T1	T2	T1 / T2
Left	5	10	5/14
Peak	6	12	6/12
Right	7	14	7/10

FIGURE 4–9

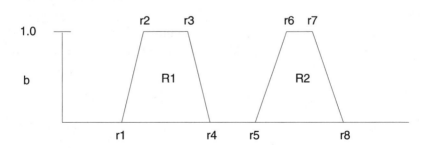

TABLE 4-7
Trapezoidal Numbers

	R1	R2
Left	5	10
Left peak	6	11
Right peak	7	12
Right	8	13

TABLE 4-8
Addition with Trapezoidal Numbers

	R1	R2	R1 + R2
Left	5	10	15
Left peak	6	11	17
Right peak	7	12	19
Right	8	13	21

TABLE 4-9
Subtraction with Trapezoidal Numbers

	R1	R2	R1 − R2
Left	5	10	−8
Left peak	6	11	−6
Right peak	7	12	−4
Right	8	13	−2

Other operations with trapezoidal numbers like multiplication and division do not necessarily yield trapezoidal numbers, so we do not discuss those operations here.

FuziCalc Financial Functions

FuziCalc provides an extensive set of financial functions. Most of them are analogous to those used in other spreadsheet programs. To extend these functions to deal with fuzzy numbers, the program imposes some limitations. Since the algorithms of many financial functions are quite complex or involve iterative solutions, fully fuzzy calculation of them involves many fuzzy operations and would produce results with large uncertainty. Instead, FuziCalc computes most fuzzy financial functions by performing multiple crisp calculations, using the effective peak and limits

TABLE 4-10

FuziCalc Financial Functions

Name	Syntax	Allowable Fuzzy Arguments
Declining balance depreciation	db(cost, salvage, life, period[,month])*	Cost, salvage
Double declining balance depreciation	ddb(cost, salvage, life, period [,factor])	Cost, salvage
Effective interest rate	effect(rate, periods)	Rate
Future value	fv(rate, nper, pmt[,pv[,type]])	Rate, number of periods, payment, present value
Interest payment	ipmt(rate, per, nper, pv[,fv [,type]])	Rate, period, number of periods, present value
Internal rate of return	irr(values[,guess])	Cells in values range
Modified internal rate of return	mirr(values, finance_rate, reinvest_rate)	All
Nominal interest rate	nominal(effect_rate, npery)	Effective rate
Number of periods	nper(rate, pmt, pv, [fv [,type]])	All except type
Net present value	npv(rate, value [, value [, ...]])	All
Outstanding principal balance	OPBal(rate, per, nper, pv [, fv [, type]]0	All except type
Payment	pmt(rate, nper, pv [,fv [,type]])	All except type
Principal portion of payment	ppmt(rate, per, nper, pv [, fv [, type]])	All except type
Present value	pv(rate, nper, pmt, [, fv [, type]])	All except type
Interest rate per period	rate(nper, pmt, pv [, fv [,type [, guess]]])	All except type and guess
Straight line depreciation	sln(cost, salvage, life [, per])	Cost, salvage
Sum-of-years' digits depreciation	syd(cost, salvage, life, per)	Cost, salvage
Variable declining balance depreciation	vdb(cost, salvage, life, start_period, end_period [, factor [, no_switch]])	Cost, salvage

Note: Optional arguments in [ ].

Source: *FuziCalc User's Guide*, version 1.5.

of each of the inputs. From these, the program forms a triangular fuzzy result. This triangular result accurately reflects the uncertainty in the estimate of the specified function.

Additionally, because of algorithmic details, some financial functions have "trouble spots" if certain argument combinations are used. (Most often the specified arguments would cause a division by zero.) When these conditions are detected, FuziCalc returns !MATH error codes. Table 4–10 lists the financial functions, their syntax, and the arguments that can be fuzzy.

Additional Applications

Although we presented only a brief FuziCalc example in this chapter, we believe it introduces the potential for using fuzzy numbers with uncertain financial variables. Readers who have examined the text's earlier material on simulation should recognize many more potential applications for fuzzy numbers. They are especially useful when the user cannot draw on historical data for probability distributions and the beliefs assigned to possible outcomes are not compatible with a neat statistical expression.

SOURCES AND RECOMMENDED READING

FuziCalc User's Guide, version 1.5. Knoxville, TN: FuziWare, Inc., 1994.

Kaufmann, A. and M. M. Gupta. *Introduction to Fuzzy Arithmetic: Theory and Applications.* Boston: International Thomson Computer Press, 1991.

SOFTWARE RESOURCES

FuziCalc version 1.51j
FuziWare, Inc.
7224 Lawford Road
Knoxville, TN 37919
Tel. 800-472-6183 or 423-588-4144
Fax 423-588-9487
Suggested retail price: $199

CHAPTER 5

Forecasting

INTRODUCTION

How much would you be willing to spend to know the future? It's a tempting prospect because that knowledge would be invaluable. Of course, we have no way of predicting the future with total accuracy. We can only make informed judgments, or forecasts, and that is the subject of this chapter.

Forecasters, particularly those who try to predict economic variables, are often the target of criticism. Former Treasury Secretary Donald Regan summed up many observers' opinions of economic forecasts when he said, "If you believe them, then you also believe in the tooth fairy."[1] Inaccurate forecasting isn't limited to economic forecasts, of course—the business press often reports product shortages and excess inventory caused by a manufacturer's failure to forecast demand accurately.

We mention these problems to stress one of the chapter's key themes: Forecasts are *estimates* that are subject to error. The forecasting methods described in this chapter do *not* produce guaranteed results. They produce reasonable estimates or ranges of estimates that the forecaster must evaluate, based on experience. With these limitations in mind, this chapter reviews several common forecasting methods and their potential applications.

FORECASTING METHODS

This chapter reviews several forecasting methods, which we can divide into causal and time-series models. Each method has its own trade-offs in terms

---

1. *Time,* August 27, 1984, p. 46.

of complexity, data requirements, and explanatory power. The first causal method we review, linear regression, relies on econometrics, which is a branch of economics that combines economic theory and statistics. Causal models assume that a relationship exists between the result (dependent variable) and another factor (independent variable). For instance, if we wanted to forecast housing prices, we could use selling price as the dependent variable with the home's square feet of living space as the independent variable. For these two variables, we assume that more (less) living space leads to higher (lower) housing prices, and our model would test that relationship.

In contrast, time-series models focus solely on the dependent variable's past values. We assume that we can discover and use patterns in the data to forecast the data's future values. As an example, if we wanted to forecast short-term interest rates, we might use the last 60 days' Treasury bill rates for our data set. Time-series models like this lack the explanatory interpretations of the causal models because there are no explanatory variables. In the short-term interest rate example, we have no variables, such as changes in inflation or money supply, to explain changes in interest rates. Therefore, we cannot examine the relationship between the independent and dependent variables. We cannot answer questions about the impact of changes in the money supply on short-term rates. In their favor, though, PC-software advances have made time-series models easier to use, and they have respectable records for short-term forecasts.

We examine several time-series methods. Extrapolation techniques fit a trend line to the data to forecast future values of the dependent variable. Smoothing methods use weighted averages of past data to develop forecasts. The general approach is to weight recent observations more heavily that those in the distant past, using the assumption that the recent past is more relevant than the distant past. The final method we discuss is the Box-Jenkins approach. This method works well with complex time series when the underlying factors like trend and seasonality are not immediately apparent.

LINEAR REGRESSION

Example: One-Variable Model

To illustrate causal, or econometric methods, we start with a simple one-variable linear regression model. In this example, your client builds homes and has asked you to develop a model that can forecast a home's selling price based on its size. He has provided you with recent selling prices (in thousands of dollars) for homes in the area and an estimate of each home's living space (in square feet). This information is listed in Table 5–1, which is modeled after Ramanathan (1992).

Your first step is to plot the data, which is always a good practice if the data can be graphed in a meaningful format. Figure 5–1 plots the dependent variable, price, on the vertical (y) axis and the explanatory variable, square feet, on the horizontal (x) axis, with a line sketched through the "center" of the data.

You can see several features in Figure 5–1. The plot shows a positive relationship between the variables, although the data points are not grouped very tightly around the line. Still, it looks like you can start the analysis safely by using a linear model. Before we run the regression and use it for forecasting, though, we review the technique's mechanics.

Regression Review

If you are comfortable with regression techniques, you can skip this section and move to the next. If you need a refresher, this section reviews the assumptions and mechanics of simple linear regression (SLR), which is also known as ordinary least squares (OLS) regression.

TABLE 5–1

Housing Prices

Observation	Price ($000)	Square Feet
1	$199.9	1,065
2	228	1,254
3	235	1,300
4	285	1,577
5	239	1,600
6	293	1,750
7	285	1,800
8	365	1,870
9	295	1,935
10	290	1,948
11	385	2,254
12	505	2,600
13	425	2,800
14	415	3,000

FIGURE 5-1

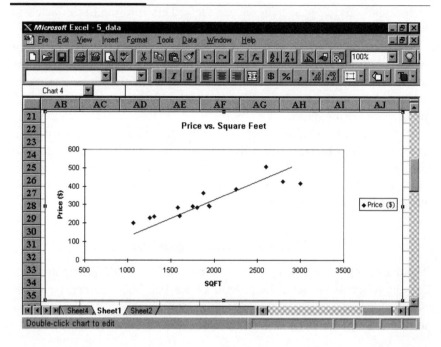

SLR models assume that a linear relationship exists between the dependent variable and the independent variable. In our example, we assume a positive linear relationship between price and size: more (less) living space means higher (lower) prices. This is an initial assumption—the true relationship might be negative, nonlinear, or even nonexistent.

The formula for a straight line is the familiar $Y = a + bX$, where Y is the dependent variable, X is the independent variable, a is the value of Y when X equals zero (also called the y-intercept), and b is the slope of the line. In our example, we have price as the Y variable, and square feet is the independent, or X, variable, which gives us the model

$$\text{Price} = a + (b * \text{Square feet})$$

We do not yet know values for a and b, but common sense tells us that b should have a positive value, as Figure 5-1 indicated: Increased space should have a positive impact on price.

In Figure 5-1 we sketched a line to represent our visual estimate of the data's center. This line represents an attempt at developing a linear regression model. If we manually calculated the values of a and b for the line, we would have the parameters we need to complete the model. If you look at the diagram, though, you will realize that we could have tried other lines, and some of those other lines might fit the data better. This is the essential technique behind linear regression: finding the line that best fits the data.

Before we see how SLR fits the line, we should explain what we mean by "best fit." As you look at the diagram, you'll notice that the line does not pass through most of the points—it misses them slightly. If a linear model specified the relationship perfectly, each data point would be on the line. We can see that doesn't happen—some points are above the line and others are below. As an SLR program fits a line through the data, it measures the vertical distance between the line and each data point. This distance represents an error, or residual, in fitting the model (the equation for the line) to the data. The goal of SLR is to find a line that misses by the least overall amount. SLR works by fitting a line to the data, squaring the residuals, summing them, and then finding the line that minimizes that sum. (Mathematically, the problem is to minimize

$$\sum_{i=1}^{N}\left(Y_i - \hat{Y}_i\right)$$

where $\hat{Y}_i$ is the regression's estimate of Y for a given value of X. The SLR derivations are in the appendix if you want to review the math.)

Because the regression model does not fit the data perfectly, it can give us only estimates of the true parameters a and b. To reflect the uncertainty in our estimates, we rewrite our original $Y = a + bX$ model as $Y = a + bX + e$. In this version, α (alpha) and β (beta) represent our estimates of the true, unobservable values of a and b, respectively, and ε (epsilon) is a random error term. This model says that price is a function of square feet and some unknown, random influences. Intuitively, this model makes sense. We know that other factors besides living space influence a home's price. These factors could include location, design, the state of the local economy, and so on. The ε term captures those unknown random influences on the selling prices.

Linear Regression Programs

Linear regression is a popular analytical technique, and you will find SLR programs in statistics software packages and spreadsheets. While the user's dialogue with each program is different, the basic information you must provide will be similar across programs. You must identify the dependent and independent variables and select the output information you want. A detailed explanation of the output follows Table 5–2.

T A B L E   5-2

Regression Results
Dependent Variable = Price

Independent Variable	Regression Coefficient	Standard Error of Coefficient	t-Score
SQFT	0.1388	0.0187	7.4068
Intercept	52.3509		
Regression Statistics			
R-squared	0.8205		
Adjusted R-squared	0.8056		
Multiple correlation	0.9058		
Standard error of estimate	39.0230		
Durbin-Watson	1.9751		
F value	54.8605		

The first part of the program's output, Regression Results, provides two pieces of information. First, it estimates the coefficients of the line that best fits the data. We use a linear model with the form, Price = $a + b$ * Square feet, where a is the y-intercept and b is the slope of the regression line. You will find these estimated values in the column, Regression Coefficients. We now can rewrite the model as Price = 52.3509 + 0.1388 * Square feet. In other words, for a home with 1,500 square feet, the predicted price is 52.3509 + 0.1388 * 1,500, or $260,550.

The second valuable piece of information is the t-score for the square feet variable, which is listed in the fourth column. This statistic helps us determine if the relationship between square feet and price is significant. In other words, does the amount of living space truly affect the house's price? As a rule of thumb, you can interpret the t-score roughly as follows: A t-score greater than ±2.0 means the variable plays a significant role in the regression. The SQFT variable has a t-score of 7.4068, indicating a significant relationship. (Technical note: You calculate the t-score by dividing the regression coefficient by its standard error, or 0.1388/0.0187 = 7.4 in this case. You can see how a smaller standard error in the denominator, which indicates a tighter model "fit," increases the t-score.)

We focus on three key statistics in the Regression Statistics part of the output in Table 5–2. (We discuss the other statistics and their calculations in the appendix.) The first is the R-squared value of 0.8205. This value tells us how well the model explains the variation in the dependent variable (Price). A high R-squared value (close to 1.00) indicates a very good fit. This regression's result of 0.8205 is good, but we might have a problem because of our small (N = 14) sample size. For small-sample cases such as this, it is better to use the adjusted R-squared statistic, which is still fairly high at 0.8056.

The next statistic we examine is the Durbin-Watson value, which tells us if there is autocorrelation in the residuals. *Autocorrelation* means the residuals (error terms) created by fitting the current model are correlated with one another. In this example, it probably means we are missing a relevant independent variable in our model. A Durbin-Watson value near 2.0 indicates no autocorrelation, while values near 0 or 4 strongly indicate autocorrelation. This regression's value of 1.9751 is very close to 2.0, so we do not worry about autocorrelation in this sample.

The last statistic we review is the F value of 54. The F value gives us information on the regression's overall significance. The high value here shows that the regression model does have significant explanatory power.

The square feet and home price model is an example of a positive linear relationship. In the following example we find a negative relationship between the independent and dependent variables. Your client's company owns and operates a chain of convenience stores, and it must decide where to place its next store. The marketing director's intuition suggests that the store should be in a high-income area because those customers generally have more discretionary income, which should generate sales of items with higher profit margins.

To test this assumption, you run an SLR using the data shown in Table 5–3, which lists each existing store's profit margin and local area median household income. The profit margin serves as the dependent variable (y-axis) with median income as the independent variable (x-axis). The regression results are shown in Table 5–3.

Surprisingly, the coefficient for income is negative, giving us the following model:

$$\text{Profit margin} = 23.599 - 0.508 * \text{Income}$$

In other words, stores located in areas with higher median incomes show lower profit margins than stores in lower-income areas. If profit margin is the key decision variable, the marketing director needs to reexamine the assumptions behind his intuition.

Model Assumptions

When we build causal models, we usually must make assumptions to simplify the model-building process. If we did not make these assumptions, even the simplest problem's complexity could be overwhelming. To use

TABLE 5-3

Store Profit

Profit (%)	Median Income
12	24
8	33
9	30
16	18
4	36
5	36
12	25
7	32
7	32
11	20
15	17
14	17
8	33
4	37
6	35

Regression Results

Dependent Variable = Profit Margin

Independent Variable	Regression Coefficient	Standard Error of Coefficient	t-Score
Income	−0.508	0.041	−12.476
Intercept	23.599		

Regression Statistics

R-squared	0.923
Adjusted R-squared	0.917
Multiple correlation	0.961
Standard error of estimate	1.133
F value	155.642

SLR, we make several important assumptions about the model and data. If any of those assumptions are significantly violated, we might be forced to transform the data or use another model. Here are brief explanations of those assumptions and their implications for our example.

Assumption 1. The model is linear ($Y = a + bX + e$), and we can identify the independent variables correctly. There are several possible violations of this assumption. First, the relationship between the dependent and independent variables might be nonlinear. Second, we might fail to include important explanatory variables, or we might include unnecessary variables. Finally, the value for *b* might change during the period being examined, while the linear model assumes a constant *b*.

Assumption 2. The model predicts a *Y* value for a given *X* value. The difference between the predicted and actual value is the residual, or error term. Figure 5–2 shows the actual versus calculated values for the housing-price data regression.

The SLR makes several important assumptions about these residuals. First, it assumes that the average, or expected value, of the residuals is zero. Next, the model assumes that the residuals follow a normal distribution with the same variance and they are not correlated with one another. If the error terms do not have the same variance, this creates *heteroskedasticity*. If the errors are correlated with one another, this condition is known as *autocorrelation*. The presence of either condition poses a problem and can invalidate the use of the SLR model.

If your data violate these assumptions, you might need to take corrective measures or consider another model. Most software packages provide details on interpreting their regression diagnostics to help you recognize potential problems.

Example: Multiple Regression

Your first home-price model does a decent job of explaining the variation in home prices with its adjusted R-squared value of 0.8056. But you would like to develop a model with greater explanatory power, so you ask your client if any other variables are worth considering. He provides two

FIGURE 5–2

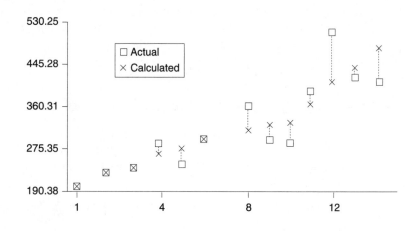

more variables for each house in the data set: the number of bedrooms and bathrooms. Adding these new explanatory variables changes the analysis from a simple linear regression to a multiple linear regression (MLR). The principle remains the same, though: You want to find a significant linear relationship between the independent and dependent variables. (Remember that a plane or a hyperplane can also describe a linear relationship— we are not limited to lines in two dimensions.) To find the relationship, you restate the model as

$$Y = a + b_1X_1 + b_2X_2 + b_3X_3 + e$$

where X_1, X_2, and X_3 represent the number of square feet, bedrooms, and bathrooms, respectively. You add the new values to the data set and rerun the regression (Table 5–4).

The new explanatory variables do not improve the results. The t-scores for bedrooms and bathrooms are low, and the new model's adjusted R-squared of 0.7868 is lower than that of the single-variable model (0.8056). Apparently, we cannot improve the model by adding these two explanatory variables. What if we try different combinations of the independent variables? Perhaps we would get better results with a model that includes only square feet and the number of bedrooms, or square feet and the number of bathrooms.

To test the various combinations, we use a technique called stepwise regression. This automated method is found in most statistics programs and systematically tests the independent variable combinations. It works by adding and deleting variables until none of the missing variables can significantly improve the model's fit. In this example the program tests the following models (adjusted R-squared values in parentheses): square feet only (.80), square feet and number of bedrooms (.805), square feet and number of bathrooms (.824), and square feet with both bedrooms and bathrooms (.786). Although we do not list each model's results here, in each instance the t-values for BEDS and BATHs were insignificant. After comparing the stepwise regression's results, you decide to use the original model

Price = 52.3509 + 0.1388 * Square feet

Forecasting with the Regression Model

After we estimate the coefficients, this model allows us to forecast house prices for a given square foot value. For instance, if your client asks for a price forecast on a 2,500 square foot house, you simply enter the square foot value into the model

Predicted price = 52.3509 + 0.1388 * 2,500 = 399.35

TABLE 5–4

Expanded Home Sales Data

Observation	Price ($000)	Square Feet	Bedrooms	Bathrooms
1	$199.9	1,065	3	1.5
2	228	1,254	3	2
3	235	1,300	3	2
4	285	1,577	4	2.5
5	239	1,600	3	2
6	293	1,750	4	2
7	285	1,800	4	2.5
8	365	1,870	4	2
9	295	1,935	4	2.5
10	290	1,948	4	2
11	385	2,254	4	3
12	505	2,600	3	2.5
13	425	2,800	4	3
14	415	3,000	4	3

Regression Results

Dependent Variable = Price

Independent Variable	Regression Coefficient	Standard Error of Coefficient	t-Score
SQFT	0.154	0.035	4.405
BEDRMS	−22.321	27.075	−0.824
BATHS	−8.788	45.447	−0.193
Intercept	125.864		

Regression Statistics

R-squared	0.835
Adjusted R-squared	0.786
Multiple correlation	0.914
Standard error of estimate	40.951
Durbin-Watson	1.9704
Number of data points	14
Number of points used	14
F value	16.904

or roughly $399,350. But how confident can you be about this forecast? We know that the values for *a* and *b* are estimates, so our forecasted price is also an estimate. (Even if we know *a* and *b* for certain, there will still be random events that influence the dependent variable.) A better solution is to develop a price *range* around the estimate. Statisticians use the formula shown below to estimate the low and high values of the range around a regression's forecast. It creates a *prediction interval* that depends on the degree of confidence the forecaster wants to have in the forecast. Most statistics programs will generate the prediction interval automatically if you provide the independent variable's value and the desired confidence level. We describe the formula in detail so you can see how it works and then show the values for the house price regression.

$$\alpha + \beta x^* \pm t_{\alpha/2,n-2} \times s \sqrt{1 + \frac{1}{n} + \frac{n(x^* - \bar{x})^2}{n\sum x_i^2 - (\sum x_i)^2}}$$

The formula has two parts. The first part, $\alpha + \beta x *$, is the point estimate we developed above. We use x^* to represent the independent variable value we want to forecast. In this case we set x^* to 2,500. The rest of the equation makes an adjustment to the point estimate to reflect the uncertainty in the forecast. Here is a brief explanation of each term:

■ $t_{\alpha/2, n-2}$ When we create the forecast range, we need to specify the degree of confidence we want to have that our forecast will fall into that range. Typical values are 95 percent, 90 percent, and so on. Higher confidence levels lead to wider ranges, which in turn mean less precise forecasts. The t-value we use is a function of the confidence level we specify and the size of our sample ($n = 14$). For a 90 percent confidence level and a sample size of 14, the t-value is 1.782. (You can find t-value tables in any statistics textbook.)

■ s The regression's standard error, which is part of the program's output. Value: 39.023

■ $\bar{x}$ The average value for our x variables SQFT.

■ $\sum x_i$ The sum of the individual x variables.

If your regression program doesn't provide prediction intervals, you can calculate these values manually. Here is the formula with the calculated values.

$$52.3509 + (.13875)(2500) \pm (39.023)\sqrt{1 + \frac{1}{14} + \frac{14(2500 - 1976)^2}{14(1,513,039) - (715,723,009)}}$$

After simplifying the formula, you get the range: 399.2259 ± 71.7296. In other words, you are 90 percent confident that the price of a house with 2,500 square feet will be between $327,433 and $471,018—quite a wide range!

We can do several things to narrow the prediction range. The first is to lower our confidence level. If we are willing to settle for an 80 percent confidence interval, the forecast range will be smaller. Another possibility is to increase our sample size, if that is feasible, with the goal of generating a lower t-statistic. Finally, your client should draw on his expertise to evaluate the forecast. His experience might lead him to modify the forecasted price, even if he can't quantify the factors that influence that decision.

Lagged Variables

In this next example, we demonstrate a regression using a lagged independent variable. Your client owns a retail business and wants to determine if her advertising has a positive impact on sales. Table 5–5 shows the data for sales revenue and advertising expenditures for the last 14 years.

You run an SLR with sales as the dependent variable and advertising as the independent variable. The results, shown in Table 5–6, are encouraging as the model has an adjusted R-squared of .869.

A natural line of inquiry is to ask about the effect of the previous year's advertising on the current year's sales because we suspect that there should be a spillover effect. To test this hunch, we use include the previous year's sales as an independent variable and show the results in Table 5–7. (Notice that we lose the first year's observation by doing this.)

TABLE 5-5

Sales and Advertising Amounts

Year	Sales	Advertising
1	65	7
2	80	6.5
3	73	7
4	86	6.5
5	88	7.5
6	92	8.5
7	101	8.5
8	95	9
9	99	10
10	103	11
11	107	9
12	117	12
13	120	14
14	140	15

TABLE 5–6

Regression Results

	Dependent Variable = Sales		
Independent Variable	Regression Coefficient	Standard Error of Coefficient	t-Score
Advertising	6.182	0.689	8.968
Intercept	40.87		
Regression Statistics			
R-squared	0.880		
Adjusted R-squared	0.869		
Multiple correlation	0.938		
Standard error of estimate	6.537		
F value	80.421		

The t-score for the lagged advertising value was significant at 2.108, but that value is just barely above the 2.0 cutoff. The model's adjusted R-squared improved slightly from .869 to .90. The conclusion: Using prior year's advertising expenditures with the current year's improves the model slightly.

The regression analyses shown here are the simplest type of causal models. In their efforts to model complex economic relationships, econometricians use a variety of much more sophisticated techniques. The drawback to using these more powerful tools is that the user needs a solid background in the underlying theory and technique to develop viable models. Therefore, we leave discussion of those techniques to the econometrics texts.

TIME-SERIES ANAYLSIS

Regression works well in the right circumstances. If you don't have data for the explanatory variables, though, you can't use regression. Also, if your data violate any of the assumptions needed to use linear regression, you have another problem. These problems occur frequently with financial data, especially time-series data. Time series are events that occur at regular intervals: daily prices, monthly sales, and so on. Because much financial data frequently fall into this category, the rest of the chapter reviews time-series methods and their applications.

Time-series techniques analyze a variable's past behavior with the goal of finding a recurring pattern. If we find a recurring pattern, it serves

TABLE 5–7

Regression Results

Dependent Variable = Sales			
Independent Variable	**Regression Coefficient**	**Standard Error of Coefficient**	**t-Score**
Advertising	3.621	1.356	2.671
Prior year advertising	3.435	1.630	2.108
Intercept	34.612		
Regression statistics			
R-squared	0.917		
Adjusted R-squared	0.900		
Multiple correlation	0.957		
Standard error of estimate	5.705		
F value	55.016		

as the basis for estimating future values. Some of these methods use a simple extrapolation process, while others develop more complex models. The key difference between econometric and time-series models is that the former use explanatory variables, while the latter use only the "dependent" variable's history. This difference eliminates the explanatory value of a time-series model, but not its forecasting value.

When you first begin working with time-series data, you should look for three features: trend, seasonality, and volatility. Analyzing these features properly is critical to getting acceptable forecasts because some forecasting methods cannot handle trends and seasonality. In the next example, we see all three elements and we demonstrate the shortcoming of the applied model.

Example: Retail Sales

Your client owns a retail business. Sales have been growing steadily over the past three years, as shown in Table 5–8. He doesn't know why sales are growing—he doesn't advertise much, so he assumes the cause is repeat business and referrals from satisfied customers. He gives you the following monthly sales figures for the past five years, with Year 5 as the most recent. (We ignore the possible impact of inflation here by assuming these figures are real, or inflation-adjusted, values.)

TABLE 5-8

Monthly Sales

	Year 1	Year 2	Year 3	Year 4	Year 5
January	65	60	80	104	105
February	60	61	80	103	129
March	67	70	78	92	99
April	72	75	85	107	127
May	80	90	90	98	116
June	80	85	95	142	169
July	72	80	90	93	113
August	70	90	96	100	117
September	80	91	100	126	141
October	85	88	105	139	172
November	90	100	120	175	202
December	100	115	130	190	220

Like many retail businesses, the firm's sales follow a cycle: December is the busiest month, followed by a slowdown in the first quarter. Your client wants to forecast next year's sales so he can plan his staffing levels. You start the analysis by plotting the firm's sales over the past 60 months in Figure 5–3.

Figure 5–3 reveals several features. First, the overall trend of sales is upward. Second, a seasonal pattern is clearly evident: Sales spike up in summer, drop off slightly in early fall, begin increasing again through December, and drop off sharply in January. Because we don't have any explanatory variables to build an econometric model, we use time-series methods to forecast next year's sales. (It might be possible to develop an econometric model for this client's forecasts, although we do not attempt it here. Economic data such as consumer confidence surveys, regional economic conditions, retail sales, and so on, are available for many areas. This public data could form the basis for a causal model.)

Analyzing Time Series

We need to review two issues before analyzing the sales figures: data structure and forecast accuracy. First we divide the observations into three sequential periods: estimation, in-sample forecast, and out-of-sample forecast. We perform this step to test any model's forecasting ability on

FIGURE 5-3

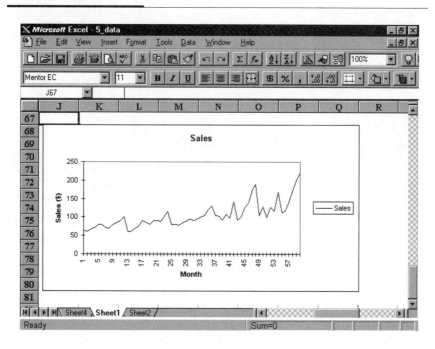

historical data before using it to forecast the future. In this case we use the first four years' sales (48 observations) as the estimation period. Next we test the model's forecasting ability on the remaining 12 data points, which cover months 49 to 60. This phase is the in-sample forecast period—think of it as a "test drive" for the model. Because we have the historical observations for this period, we can compare the model's forecast to the actual values. If the model fits the in-sample data well, we will have more confidence in its ability to predict future values. If the forecast model fits these points poorly, we go back to the first 48 observations and fit a new model, repeating the process until the fit satisfies us.

The issue of model "fit" is important because different goodness-of-fit measurement techniques can lead to different conclusions about a model's forecasting ability. Statisticians and econometricians have developed several model selection criteria, and you should check to see which criteria your software program uses. Goodness-of-fit criteria generally share a common foundation, which is the sum of a model's errors or squared errors. We saw earlier (Figure 5–2) that the difference between a model's fitted value and the actual value creates an error, or residual. By examining those errors, usually by summing them or their squares, we see how closely the model fits the data. (The summed squared errors are known as sum of squared errors [SSE], error sum of squares [ESS], or sum of squared residuals [SSR], depending on the program's notation.) A good forecast will have a small SSE, while a poor fit will show a larger value.

The four measures in Table 5–9 are the most commonly used to evaluate a forecasting method's accuracy. We demonstrate their use in the next section.

Extrapolation

In Figure 5–1 we fitted a line through the data to see if a linear relationship existed between the independent (square feet) and dependent (price) variables. This same technique of line, or curve, fitting can be used with time-series data by plotting the observations (y-axis) over time (x-axis). We are not restricted to linear functions—as Table 5–10 shows, many of the standard extrapolations are nonlinear. The goal is to find a smooth curve that can account for the underlying trend. Table 5–10 lists the most common curves fitted to time-series data. (Remember that these models do not use independent explanatory variables; instead, Y_t is function of time t.)

At this stage the goal is to find a curve that forecasts well during the in-sample period. We start with the linear function, and our first step is to estimate values for a and b from the observation period data. We do this by regressing each period's sales against its t (time) value. This gives us the model: $\hat{Y}_t = 60.74 + 1.45t$. We use this model to forecast the values for the period covering months 48 through 59. In Table 5–11 we list the actual values, the forecast values, the forecast error, and the squared forecast error for the linear function to demonstrate the extrapolation technique.

TABLE 5–9

Goodness-of-Fit Measures

Measure	Formula
Mean absolute deviation (MAD)	$\sum |e| / n$
Mean squared error (MSE)	$\sum e^2 / n$
Root mean squared error (RMSE)	$\sqrt{\text{MSE}}$
Mean absolute percentage error (MAPE)	$\dfrac{\sum |e| / A}{n}$

Note: e = error (forecast − actual); n = number of observations; A = actual value.

TABLE 5-10

Common Extrapolations

Linear:	$Y_t = \alpha + \beta t + \varepsilon_t$
Quadratic:	$Y_t = \alpha + \beta_1 t + \beta_2 t^2 + \varepsilon_t$
Cubic:	$Y_t = \alpha + \beta_1 t + \beta_2 t^2 + \beta_3 t^3 + \varepsilon_t$
Logarithmic:	$Y_t = \alpha + \beta \log(t) + \varepsilon_t$
Exponential:	$Log(Y_t) = \alpha + \beta t + \varepsilon_t$

TABLE 5-11

Forecast versus Actual

Period	Actual Value	Forecast	Forecast Error	Absolute Error	Squared Error	Percentage Error
48	105	130.34	25.47	25.47	648.96	0.2429
49	129	131.79	3.07	3.07	9.45	0.0239
50	99	133.24	34.73	34.73	1206.50	0.3526
51	127	134.69	7.99	7.99	63.90	0.0631
52	116	136.14	20.19	20.19	407.62	0.1741
53	169	137.59	−31.64	31.64	1000.84	0.1869
54	113	139.04	26.14	26.14	683.41	0.2316
55	117	140.49	23.92	23.92	572.03	0.2052
56	141	141.94	1.15	1.15	1.33	0.0082
57	172	143.39	−28.83	28.83	831.18	0.1674
58	202	144.84	−56.77	56.77	3223.20	0.2816
59	220	146.29	−73.71	73.71	5433.16	0.3350
Sum				333.63	14081.59	2.2726

Using the formulas from Table 5–9 gives us the results for the linear model, shown in Table 5–12.

We fit only the linear model here, but the approach is the same with the other models. We use the observation period to generate the needed parameters and then use those parameters to generate in-sample forecasts. We compare the forecasts to the actual values and select the model that performs best according to the forecast accuracy measure we choose.

Although simple extrapolation methods are easy to use, most fore-casters use the curve-fitting technique as a first step in their analysis, not as a stand-alone method. The method has little forecasting accuracy with

TABLE 5-12

Forecast Error Measures

Measure	Value
Mean absolute deviation (MAD)	333.63/12 = 27.80
Mean squared error (MSE)	14081.59/12 = 1173.47
Root mean squared error (RMSE)	(14081.59/12)^1/2 = 34.26
Mean absolute percentage error (MAPE)	2.2726/12 = .1894

seasonal data, which we had here, and its only value is in identifying an underlying trend in the data. Apart from that use, we do not recommend it as a forecasting technique.

Moving Averages

With the simple moving average (SMA) method, we use the n most recent data points as our forecast inputs. The formula for an n-term SMA, which we denote by SMA(n), is

$$Y(t) = \frac{1}{n}\left(Y_{t-1} + Y_{t-2} + \cdots + Y_{t-n}\right)$$

where the current level Y_t of the series is defined as the average of the last n observations. For example, if we use a four-period moving average, SMA(4), the formula is

$$Y(t) = \frac{1}{4}\left(Y_{t-1} + Y_{t-2} + Y_{t-3} + Y_{t-4}\right)$$

Here is an example of an SMA(4) using our sales data from the previous example. In Table 5–13 we list the formulas for the forecasts of periods 48, 49, 50, and 51 to demonstrate how the average rolls forward with each new period. Table 5–14 shows the forecast results, and Table 5–15 calculates the goodness-of-fit statistics.

The SMA method has two major problems. First it cannot account for trend and seasonality. Second it does not allow extended out-of-sample forecasts. As you can see with this data, we can predict only as far as the 60th period by using the average of periods 56 to 59. After that, we have no more historical data for extrapolation. (Technically, we cannot forecast past the 48th month if we use months 48 to 59 as our in-sample test data. This method would give us a level forecast of 157.50 (the same

TABLE 5-13

Moving Average Formulas

Period	Formula	Values
48	¼(periods 44 + 45 + 46 + 47)	¼(126 + 139 + 175 + 190)
49	¼(periods 45 + 46 + 47 + 48)	¼(139 + 175 + 190 + 105)
50	¼(periods 46 + 47 + 48 + 49)	¼(175 + 190 + 105 + 129)
51	¼(periods 47 + 48 + 49 + 50)	¼(190 + 105 + 129 + 99)

TABLE 5-14

Forecasts with SMA(4)

Period	Forecast	Actual	Forecast Error	Absolute Error	Squared Error	Percentage Error
44		126				
45		139				
46		175				
47		190				
48	157.50	105	52.63	52.63	2,770.41	0.50
49	152.22	129	23.50	23.50	552.27	0.18
50	149.65	99	51.14	51.14	2,615.30	0.52
51	130.52	127	3.83	3.83	14.64	0.03
52	114.70	116	−1.25	1.25	1.57	0.01
53	117.47	169	−51.76	51.76	2,679.02	0.31
54	127.59	113	14.70	14.70	215.99	0.13
55	131.19	117	14.62	14.62	213.74	0.13
56	128.66	141	−12.13	12.13	147.02	0.09
57	134.87	172	−37.35	37.35	1,394.97	0.22
58	135.62	202	−65.99	65.99	4,355.17	0.33
59	157.80	220	−62.20	62.20	3,869.05	0.28
Sum				391.10	18,829.15	2.7192

TABLE 5-15

Goodness-of-Fit Measures for SMA(4)

Measure	Value
Mean absolute deviation (MAD)	391.2/12 = 32.59
Mean squared error (MSE)	18829.15/12 = 1569.1
Root mean squared error (RMSE)	$(18829.15/12)^{1/2} = 39.61$
Mean absolute percentage error (MAPE)	2.7192/12 = .2266

as month 48) for months 48 to 59. We use those months in the calculations to demonstrate the moving average method.)

Exponential Smoothing

Exponential smoothing (ES) methods are the most sophisticated forecasting approach we have examined so far. Like the SMA, ES methods use weighted past data to generate forecasts. Unlike the SMA, though, which weights all past data points equally, the user can control the weights in ES. If the recent past is considered more important than the distant past, those recent data points can be weighted more heavily. ES methods can also account for trend and seasonality, making these methods very flexible.

Here is the formula for the simplest form of ES, which does not accommodate an underlying trend or seasonality in the data:

$$\hat{Y}_t = \alpha Y_{t-1} + (1 - \alpha)\tilde{Y}_{t-1}$$

Notation

$\hat{Y}_t$ = Smoothed value used for forecast.

α = Weighing constant.

Y_{t-1} = Most recent observation.

In other words, the forecast for the next period will be a weighted combination of the previous period's observation and smoothed value. The value for α can range from 0 to 1, with a larger value placing more weight on the most recent data.

Figure 5–4 shows both raw and smoothed data from the sales figures for periods 48 to 59. The value for α was set at .5, and we used Microsoft Excel to calculate the smoothed values listed in column C. (The first value of 105 in C2 is not a calculated value—we included it to make the graph smoother. The smoothed values start in cell C3, and the formula in each cell uses the ES formula. For example, cell C8 has the formula

=0.5*B7+0.5*C7

As you can see from Figure 5–4, the plot of the smoothed values is much less jagged than the raw data plot.

We know that the sales data have both trend and seasonality, so this simple ES method is inappropriate. To handle these additional features, we need a more complex model. We can choose from two main families of models: Holt and Winters. Holt's ES allows for an underlying trend in data by adding a second parameter to the model. The Winters ES models

FIGURE 5–4

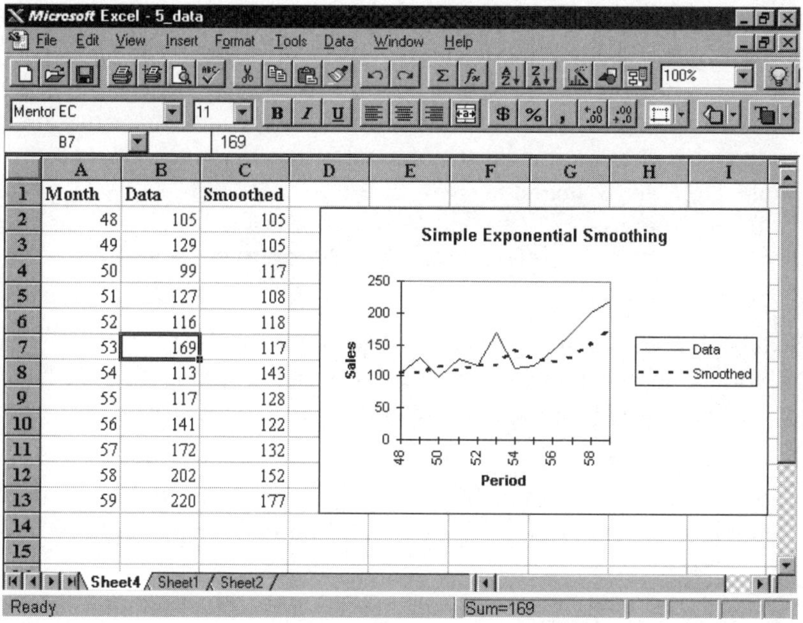

can accommodate both trend and seasonality. By including these models, we now must consider over two dozen ES methods, which raises the obvious question, How do I know which ES model works best with my data? An even broader question is, How do I know that ES models are the best technique for my data? One solution would be to run multiple models and compare the goodness-of-fit statistics for the resulting in-sample forecasts. That method is feasible and we demonstrate it in the next section, but for many users it requires more time and forecasting expertise than available. A better alternative is to harness the PC's power to let the forecasting software select the best model. In the next section we look at this solution, which takes the form of automated forecasting software.

FORECASTING SOFTWARE: FORECAST PRO

Our goal is to find a model that provides the best-fitting, in-sample forecasts, but that can be a daunting task. Fortunately, software is now available that examines the data using an expert system and decides which model is appropriate. For the rest of this chapter, we use Forecast Pro from Business Forecast Systems, a program that offers this automated modeling feature.

You can work with Forecast Pro in two ways. The first method uses the program's expert system to examine the data and recommend a forecasting model. The other approach is to use the program's built-in features to run a "manual" analysis. Using this method, the user can choose from several models: moving averages, exponential smoothing, Box-Jenkins, and dynamic regression. In the next section, we demonstrate the manual approach by creating forecasts of the sales data using three ES methods: simple, Holt, and Winters.

Manual Methods

Step 1: Divide the data.
We tell the program to hold back 12 data points (one year of data) that we will use for our in-sample forecasts. As you can see in Figure 5–5, the program breaks the data at the beginning of 1995, the last year in the data set.

Step 2. Select and evaluate the model.
To illustrate the program's output, we apply the three ES models sequentially: simple, Holt, and Winters. Here are the numerical and graphical results

FIGURE 5–5

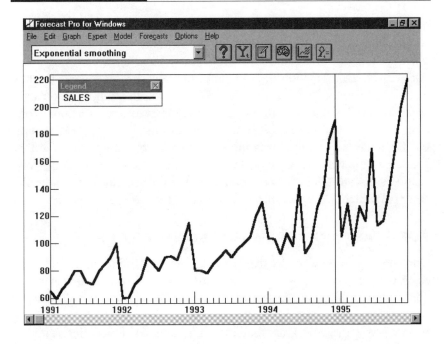

from fitting each model to the data. (The diagnostic results that have not been described previously are explained following the first set of results.)

Model 1. Simple exponential smoothing: no trend, no seasonality
Confidence limits proportional to level

Component	Smoothing Weight	Final Value
Level	0.80000	185.49

Standard Diagnostics

Sample size 48	Number of parameters 1
Mean 94.7	Standard deviation 26.71
R-squared 0.6372	Adjusted R-square 0.6372
Durbin-Watson 1.949	Ljung-Box(18)=28.8 P=0.9492
Forecast error 16.09	BIC 16.58
MAPE 0.1199	RMSE 15.92
MAD 11.65	

FIGURE 5–6

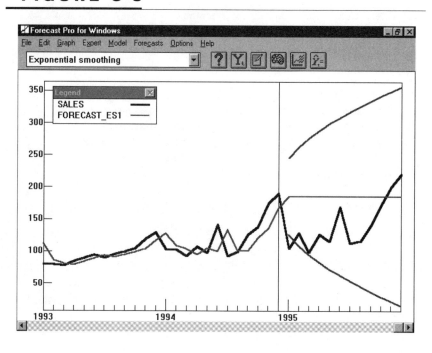

Terminology

Smoothing weight Optimal value of α (selected by the program).

Ljung-Box statistic Measures overall autocorrelation of the fitted errors. Two asterisks to the left of the statistic indicate significant autocorrelation, and the model may be invalid for the data.

Bayesian Information Criteria (BIC) An approximate measure of the forecasting performance to expect from the model. The model that produces the smallest BIC is likely to provide the best forecasting performance for the data set. Forecast Pro uses the BIC as its default model-selection criterion.

Figure 5–6 is divided into two sections: estimation data (pre-1995) and in-sample test data (1995), which we use to test the model's forecasts. Because the simple ES model does not account for trend or seasonality, the forecast is a flat line. Obviously, this model has little forecasting value with this data.

Model 2. Holt exponential smoothing: linear trend,
            no seasonality
            Confidence limits proportional to level

Component	Smoothing Weight	Final Value
Level	0.75342	184.49
Trend	0.01506	2.1234

Standard Diagnostics

Sample size 48	Number of parameters 2
Mean 94.7	Standard deviation 26.71
R-squared 0.6457	Adjusted R-squared 0.638
Durbin-Watson 1.925	*Ljung-Box(18)=33.07 P=0.9836
Forecast error 16.07	BIC 17.06
MAPE 0.119	RMSE 15.73
MAD 11.47	

This model uses two smoothing weights: one for the level and one for trend. When we compare goodness-of-fit statistics between this model and the simple ES, we see that this model is an even weaker performer. The reason is evident in Figure 5–7: Including a trend line takes the forecast values further away from the actual 1995 values, increasing the forecast error term.

FIGURE 5-7

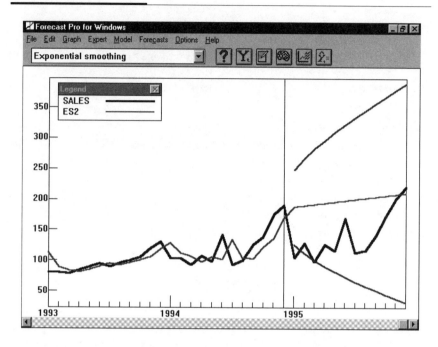

Model 3. Multiplicative Winters: linear trend, multiplicative seasonality
Forecast model for SALES
Automatic model selection
Multiplicative Winters: linear trend, multiplicative seasonality
Confidence limits proportional to indexes and level

Component	Smoothing Weight	Final Value
Level	0.09743	134.55
Trend	0.30065	3.1554
Seasonal	0.99992	

Seasonal Indexes

January to March	0.99043	0.95312	0.83312
April to June	0.94195	0.85135	1.18118
July to September	0.76721	0.82200	1.01901
October to December	1.10109	1.34350	1.41207

Standard Diagnostics

Sample size 48	Number of parameters 3
Mean 94.7	Standard deviation 26.66
R-squared 0.8595	Adjusted R-squared 0.8533
Durbin-Watson 1.405	Ljung-Box(18)=12.34 P=0.171
Forecast error 10.21	BIC 11.16
MAPE 0.06782	RMSE 9.888
MAD 6.935	

This model allows for seasonal fluctuations and shows the seasonal adjustment factors. This model generates the lowest BIC statistic of the three ES models, and as Figure 5–8 shows, its forecasts come closest to the actual 1995 data.

Table 5–16 lists the forecasts and actual values for the 1995 (in-sample) data. The program also provides a 95 percent confidence interval around the forecast, and the upper and lower limits for the interval are listed with the data.

Expert Mode

Our comparison of the three ES methods was based on the assumption that it was the best model to use. But how can we be sure that our assumption was correct? We would have more confidence in the initial choice of

FIGURE 5–8

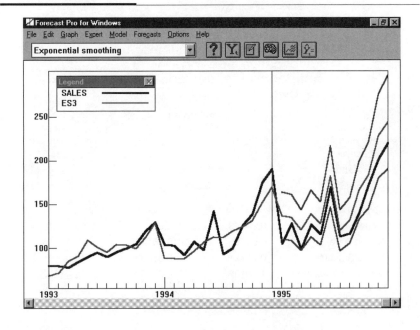

TABLE 5-16

Forecasts of Sales from Base Period 1994-12
Multiplicative Winters method

Period	Lower 2.5	Forecast	Upper 97.5	Actual
1995-01	109.745	136.704	163.662	105
1995-02	108.382	134.528	160.675	129
1995-03	97.344	120.534	143.724	99
1995-04	112.490	139.114	165.737	127
1995-05	103.461	127.945	152.429	116
1995-06	146.557	181.465	216.374	169
1995-07	96.694	120.025	143.357	113
1995-08	105.719	131.720	157.722	117
1995-09	132.939	166.456	199.973	141
1995-10	145.279	183.017	220.755	172
1995-11	179.658	227.953	276.247	202
1995-12	90.296	243.430	296.563	220

the ES method if we had extensive forecasting experience, but even if we had that experience, doesn't it make sense to compare results with other models? It does, and this is where a program like Forecast Pro becomes more valuable. The program offers an expert mode that evaluates the data and recommends a forecasting model. Figure 5–9 shows the program's output after examining the sales data (using all 60 data points).

In Figure 5–9 the program describes its data examination results in understandable language and states its recommendation clearly. Forecast Pro recommends we use an exponential smoothing method. The output also describes the results of its comparison between exponential smoothing and Box-Jenkins, using the out-of-sample MAD as its criterion. Although the Box-Jenkins did not score as well in this example, the method is used widely in forecasting, and we discuss it in the next section.

Box-Jenkins Method

The Box-Jenkins method consists of a group of forecasting models. The autoregressive (AR) models use the variable's past values in developing the forecast, while the moving average models use past forecast errors. These methods are combined in the autoregressive integrated moving average (ARIMA) method. The ARIMA model's parameters are usually

FIGURE 5-9

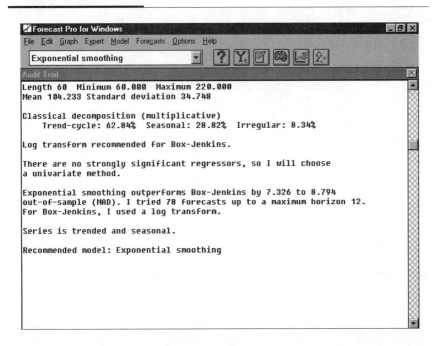

given in the format ARIMA (p,d,q) (P,D,Q). The lowercase letters signify the model's autoregressive (p), moving average (q), and differencing factors (d), while the uppercase letters stand for the same factors, but on a seasonal basis. The idea behind the Box-Jenkins method is that stable correlations exist among the data and these correlations can be extrapolated for forecasting. Box-Jenkins can provide better forecasts than exponential smoothing when you have a fairly long data series (more than 40 points) that is not too volatile.

One drawback of using the Box-Jenkins method is that the user needs fairly extensive experience to implement it successfully. As we demonstrate in the next section, selecting the proper model calls for interpretations and judgments that could intimidate the novice and create the opportunity for error. Developing the model also can be time-consuming, because the user must diagnose each model to judge its forecasting power. The new generation of forecasting software like Forecast Pro eliminates the need for extensive user experience by automating the data evaluation, model selection, and testing stages. The software removes many of the stumbling blocks to using the Box-Jenkins method, making it more accessible to a wider range of users.

In the next section, we demonstrate the basic elements of manually developing a Box-Jenkins model to highlight the concepts and steps behind the method. We then use Forecast Pro's automated model building feature to develop forecasts for the sales data that we used in the previous examples. After comparing the time and effort required to use the manual versus the automated method, we believe you will appreciate the efficiency of automation.

Building the Model

Box-Jenkins users follow an established procedure in building their forecasting models. Here are brief descriptions of each step.

Step 1: Examine the Data

As with the previous models, we examine the data plot to look for evidence of trend and seasonality. This step is especially important in a Box-Jenkins model. This method requires that the data be stationary, which means that the data do not follow a trend or have seasonal factors and that the variance of the data should be constant over time. Because most business and economic data are not stationary, we first must transform the data. The usual techniques for making the data stationary are differencing and transformation. Table 5–17 is an example of how differencing can transform data with a trend into stationary data.

The original data (Y_t) shows a clear upward trend. But when we take the difference between Y_t and Y_{t-1}, we see in the fourth column that the differenced series is stationary. In some cases we might have to difference a series twice, but two is usually the maximum number of steps needed for financial data. Transforming the data can also make it stationary. For example, if the data show exponential growth, taking the log of the data can make it stationary.

TABLE 5–17

Differencing Data

T	Y_t	Y_{t-1}	Y_t-Y_{t-1}
1	100		
2	112	100	12
3	120	112	8
4	130	120	10

Step 2: Identify the Model

The Box-Jenkins user can select several variations of the model. To select the proper one for the data, the user first reviews the plot of the data's autocorrelations. Autocorrelation (AC) measures the relationship between data points in a series, and the user looks for an identifiable pattern in the AC plot. The AC plot for the sales data is found in Figure 5–10.

The user must now interpret the plot in Figure 5–10 to determine the model's initial parameters by relying on experience or published examples of known AC patterns. You can see why this method could discourage inexperienced users: If the pattern is not immediately identifiable, they must rely on their judgment, an unpleasant prospect for the novice.

Next the user applies an initial model and examines the residuals from that model in the partial autocorrelations (PAC) plot. We show the sales PAC plot in Figure 5–11 from a simple moving average model created in Forecast Pro. Once again, the user must interpret the plot to set the Box-Jenkins model's parameters.

Step 3: Diagnose the Model

After building the model, the next step is to use it for in-sample forecasting. This allows the user to estimate the goodness-of-fit statistics reviewed earlier in the chapter. Most users will diagnose multiple models to compare their results.

FIGURE 5–10

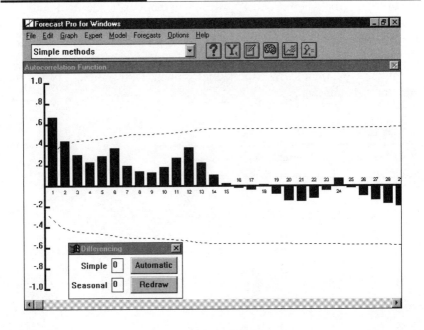

FIGURE 5–11

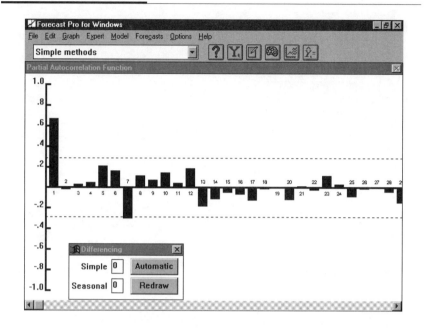

Step 4: Use the Model

After deciding which model works best, the user can begin generating out-of-sample forecasts.

Using Automatic Model Selection

These steps are not very difficult for experienced Box-Jenkins users. To a novice or infrequent users, though, the process can be intimidating, especially when they must use their own judgment to set the model's parameters. Automated model-building software eliminates this problem by examining the data, testing a range of parameters, and recommending a model based on an objective goodness-of-fit statistic. As we showed earlier in Figure 5–9, the Forecast Pro program recommended a log transformation of the data for Box-Jenkins. Here are the forecast results and graph (Figure 5–12) based on that method.

Forecast Pro Output
Forecast Model for SALES (log transform)
Automatic model selection
ARIMA(0,1,1)*(0,1,0)

Term	Coefficient	Std. Error	t-Statistic	Significance
b[1]	0.8358	0.0764	10.9407	1.0000

FIGURE 5-12

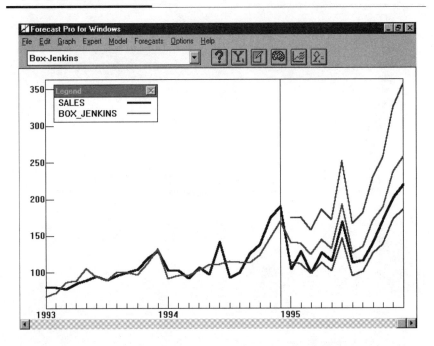

Standard Diagnostics

Sample size 47	Number of parameters 1
Mean 112.2	Standard deviation 35.21
R-squared 0.8736	Adjusted R-squared 0.8736
Durbin-Watson 1.787	Ljung-Box(18)=14.65 P=0.3142
Forecast error 12.52	BIC 12.9
MAPE 0.07485	RMSE 12.39
MAD 8.7	

We compare the diagnostic statistics from the exponential smoothing models and the automated Box-Jenkins forecasts in Table 5–18. Based on those results, the Winters exponential smoothing was more accurate than the ARIMA model. In recommending methods, Forecast Pro software uses the BIC score to select the appropriate model within a family (for example, the best exponential smoothing or best Box Jenkins model). To make comparisons across model families, it creates a holdout sample, calculates its MDA, and uses this statistic for interfamily comparisons. If you use an automated forecasting program, you should be aware of the program's ranking criteria.

TABLE 5–18

Comparison of Results

Test Statistic	Exponential Smoothing: Simple	Exponential Smoothing: Holt	Exponential Smoothing: Winters	Box-Jenkins: ARIMA (0,1,1)(0,1,0)
MAPE	0.12	0.12	0.07	0.07
MAD	11.65	11.47	6.94	8.7
RMSE	15.92	15.73	9.89	12.39

SUMMARY

Traditionally, forecasting has been as much of an art as a science. Forecasters frequently needed to exercise extensive judgment in developing their models, and experts frequently disagreed about the best approach for a particular data set. Automated forecasting software such as Forecast Pro uses expert systems to evaluate data, select, and test models. While automation does not relieve the user of the need for intelligent judgment, it does give the forecasting novice increased access to more sophisticated and powerful models.

SOURCES AND SUGGESTED READING

Goodrich, R. L. *Applied Statistical Forecasting.* Belmont, MA: Business Forecast Systems, Inc., 1992.

Kennedy, P. *A Guide to Econometrics.* 3rd ed. Cambridge, MA: MIT Press, 1992.

Pindyck, R. S. and D. L. Rubinfield. *Econometric Models and Economic Forecasts.* 3rd ed. New York: McGraw-Hill, 1991.

Ramanathan, R. *Introductory Econometrics with Applications.* 2nd ed. New York: Harcourt Brace Jovanovich, 1992.

Shim, J. K.; J. G. Siegel; and C. J. Liew. *Strategic Business Forecasting.* Chicago: Probus, 1994.

SOFTWARE RESOURCES

Forecast Pro for Windows
Business Forecast Systems, Inc.
68 Leonard Street
Belmont, MA 02178
Tel. 617-484-5050
Fax 617-484-9219
URL: http://ourworld.compuserve.com/homepages/forecastpro
Suggested retail price: $595
Free demo disk available

Microsoft Excel
Microsoft Corporation
One Microsoft Way
Redmond, WA 98052-6399

CHAPTER 6

Artificial Neural Networks

INTRODUCTION

Artificial neural networks have become popular in recent years. As the technology has gained acceptance, finance practitioners such as accountants, investment managers, and credit analysts have developed successful applications of neural networks. It is not just the smaller, more adventurous companies adopting the technology, either—several of the world's largest financial service firms have been among the most active developers.

In this chapter we examine neural networks and discuss their potential applications for financial advisors. Although neural net programs can be described accurately as a "black box" technology, a novice can use commercially available software successfully, assuming she understands the problem under study. As we show, judicious selection and manipulation of the data used for input is a critical factor in building a reliable network. Therefore, a user can compensate for inexperience with the technology by having a good grasp of the problem. Also, the material in this chapter emphasizes network development and applications instead of theory. We believe that approach makes the technology more accessible to the reader.

NETWORK ELEMENTS

Artificial neural networks are an attempt to simulate part of the brain, which has billions of cells called neurons. A neuron is composed of dendrites, which provide input to the cell's body (nucleus), and an axon, which conducts signals from the cell's body to other neurons. The connecting points between the neurons are known as synapses. The synapses do more than just conduct signals between neurons, though. They can increase or decrease a signal's intensity (increase its "weight"), causing it to excite or inhibit the neuron receiving the signal. As a neuron receives incoming signals, it decides if the level of stimulation is sufficient to cause it to become excited. An excited neuron will create an output signal, while an inhibited neuron does not generate a signal. (Think of the reflex test a doctor gives you when she taps on your knee with a rubber hammer. If she taps you very lightly, your knee might not react. If she taps you forcefully enough, the reflex occurs and your leg snaps out. The tap corresponds to the incoming signal: If it excites the receiving cells sufficiently, they generate an output.)

Each neuron receives and sends out signals of one kind: sound response, motor activity, and so on. When the neurons combine in groups, they allow us to perform a wider range of complex actions. What we recognize as learning takes place by changes to the synapses. According to Lawrence (1993), "The general opinion is that neurons 'learn' as a function of the signals that they receive. The synapses change over time as signals are received, and this constitutes learning. Knowledge is 'captured' in bits and pieces by the weights synapses attach to incoming signals."[1]

An artificial neural network uses software in an attempt to replicate the neuron's behavior. The network's neurons, also known as processing elements or nodes, have the structure shown in Figure 6–1.

Figure 6–1 shows the neuron receiving inputs, denoted by the X_i, which are processed in the summation function. After processing the inputs,

FIGURE 6–1

An Artificial Neuron

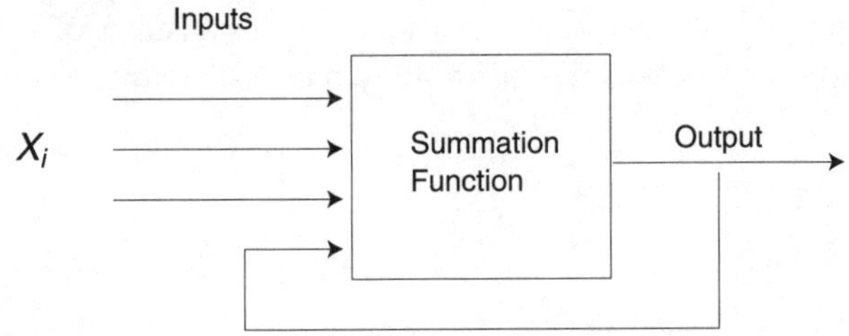

---

[1] J. Lawrence, *Introduction to Neural Networks* (Nevada City, CA: California Scientific Press, 1993), p. 81.

the neuron sends an output signal, which can be a final product or can go to other neurons. Many networks also have a feedback loop, shown in Figure 6–1 as the line from the output back to the node. As we see shortly, networks learn from their errors, and the feedback facilitates this function.

An individual node does not have much processing power, but nodes can be linked together. A common network structure is to have three layers: input, intermediate, and output. As Figure 6–2 shows, each input node can connect to each intermediate node, which in turn connects to each output node. The intermediate nodes are often called the hidden layer, and they make the connection between the input and output layers.

NETWORK SIGNAL PROCESSING

Although Figures 6–1 and 6–2 may appear complex, an example will show that their mechanics are straightforward. Let's assume the processing element in Figure 6–1 receives input signals from two sources. We denote the first signal by X_1 and the second by X_2. Each signal carries a weight, W_1 for the first signal and W_2 for the second, and a higher weight means a relatively stronger signal. (As we show shortly, these weights are subject to change, so their initial values are not critical.) For this example, we assign the values shown in Table 6–1.

As these signals reach the processing element, their weighted values are summed: $(2 * .3) + (1 * .1) = .70$. This is equivalent to using the formula

$$Y_j = \sum_{i=1}^{n} X_i W_{ij}$$

where Y is the weighted sum of the element's inputs. After the processing element calculates the weighted sum of its incoming signals, it changes

FIGURE 6–2

Neurons Connected in Network

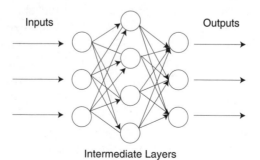

Intermediate Layers

TABLE 6–1

Input Signals

Signal	Value	Weight (W)
X_1	2	.3
X_2	1	.1

the inputs into an output signal by using a transformation, or transfer, function. This function modifies the output signal to make it more manageable by placing it in a narrow range, usually between –1 and 1 or 0 and 1. There are several types of transfer functions. Some apply a linear operation to Y, while others apply a step, or threshold, function, which works like an on-off switch. With a step function, if Y is below a certain level, .50 for example, the signal will be too weak to produce an output (the switch is "off"). If Y reaches the threshold level, the processing element produces an output (the switch is "on"). A popular nonlinear transfer function is the sigmoid function, which uses the formula

$$\frac{1}{1+e^{-y}}$$

In the previous example, Y (the signals' weighted sum) has a value of .70, resulting in an output

$$\frac{1}{1+e^{-.7}} = .668$$

HOW NETWORKS LEARN

We mentioned earlier that the brain learns by making changes to the synapses between neurons. Neural nets work in a roughly equivalent manner. To teach or train a network, the user presents it with inputs and corresponding outputs. Suppose that we wanted to train a network to forecast the direction of change (up or down) in the next day's Dow Jones Industrial Average (DJIA). Our data set might look something like Table 6–2.

The values of Table 6–2 are irrelevant at this stage, but the matching of inputs and output is important. We present the neural net with inputs (changes in gold, oil, and bond prices) and an associated output: change in the DJIA. Each day's set of numbers represents a training example or fact. The network takes the input data and creates an output based on that particular input data. If a difference occurs between the network's estimate of the

TABLE 6-2

Neural Net Inputs

Day	Gold*	Oil*	Bonds*	Change in DJIA
−1	+.50	+.25	+.30	−12.60
−2	−.75	+.10	−.50	+33.25
~	~	~	~	~
−365	+1.50	+1.00	+.50	−44.00

*Percentage change in price or yield.

output and the actual value, the network adjusts the weights between its neurons. It repeats this process of adjusting its weights until the errors reach an acceptable level. There are several different methods for adjusting the weights, but we do not cover that material here. Most neural net software programs use one of the more popular methods as a default, and that default selection is usually a good starting place for most networks.

This method of network learning by example and repetition is known as "back propagation." Lawrence provides a colorful example that illustrates the method. Imagine that you are trying to teach a network to recognize vegetables based on their characteristics. If you give the network the inputs "large, round, orange, vegetable," you want the response "pumpkin." What happens if the network does not respond with pumpkin?

> Suppose our untrained network initially decides that a large, round, orange vegetable is a zucchini. The training example, which has the correct output, indicates the vegetable is really a pumpkin. The network compares the network output and the training example output and then makes changes to its internal connections (weights) so that the next time it sees the same inputs, it will be more likely to produce the correct answer. The connections are adjusted so that the inputs are associated more strongly with the pumpkin output and less strongly with the zucchini output. This training is repeated for a set of examples until the network learns the correct answers. Once the network is trained using pre-selected inputs and outputs, we can run it on new information (without any supplied outputs) and have it recognize, generalize, or predict the answer for us.[2]

In summary, neural networks learn by association. To train a network, the user presents it with matched pairs of inputs and outputs. The network makes multiple passes through the data until it can associate the

2. Ibid., p. 7.

inputs and outputs with a user-selected degree of accuracy. To check the network at this stage, most users test it against a new set of facts with known outcomes. If the network performs well with these new facts, it is ready for actual use. We describe these steps in more detail when we create sample networks.

NETWORK STRENGTHS AND WEAKNESSES

The black-box operations of a network's method take place in the hidden layers. Because we normally do not see the changes to the program's weights, we do not really know what the program is doing. From one perspective, that situation is acceptable: "As long as the network generates the correct answer, I don't care how it reached that answer." If you can live with that lack of knowledge about the method used to reach an output, then this aspect of a neural net's operation will not concern you. Other users are more interested in how the network reaches its output, though, especially with economic models, where the network's weights might ignore, or contradict, existing theory.

Because of this lack of transparency, networks work well in situations where you believe a relationship exists among the inputs and the output(s), but you don't know what that relationship is. Klimasauskas (1991)[3] identifies three areas in which neural nets work best: classifying data, modeling and forecasting, and signal processing. Examples of classifying activities include credit approval, stock picking, and automated securities trading. Networks are used to model and forecast interest rates, while speech recognition is an example of a signal processing use.

Neural nets do not work as well in situations that demand precise answers. For those situations that demand numerical precision, the user will get better results with spreadsheets and other "numerically correct" programs. Another potential problem with neural nets is that they cannot guarantee an optimal solution to every problem, which might be caused by the nature of the problem or reflect improper network design.

In spite of these potential problems, users have adopted neural networks for a wide range of financial applications. Trippi and Turban (1993) include articles covering the following areas:

Analysis of financial condition.

Business failure prediction.

---

3. In *Neural Networks in Finance and Investing,* R.R. Trippi and E. Turban, eds. (Chicago: Probus, 1993).

Debt risk assessment.

Security market applications.

Financial forecasting.

Articles in Freedman, Klein, and Lederman (1995) include those areas and accounting applications, as well. Academics in finance also are showing interest in the technology, with research papers on networks appearing regularly at finance conferences.

These developments should encourage the financial advisor who is considering adopting the technology for internal use or for client applications. As we show in the following sections, though, developing a successful neural network requires a dedicated effort. Learning to use the software is no longer an issue because the programs have developed easy-to-use interfaces. The real challenge is in selecting and transforming data and then finding the network parameters that work best for your application. Assuming the absence of beginner's luck, this procedure requires a period of experimentation with no guarantee of success. Based on the widespread acceptance of neural nets, however, this effort apparently has been worthwhile for many financial users.

DESIGNING A NETWORK

We stated earlier that proper design is critical to a network's success. We briefly introduce the design process in this section. Our source for this material is the *BrainMaker Professional User's Guide and Reference Manual* (4th edition). The BrainMaker line of neural network software is produced by California Scientific Software, and we use the professional version (denoted by BMP) of the program to develop this chapter's examples.

The Seven-Step Design Process

A logical design process can help the network development process go more smoothly. The BMP manual suggests the following seven-step process.

1. Decide what you want your neural network to predict or recognize.
2. Decide what information you want BrainMaker to use for its predictions.

These first two steps may sound obvious, but until you decide what you want the network to accomplish and what data you will supply, you can't build a network. For example, if you want to predict a particular stock's price, you might include the stock prices of its competitors, prices of critical materials the company uses in production, a market index, an interest-rate indicator, and so on. Deciding what information to provide is not easy: You don't want to overlook any important factors, but at the same time you shouldn't include data that has no logical place in the input set. If you include too little relevant data, the predictions will be poor. Include too much (the "kitchen sink" approach), and you can confuse the network. Obviously, this step requires you to use your experience and knowledge of the problem, and you probably will want to readjust your input set as you experiment with the network.

3. Get some data. BMP and most other neural net software allow you to input data directly, and most programs can accept ASCII, spreadsheet, and database files (numerical data only). We discuss the amount of data you should use shortly.

4. Build a network. BMP groups its data in a spreadsheet format with the data organized by columns. (The rows hold the training facts.) After you enter the data, you must identify each column so the program can distinguish between input and output data. BMP also allows annotation data for descriptive purposes, but this data is not used by the network.

5. Train the network. In this step the network looks at the training facts, produces its output, and begins correcting its weights in an effort to improve its results. When the network's output errors become acceptably small, the network stops training.

6. Test the network. It is important to reserve some of the training facts so you can test the network on known results. Occasionally, a network will do a very good job with its training data set but will perform poorly outside the training set. Keeping some of your data in reserve for testing allows you to look for problems of that nature.

7. Run the network. If the trained network tests satisfactorily, it is ready for use.

SAMPLE NETWORKS

Now that we have reviewed the basic elements of neural network design and operation, we can begin to examine applications. We present the applications in order of increasing complexity. The first application of developing a credit-scoring network is based on an example developed by

Klimasauskas (1991). We use this example to describe the data gathering and network design process, although we do not build the network. The second application demonstrates BrainMaker's ability to assess real estate values, and the third uses BMP to forecast a financial market index.

Example: Credit Approval

Any organization that sells to customers on credit faces a risk that customers will not pay their bills. This presents a dilemma because issuing credit is a proven way to increase sales. As a result, most firms use a credit-screening or scoring process in an effort to avoid issuing credit to customers whose profile indicates a high risk of nonpayment. Banks and other financial firms use neural nets extensively to identify poor credit risks, and this section outlines the network development process. This network's goal is to assign a credit-risk rating (good, poor, or indeterminate) to each applicant.

The Input Data

The credit granting process usually starts with the applicant completing the creditor's standardized application form. Table 6–3 lists the typical information that the creditor will request from the applicant.

As you can see, several original data types are nonnumeric. Although we could designate some of them as annotations, we want to include others in the analysis. To use these data fields, we must transform them into formats the network can use, typically in the 0 to 1 range. There are several accepted methods for transforming data, depending on the nature of the entry. The simplest is the Yes/No category: 1 for yes, 0 for no. Other items can take only a limited number of values. Under marital status, for example, the respondent must answer married, divorced, widowed, or singled. To match the applicant's status, each category receives a yes (1) or no (0) input. Categories that take digits, like income and number of late payments in past year, can be rescaled to the 0 to 1 range.

Network Parameters

After the training data are prepared and a test sample is reserved (roughly 10 percent of the facts), the user must make several decisions about the network's parameters. Klimasauskas provides a list of the key parameters, which we partially reproduce in Table 6–4.

We discuss these parameters in more detail when we begin to work with BMP. We can provide several rules of thumb for several of the param-

TABLE 6-3

Typical Credit Application Information

Data Item	Original Data Type
Name	character
Address	character
Zip code	digit
Own residence	Yes/No
Years at residence	digit
Home telephone	text
Marital status	text
Social Security number	text
Driver's license number	text
Employer	text
Occupation	text
Years with employer	digit
Employment income	digit
Other income	digit
Checking account	Yes/No
Savings account	Yes/No
Other charge cards	digit
Number of late payments in past year	digit

eters, though. For hidden layers, start with a single layer—that's usually enough for most problems. In deciding how many hidden-layer neurons to have, start with either slightly fewer than half the number of input and output neurons, or 5 to 10 percent of the number of training facts. These rules will help you get started, and you can make changes as needed later.

NEURAL NETWORK SOFTWARE: BRAINMAKER

Example: Real Estate Appraisal

In this example, we begin using BMP to produce forecasts of real estate selling prices. Neural networks have been used successfully to appraise real estate, with some practitioners claiming 90 percent accuracy in forecasting sales prices. This result is impressive, considering the wide range of values for a single property that the traditional expert appraisal method often produces.

TABLE 6–4

Back-Propagation Network Parameters

Problem-Specific Parameters	
Number of inputs to network	
Number of outputs from network	
Network Decisions	
Type of transfer function	Hyperbolic tangent, sigmoid, sine
Learning rule	Delta rule, cumulative delta rule, normalized cumulative delta rule
Topology	Number of hidden layers, processing elements per layer

The data for this network were supplied to California Scientific Software by one of its customers who trained his network to appraise real estate in the New York area. Table 6–5 lists the data categories by name, description, and the range of values the data took. The database holds 217 sales.

BMP provides a separate data manipulation program called NetMaker, which we use to prepare the data for BMP. Figure 6–3 shows part of the real estate data after it has been entered into NetMaker. Each column represents a data type, and each row represents the information for a home.

The text NotUsed above the data field's name in each column signifies that the column has not yet been identified as output or input. In this network the data marked SalePrice will be our output with the other columns used for input. To identify the SalePrice column as the output, we click on the SalePrice field name, go to the Label pull-down menu and select Mark Column as Pattern. (BrainMaker identifies the output by the name Pattern.) Next we mark the remaining columns as inputs. Figure 6–4 shows the result of marking the columns.

We have completed the file preparation work, so we save the file, close NetMaker, and go to the BrainMaker program. We load the real estate data, which produces the screen in Figure 6–5.

This is the first time we have shown the BMP screen, so a brief explanation of its elements is in order. We start with the first line directly below the pull-down menus. (We discuss those menus as we use them in this and the following example.)

TABLE 6-5

Real Estate Database Description

Name	Description	Range
SALEPRIC	Actual sale price of home	$103,000–250,000
DWLUN	Number of dwelling units	1–3
RDOS	Reverse date of sale (months since sale)	0–23
YRBLT	Year built	1850–1986
TOTFIXT	Number of plumbing fixtures	5–17
HEATING	Heating system type	2 or 3
WBFPSTKS	Wood-burning fireplace stacks	0–1
BMNTGAR	Basement/garage	0–2
ATTFRGAR	Attached frame garage area	0–228
TOTLIVAR	Total living area	714–4185
DECK/OFP	Deck/open porch area	0–738
EENCLPOR	Enclosed porch area	0–452
NBHDGRP	Neighborhood group	1 or 2
RECROOM	Recreation room area	0–672
FINBSMT	Finished basement area	0–810
GRADE%	Grade factors	0.85–1.08
CDU	Condition/desirability/usefulness	3–5
TOTOBY	Total other value (building and yard)	0–16400

Line 1

Waiting: BMP is inactive and waiting for instructions.

Facts: EMRE2.fct is the name of the fact file we will use for training. It contains 90 percent of the total facts available, with the remaining 10 percent reserved for testing.

Learn: The network's learning rate, which determines how large an adjustment BMP will make to its weights as it learns. The default is 1.00, and we will start with that value.

Tolerance: The amount of error that BMP will accept before making corrections to the network. The default tolerance is .100, or 10 percent, which means that the output must be within 10 percent of the actual to be considered a "good" output.

Line 2

Fact: Number of the fact being processed to train the network. BMP processes one fact at a time until it cycles through the entire

FIGURE 6-3

NetMaker Professional - RE.DAT									_ 🗗 ✕
File Column Row Label Number Symbol Operate Indicators									
NotUsed NotUsed NotUsed NotUsed NotUsed NotUsed NotUsed NotUsed NotUsed									
	ALEPRI	DWLUN	RDOS	YRBLT	TOTFIXT	HEATING	BFPSTK	MNTGA	TTFRGA
1	140000	1	13	1920	5	2	0	0	0
2	155000	1	5	1900	5	2	0	0	0
3	200000	2	3	1910	10	2	0	0	0
4	157000	1	18	1930	7	2	1	0	0
5	171000	1	18	1930	6	2	1	0	0
6	170000	1	10	1900	8	2	0	0	0
7	168000	1	22	1955	8	2	0	0	0
8	145000	1	1	1910	5	2	0	0	0
9	155000	2	23	1920	10	2	0	0	0
10	167000	2	14	1926	10	2	0	0	0
11	172000	3	16	1900	15	2	0	0	0
12	172000	2	22	1920	9	2	0	0	0
13	155000	1	13	1920	5	2	0	0	0
14	232000	3	11	1900	15	2	0	0	0
15	240000	3	0	1900	15	2	0	0	0

FIGURE 6-4

NetMaker Professional - RE.DAT									_ 🗗 ✕
File Column Row Label Number Symbol Operate Indicators									
Pattern Input Input Input Input Input Input Input Input									
	ALEPRI	DWLUN	RDOS	YRBLT	TOTFIXT	HEATING	BFPSTK	MNTGA	TTFRGA
1	140000	1	13	1920	5	2	0	0	0
2	155000	1	5	1900	5	2	0	0	0
3	200000	2	3	1910	10	2	0	0	0
4	157000	1	18	1930	7	2	1	0	0
5	171000	1	18	1930	6	2	1	0	0
6	170000	1	10	1900	8	2	0	0	0
7	168000	1	22	1955	8	2	0	0	0
8	145000	1	1	1910	5	2	0	0	0
9	155000	2	23	1920	10	2	0	0	0
10	167000	2	14	1926	10	2	0	0	0
11	172000	3	16	1900	15	2	0	0	0
12	172000	2	22	1920	9	2	0	0	0
13	155000	1	13	1920	5	2	0	0	0
14	232000	3	11	1900	15	2	0	0	0
15	240000	3	0	1900	15	2	0	0	0

FIGURE 6-5

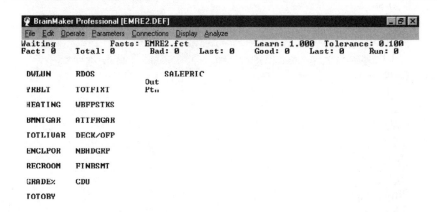

training set. If the network is not trained within the tolerance level, it returns to the first fact and starts back through the training set.

Total: Cumulative number of facts processed.

Bad: Number of facts whose error exceeded the training tolerance in the current pass.

Last: Number of bad facts in the previous pass.

Good: Number of facts meeting the training tolerance in the current pass.

Last: Number of good facts in the previous pass.

Run: Number of iterations, or passes, through the training facts.

The information in the screen's first two lines allows the user to track the network's training progress. As the network learns, the number of good facts should increase while the number of bad facts decreases simultaneously. (The number of good facts plus bad facts equals the total number of available facts, so a change in one value is reflected in the other.)

Dropping down two lines in Figure 6–5, the left side of the screen lists the network's inputs. Moving to the center of the screen, we see SALEPRIC, the network's designated pattern (output). Two fields appear below it: Out, the network's output, and Ptn, the actual value provided with the training fact.

Before training the network, we must set several parameters or use the default values. The first decision is how many hidden neurons to use. The rule of thumb is one-half the sum of inputs and outputs $(17 + 1) / 2 =$ 9, so we start with nine hidden neurons. Next, we adjust the training and testing tolerance to .20 from the default levels of .10 and .40, respectively, to allow the network to train more quickly. Finally, we instruct the network to save the results from every fourth run. Before training the network, we have it load the first training fact to illustrate the input and output fields, which appear in Figure 6–6.

In Figure 6–6, each input field's value appears immediately below its name, and the output and pattern values appear next to their field names. In line 2 the Fact field has a value of 1, indicating the first fact in the file.

We are now ready to train the network. Each run will have 195 facts, with 22 reserved for testing. BMP allows you to visually monitor the network's training progress, and we select that option. Figure 6–7 shows the training results.

In line 1 of Figure 6–7, we see that the total processing time was 28 seconds. (These results were achieved on a Pentium 133 with 32MB RAM—results vary by system.) The network evaluated a total of 29,445 facts on 151 runs, getting three facts wrong (Last: 3) on the previous training run. On the final run, all the outputs were within the tolerance level (Good: 195).

The lower half of Figure 6–7 illustrates the training runs' progress graphically. The histogram shows the entire run's distribution of errors. The horizontal axis is the error level and the vertical axis is the frequency of an error. As the network trains, the errors should become smaller, causing the bars on the left side of the graph (the smaller errors) to grow. The line chart on the bottom of Figure 6–7 shows each run's error level sequentially, with the run number on the x-axis and the error (RMS) on the y-axis. Assuming that the network is training properly, the line should move downward as the number of runs increases, as it does in Figure 6–7.

FIGURE 6–6

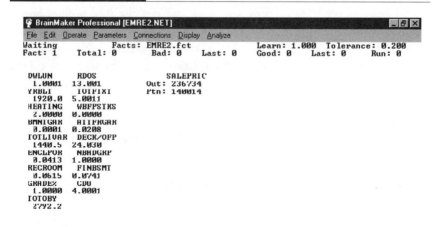

FIGURE 6-7

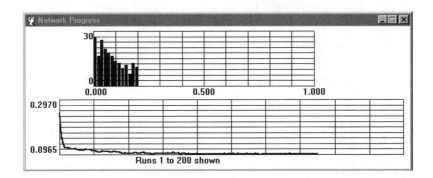

BMP also provides statistics that let the user track how well the network trained during each run. Figure 6–8 displays the average error and RMS error on the y-axis, with the number of runs plotted on the x-axis. We want to find a training run that produced both a low average error and a low RMS error. A visual inspection of Figure 6–8 suggests that we look at the runs in the low 20s, just beyond the 19.750 on the x-axis.

To inspect these runs, we modify the plot to show the first 25 runs in Figure 6–9. As suspected, run 22 produced two low values for the average error (0.00760) and the RMS error (slightly under 0.1075). Based on our review of Figure 6–9, we decide to use the weights produced in run 22, and we save that network.

Now that we have a trained network, we can use it to predict house prices. We start by placing the property's values for the inputs in their respective input fields. BMP allows users to do this manually or to read in new fact files. Figure 6–10 shows the result of giving the network a new set of inputs. The home's predicted selling price, listed in the output field of Figure 6–10, is $160,148.

Example: Financial Forecasting

Forecasting financial results, such as stock or commodity prices and changes in market indexes, is a widespread application of neural net technology. It is consistently a popular topic in articles discussing networks,

FIGURE 6-8

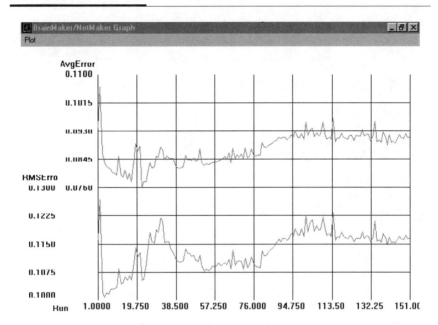

FIGURE 6-9

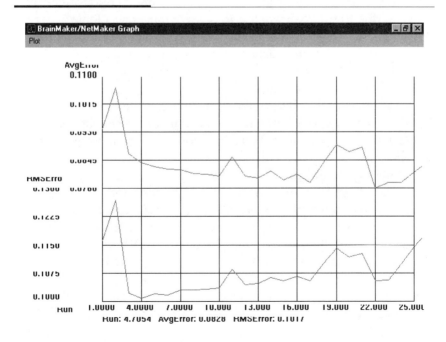

FIGURE 6-10

```
BrainMaker Professional [EMRE3.NET]                                _ 8 X
File  Edit  Operate  Parameters  Connections  Display  Analyze
Waiting           Facts:  rein.in              Learn: 1.000  Tolerance: 0.200
Fact: 1    Total: 4290    Bad: 0    Last: 0    Good: 0    Last: 0    Run: 22

  DULJIN      RDOS             SALEPRIC
  2.0001     13.001        Out: 160148
  YRBLI      TOTPIXI        Pt.
  1950.0     5.0011
  HEATING    WBFPSTKS
  2.0000     0.0000
  BMNIGAR    ATTFRGAR
  0.0001     200.02
  TOTLIUAR   DECK/OFP
  1300.7     112.13
  ENCLPOR    NBHDGRP
  0.0413     1.0000
  RECROOM    FINBSMT
  90.131     200.00
  GRADEX     CDU
  1.0000     4.0001
  TOTORY
  1.5014
```

and for many users it is the Holy Grail of applications. The interest is entirely understandable: Investors are always seeking trading advantages, and if a neural net can improve a trader's results, then the motivation for experimenting with networks becomes obvious.

In this section we build a financial forecasting network that illustrates some of the design issues involved with this type of forecast. The network attempts to predict the change in price for a fictitious stock market index, the BD100. We will use 10 types of input data (Table 6–6) with 185 examples. Some of the data are lagged, which means we must do more extensive pretraining data manipulation than in the previous examples. Although the BD100 index is a fabrication, the example is based on an existing forecasting network.

It is often a good idea to plot the data that you are investigating. In Figure 6–11 we use days for the x-axis and plot the value of the BD100 on the y-axis. The index is volatile, but shows an overall upward trend in its value.

Although we do not reproduce the graphs here, we also examine the other price fields (price1 and price2) for trends. Both series showed upward trends. Trends like this are common in financial data, and they can cause problems for the network. To avoid problems, you should modify the data by using the change from one observation to the next, not the absolute values. We use NetMaker's built-in data manipulation features to modify the data for these three items, creating a "difference" column for each. Figure 6–12 shows the results of differencing the BD100, price1, and price2 columns. The difference columns are labeled BD100D,

TABLE 6–6

Original Network Data

Data Item	Description
day	Day number (1 = oldest)
BD100	Index value
price1	Price of another asset
price2	Price of another asset
index1D	Change in value of market index
index2D	Change in value of market index
line	Technical analysis indicator
strength	Technical analysis indicator
utilD	Change in value of market index
transpD	Change in value of market index

price1D, and price2D, respectively, and are shown adjacent to the original data columns. (If the concept of differencing is not clear, think of it as the change from the value in row 1 to the value in row 2. For example, the value for BD100 [row 2] is 88 less than that for BD100 [row 1], so we enter a –88 in row 2 of the BD100D column. If you plot the difference column, it should show a fairly flat line.)

Another useful pretraining data check is to look for cycles in the data. Some data exhibit regular patterns as a result of recurring influences. We can use NetMaker's cyclical analysis chart to look for evidence of cycles in the BD100 data (not the differenced data). Figure 6–13 shows the result of that analysis.

In examining Figure 6–13, we want to find the shortest major cycle so we can train the network to predict one cycle ahead. The graph's largest peak occurs after the x-axis value of 47.625, roughly at a frequency of 51. To translate this frequency into a time format that we can use, divide the number of days used in the data by the frequency. In this example the value is 185 / 51, or roughly four days, which means that we need to create a training pattern that forecasts the value of BD100D four days in the future. Therefore, we create a new column that shifts the values in BD100D up four rows. Table 6–7 lists several values from the old and new (BD+4) columns.

The next data transformation is designed to eliminate some of the "noise," or short-term volatility, that occurs in time-series data. We smooth the BD100D data by creating a column with moving-average values. As a

FIGURE 6–11

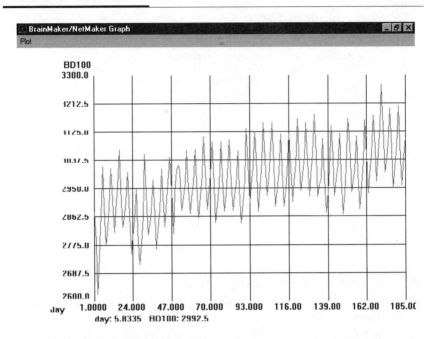

FIGURE 6–12

	day	BD100	BD100D	price1	price1D	price2	price2D	index1D	index2D
1	1	2877	0	38.77	0	46.77	0	14.68	-5.4
2	2	2789	-88	39.07	0.3	46.88	0.11	20.69	-3.55
3	3	2622	-167	39.47	0.4	47.11	0.23	23.66	0.15
4	4	2739	117	39.85	0.38	47.36	0.25	24.87	5.7
5	5	2870	131	40.34	0.49	47.66	0.3	28.02	13.55
6	6	3017	147	40.72	0.38	47.74	0.08	-12.89	9.61
7	7	2892	-125	40.61	-0.11	47.81	0.07	-17.9	5.91
8	8	2774	-118	40.55	-0.06	47.87	0.06	-18.01	-1.93
9	9	2829	55	40.52	-0.03	48.02	0.15	-11.84	0.15
10	10	2891	62	40.49	-0.03	48.16	0.14	-10.88	0.15
11	11	3011	120	40.48	-0.01	48.3	0.14	-4.08	-2.07
12	12	2910	-101	40.46	-0.02	48.61	0.31	-2.06	-4.29
13	13	2814	-96	40.52	0.06	49.01	0.4	-0.84	-6.51
14	14	2886	72	40.6	0.08	49.38	0.37	0.63	-6.51
15	15	2954	68	40.65	0.05	49.56	0.18	-0.07	-6.51

FIGURE 6–13

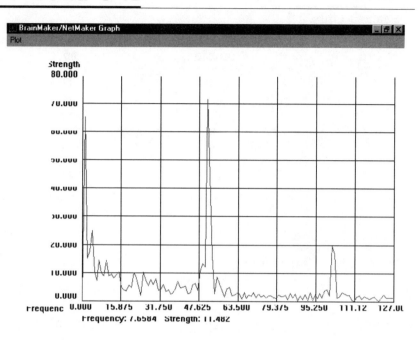

rule of thumb, the moving-average period should be no more than half the cycle (which was four days), so we create a moving-average with a period of two days. Table 6–8 lists the first few rows in the new column, which we label BDavg2.

Checking Data Correlations

This next step is not required for building a network, but it can help improve a net's forecasting ability. Intuitively, it makes sense to include as inputs those data items that show some correlation with the (original) BD100 series. We can use BMP to compare the correlations, and the first input we use is index1D. Figure 6–14 shows the correlation graph. The y-axis is the strength of the correlations, which ranges from –1 to +1. The x-axis is the time period (in days), and it is divided into two parts. Values less than zero represent the past, while x-axis values greater than zero are the future.

Most correlations are calculated at a single point, so this approach warrants explanation. We usually calculate the correlation between data series by using contemporaneous dates:

Date	Series 1	Series 2
1	value for day 1	value for day 1
n	value for day n	value for day n

TABLE 6-7

Shifted Data

Day	BD100D	BD+4
1	0	131
2	−88	147
3	−167	−125
4	117	−118
5	131	55
6	147	62
7	−125	120

TABLE 6-8

Moving-Average Data

Day	BD100	BDavg2
1	0	0
2	−88	−44
3	−167	−127.5
4	117	−25
5	131	124
6	147	139
7	−125	11

By shifting the dates, though, we can calculate leading and lagging correlations. A zero lag means we are using contemporaneous events—they happen at the same time. A positive lag means the first data series changes after the second series, and a negative lag means the first series changes before the second. For example, if we wanted to calculate a negatively lagged correlation (lag = j), we would use the following dates:

Date	Series 1	Series 2
1	value for day $1 - j$	value for day 1
n	value for day $n - j$	value for n

Figure 6–14 provides a summary snapshot of the index 1D lag. We are looking for inputs that can help predict BD100, so we focus on the left side of the graph where the negative lags are plotted. Using BMP's

FIGURE 6–14

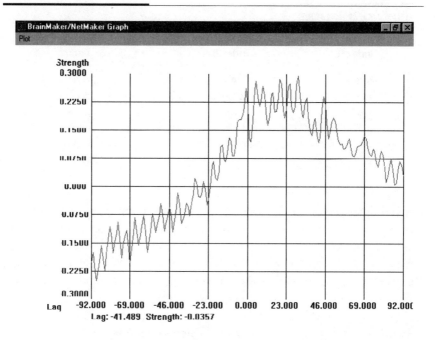

exploratory tools, we see a correlation of .25 at the −1 day lag. (This is the peak directly to the left of the zero x-axis value.) We will use any input that shows a correlation over .20, so we use index1D with a one-day lag as a new input, ind1-1.

We repeat this process of checking for possible correlations with the remaining inputs. Instead of creating new inputs with one-day lags, though, we use four-day lags to match the cycle we noted earlier. (We also create an ind1-4 field.) The final step in manipulating the data is to "clean up" the rows where the differencing created repeat data. We do not show the steps here, but the end result is that we delete nine rows, leaving 176 facts out of the original 185. The final data set has the field BD+4 as its output, and we list the inputs in Table 6–9. Figure 6–15 shows the data fields as they appear on the BMP screen.

Before training the network with these inputs, we want to comment on the network design process. To the casual reader, the steps we have taken so far in creating the networks in this chapter probably appear fairly easy. The reason they appear easy is that we are repeating steps others have already taken to design and test these networks. In a sense, we are following the trail they blazed through the woods to reach the destination. If you decide to create a network on your own, you probably will experience a

TABLE 6-9

Network Inputs

index1D	index2D	line
streng	utilD	transpD
BD100D	price1D	price2D
BDAvg2	ind1-1	ind1-4
ind2-4	line-4	stren-4
util-4	tran-4	BD-4
pric1-4	pric2-4	BDavg-4

much higher level of frustration, especially with your early efforts. Depending on the problem you are trying to solve, you might have to examine dozens of alternative structures to find a combination that produces the results you want. If that happens, try not to become frustrated. Keep notes on your models and their results so you don't duplicate any previous work. Visit the library and study published articles on network design—you might benefit from other users' findings. Thinking of your network as an ongoing experiment in which you are trying to improve the results should help you keep a long-term perspective.

We train the new network with a tolerance of .20. Once again, training time will depend on your PC, but this small network should not take long. After the network trains successfully, we use the reserved data (10 percent of inputs) to test it. We had 18 test facts, and the network produced a "good" result on 17 of them.

Tuning the Network

BMP includes several features that allow the user to tune the network for better performance. One feature, Tolerance Tuning, progressively lowers the network's error tolerance. Figure 6–16 shows the Training Control Flow dialogue box where we set these parameters.

In the upper-left corner of Figure 6–16, in the section marked Tolerance, we set the Start Training Tolerance level to .40 with a "Lower tolerance, multiply by" factor to .90. These settings mean that when the network starts training, it will correct only those errors greater than .40. When all the facts are good (within .40), the network sets a new tolerance level of .36 (.40 × .9). It repeats this process until all the facts are within a minimum tolerance that we specify, .15 in this case (set in "If Tolerance Tuning: Minimum Tolerance" box). After the network completes its training, we run it on the test facts, and once again it scores good on 17 of 18 facts.

FIGURE 6–15

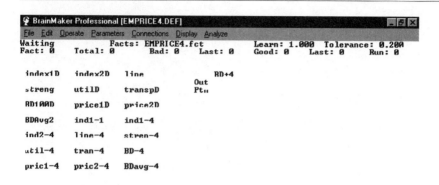

FIGURE 6–16

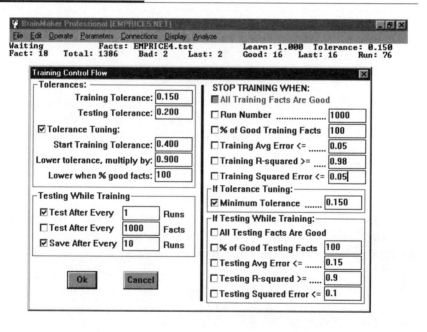

We can see the network's training progress in Figure 6–17, where the x-axis represents the number of runs. The graph shows the number of bad facts in the upper half. At first, the network produced more than 12 bad patterns per run, but that number quickly dropped off. The lower half of Figure 6–17 shows the average error, which also started high but decreased rapidly as the network learned.

As we did in the previous example, we examine the plots to find the runs with a low number of errors and low average error. Run 70 qualifies

FIGURE 6–17

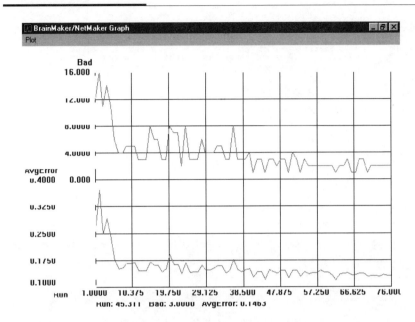

on both counts, with a bad score of 1.0 and an average error of roughly
.1291. We reload run 70 into BMP, train it, and save it as our new network.
It is now ready to use for forecasting.

Maintaining a Network

Because the factors influencing the financial markets can change over time,
it is a good idea to periodically retrain a forecasting network by replacing
the oldest data with new inputs. For example, if you work with weekly
financial forecasts, each week has five trading days. You would delete the
five oldest facts and add five new ones. Regular retraining will help retain
your networks' forecasting ability as market influences change.

DESIGN ISSUES

In this section we discuss several important network design issues and potential problems that can occur with networks. As we have stressed throughout
the chapter, the network's data and design are critical to its success.

Data

When presenting data to a network, users may be tempted to use the kitchen-
sink approach, that is, to include every data item that they think might have

an impact on the output. This approach is tempting because neural networks are promoted on their ability to recognize and subsequently ignore irrelevant data. Although the network eventually will learn to ignore the irrelevant data, having to examine it will slow the network's performance.

For example, typical inputs for a stock market index forecasting network would include some data that track commodity prices and other data that measure interest rates. One measure of commodity behavior, like the price of crude oil, is probably sufficient. It is doubtful that the network will perform much better by also including other commodity prices such as precious metals' prices, especially if the commodities' prices are highly correlated. Similarly, one measure of long-term interest rates is adequate. Having two closely related data sets, like long-term government and long-term corporate bonds, probably will slow the network's training performance.

Network Size

The goal of training is to develop a network that has the ability to work well with facts it has never seen. A network that performs well with the training facts but poorly with the test data has little value as a forecasting tool. One possible cause for poor performance is the network's ability to memorize training facts, which can be caused by using too many connections or having too few training facts. To avoid memorization, keep your networks as small as possible. Start with one hidden layer, and follow the rule of thumb given earlier on the number of hidden nodes to use.

Problem Networks

Even carefully designed networks can experience problems. If a network is not training properly, for example, there could be problems with the data or the training parameters. The learning set could have contradictory data facts, or you might have set your error tolerance level too low. You might need to rescale your data or add more hidden neurons. The documentation for neural net software like BMP usually provides suggestions for resolving network problems, and on-line resources are available as well. Ultimately, though, the best solution for network problems is user experience. Although neural net software is easy to use, there is still no substitute for user experience.

NEURAL NETS VERSUS EXPERT SYSTEMS

Neural networks and expert systems are frequently included together under the general category of machine, or artificial, intelligence. A natur-

TABLE 6–10

Expert Systems versus Neural Networks

Application	Neural Network	Expert System
Investment strategies		X
Prediction of financial trends	X	
Loan application analysis	X	X
Real estate price valuation	X	
Estate planning		X

al question for those readers who have completed Chapter 2 is, Which program should I use? As expected, the answer is, It depends. If the problem calls for sequential logic, an expert system is better. If the problem involves finding a pattern among the data, a neural network is more appropriate. It does not necessarily have to be an either-or decision, though. Depending on the situation, you might want to use both methods in searching for a solution. Lawrence (1993) offers some relevant advice in Table 6–10 for financial applications.

SOURCES AND SUGGESTED READING

BrainMaker Professional User's Guide and Reference Manual. 4th ed. Nevada City, CA: California Scientific Software, Inc., 1993.

Freedman, R. S.; R. A. Klein; and J. Lederman, eds. *Artificial Intelligence in the Capital Markets.* Burr Ridge, IL: Irwin Professional Publishing, 1995.

Lawrence, J. *Introduction to Neural Networks.* 5th ed. Nevada City, CA: California Scientific Press, 1993.

Trippi, R. R. and E. Turban, eds. *Neural Networks in Finance and Investing.* Chicago: Probus Publishing, 1993.

Trippi, R. R. and J. K. Lee. *Artificial Intelligence in Finance & Investing.* Burr Ridge, IL: Irwin Professional Publishing, 1996.

SOFTWARE RESOURCES

BrainMaker Professional
California Scientific Software
10024 Newtown Road
Nevada City, CA 95959
Tel. 800 - 248-8112
Fax 916-478-9041

Suggested retail prices
BrainMaker Professional (DOS or Windows): $795
BrainMaker (DOS, Windows, or Macintosh): $195

CHAPTER 7

Optimization

INTRODUCTION

If you asked a business owner or manager to describe the most important financial goal for the business, he probably would answer, "We want to earn the highest profit we can." Meeting that goal seems easy enough: Produce the maximum number of products that generate the highest profit per unit. It often happens, though, that the business is unable to produce as much of a particular product as it would like. Most firms have limits on the amount of capital they can access, the amount of labor and materials they can use in production, and so on. These resource limits impose constraints on production and the business must try to maximize profits within those constraints.

Individuals also must make economic decisions, and most of these decisions are constrained. For example, most of us desire unlimited amounts of goods and services, but our income and available credit limit the amount we can spend. Our goal as consumers then becomes maximizing the satisfaction we get from the goods and services we can afford. (You might remember this concept from your introductory economics classes as the utility maximization problem.) Designing an investment portfolio is another example of a constrained decision. The ideal investment would earn a high return while incurring very little risk. We know that the capital markets don't work that way, and investments that offer potentially high returns almost always have high risk. This relationship between risk and return forces the investor to impose a limit on the amount of risk he will accept in his portfolio. Having stated that limit, the investor then searches for the highest return portfolio that satisfies the risk constraint. (Investment advisors will recognize this as the Markowitz efficient frontier problem: How do you maximize expected return for a given level of portfolio risk?)

Each of these examples describes an optimization problem. Despite their different settings, they share several features. First, each requires the decision maker to state a goal: maximize profits, utility, or portfolio return. Second, the decision maker must recognize any constraints that apply: limited production resources, income, and tolerance for risk. These features are common to many decisions and they lead to the central theme of optimization: Given the constraints, what is the best, or optimal, solution I can find?

These are examples of maximization problems, but optimization techniques also are used in minimization problems. In many businesses, management gives the factory director a production target for the period. Because he is told how many units to produce, the director is not concerned with maximizing production. Instead, he focuses on minimizing production costs, given the constraints on labor and material supplies and prices that he faces. Investors can take a similar minimization approach to portfolio design. An investor who has a target return for his portfolio will want to earn that return while incurring the least possible risk. Of course, we are assuming that the plant manager in this example has incentives to minimize production costs and that the investor here is risk averse. Optimization would be a wasted effort if the plant manager were not concerned with costs or if the investor ignored risk.

Having recognized the impact of the constraints, the decision maker can choose from several methods to find an optimal solution to his problem. The simplest approach is trial and error in which he tries combinations of the constrained resources and ranks their results. This method can work for very simple problems, but it has some drawbacks. First, there is no guarantee of finding the optimal solution. You hope that the solution is close to optimal, but you can not verify that. Second, even simple optimization problems can pose mathematical difficulties. In the investment portfolio example, finding an optimal portfolio for a given level of risk involves statistical and matrix calculations. Once you consider more than two or three assets for the portfolio, the calculations become tedious and time-consuming.

The decision maker can also approach optimization problems graphically. As we demonstrate shortly, this method works for simple problems, and it is a useful tool for illustrating the optimization process. Once the problem moves beyond the two or three dimensions that can be graphed on a page, though, you cannot use this approach.

The third approach to solving optimization problems requires computerized mathematical techniques known as linear programming (LP) and nonlinear programming (NLP). These tools require the user to describe his problem mathematically, but as we show shortly, the PC-based optimization programs shield the user from much of the underlying math. The user's role is to state the problem correctly so the program can find the optimal solution. This involves identifying the goal (for example, maximize the portfolio's expected return), describing any constraints (portfolio variance must be less that 20 percent), and identifying decision variables (investment allocation). This chapter focuses on the use and potential applications of the PC-based LP and NLP methods.

EXAMPLE: LINEAR PROGRAMMING

The following example demonstrates the stages for developing an LP model. After we set up the problem, we examine the trial-and-error, graphical, and software-based approaches to solving it.

Step 1: Describe the Problem Clearly

Your client's company, Custom Woodwork, Inc., makes two types of customized wooden furniture: chairs and chests. Each piece is handmade to the customer's specifications and sells for several thousand dollars. Customers include museums and collectors. Your client can sell everything he makes, and he wants to maximize his profit by optimizing the production mix. Here are the profit and production details on each product.

	Chairs	Chests
Profit/unit	$750	$1,200
Labor required	40 hours	60 hours
Wood required	30 board feet	70 board feet

The business faces several constraints on production. First, the staff consists of five craftsmen, and the total labor available for the year is 11,250 hours. Second, the furniture requires a special type of wood, and your client can buy only 10,000 board feet per year. Given these profit contributions and constraints, how many chairs and chests should your client make?

The two last paragraphs state the optimization problem in plain English. If you can't state the problem in understandable language like this, you will have difficulties developing the LP model. Your description should include a statement of the optimization's goal (maximize his profit), the decision variables (number of chairs and chests to make), and the relevant constraints (labor and wood required and available). When you have identified those items clearly, you can express the problem in the form needed for the LP program.

Step 2: Express the Problem Mathematically

Before expressing the problem mathematically, we introduce the terminology that is used to describe LP problems.

Decision Variables The model's variables that the decision maker controls are called the decision variables. In this example your client must decide how many chairs and chests to make, so these are the model's decision variables. In an investment portfolio problem, the amounts (or weights) allocated to each investment are the decision variables.

Objective Function You probably don't think of a firm's profit as a mathematical function, but it can be described that way. In this example, total profit is a function of two quantities: profit per unit and number of units sold. In terms of chairs and chests, we can express this relationship as

$$\text{Total profit} = (\# \text{ of chairs sold} * \text{profit per chair})$$
$$+ (\# \text{ of chests sold} * \text{profit per chest})$$

If we let C1 represent the number of chairs sold and C2 be the number of chests, we can use the profit figures we have to rewrite the total profit function as

$$\text{Total profit} = (C1 * \$750) + (C2 * \$1,200)$$

The goal is to maximize profit, which we can state as

$$\text{Maximize } (C1 * 750) + (C2 * 1,200)$$

This last statement is the problem's objective function. It expresses the relationship between total profit, the number of each item produced, and the profit per item. To use the LP method, you express the problem's objective function as a linear combination of the relevant decision variables, C1 and C2 in this case. The linear combination requirement means that the objective function does not contain any terms in which a variable (like C1) is multiplied or divided by itself or any other variable. (We review nonlinear models later in the chapter.) Using the same variables, here is an example of a nonlinear objective function:

Maximize (C1 * C2/C1 * 750) + (C2 * 1,200)

If you don't express the objective function properly, your solutions will be wrong or the program might not find a solution.

Constraints The easiest way to express the model mathematically is to examine each part separately. We already stated the objective function as

Maximize (C1 * 750) + (C2 * 1,200)

Next, we need to express the constraints as linear combinations of the decision variables. The first constraint says that the business cannot use more than 11,250 hours of labor annually. Each chair (C1) requires 40 hours of labor, and each chest (C2) requires 60 hours. Therefore, the total amount of labor used will be

Labor used = (C1 * 40) + (C2 * 60)

Because the hours of labor used cannot exceed 11,250, we can express the constraint as:

(C1 * 40) + (C2 * 60) <= 11,250

The second constraint limits the company to using 10,000 board feet of wood per year. Each chair uses 30 board feet, while each chest requires 70 board feet. Using the same method as we did with the labor constraint, we can express this relationship as

Wood used = (C1 * 30) + (C2 * 70) and (C1 * 30) + (C2 * 70) <= 10,000

The model needs one more set of constraints. The optimal solution occasionally can include a negative value for one or more decision values. While that might be a mathematically correct solution, it is nonsensical for a manufacturer: How do you produce negative chairs? (A negative value makes sense with investment portfolio problems because you can sell securities short, which is equivalent to a negative investment.) To prevent negative solutions for the decision values, we need the following additional constraints:

C1 >= 0
C2 >= 0

The Problem Now that we have expressed the objective function and the constraints mathematically, we have the ingredients needed for a LP optimization problem:

Maximize (C1 * 750) + (C2 * 1,200)
Subject to
(C1 * 40) + (C2 * 60) <= 11,250
(C1 * 30) + (C2 * 70) <= 10,000
C1 >= 0
C2 >= 0

Step 3: Solve the Problem

Once you state the problem mathematically, you are ready to solve it. In this section we look at the three methods for solving a simple LP problem: trial-and-error, graphical, and software-assisted.

Trial-and-Error Method

With this method you take out your calculator or spreadsheet and examine the impact that different product mixes have on profits and the model's constraints. In this example chests have a higher profit margin than chairs ($1,200 versus $750), so it makes sense to start the analysis with an all-chests product mix. First we estimate the maximum number of chests we can produce. We have 11,250 labor hours available. Each chest requires 60 hours, which gives us a maximum production of 187 chests for the year (11,250/60 =187.5, rounded down to 187). Under the wood constraint, though, we can produce just 142 chests (10,000 board feet/70 board feet per chest = 142.8 chests), so our maximum production is 142 chests. The following table displays the results of producing 142 chests:

Profit	$170,400 (142 * $1,200)
Excess wood	60 board feet [10,000 – (142 * 70)]
Excess labor	2,730 hours [11,250 – (142 * 60)]

Your client is comfortable with the leftover wood, but the excess labor concerns him because each of the five workers has 546 excess hours (2,730/5) for the year. He can't risk layoffs, and he certainly can't afford that much wasted time. You begin to experiment with the product mix to see if you can't reduce the excess labor by making fewer chests and including chairs. For the next trial, you try 120 chests and 50 chairs. The results:

Profit	$181,500 [(120 * $1,200) + (50 * $750)]
Excess wood	100 board feet [10,000 – (120 * 70) – (50 * 30)]
Excess labor	2,050 hours [11,250 – (120 * 60) – (40 * 50)]

It's an improvement. Profit increased by over $11,000, excess wood increased only slightly, and excess labor dropped almost 700 hours.

Reducing the number of chests was the right decision, so you continue along that line for the next estimate by producing 100 chests and 100 chairs. The results continue to improve:

Profit	$195,000 [(100 * $1,200) + (100 * $750)]
Excess wood	0 board feet [10,000 − (10 * 70) − (100 * 30)]
Excess labor	1,250 hours [11,250 − (100 * 60) − (100 * 50)]

You probably are beginning to see the weakness of this method. Although each new trial has improved the results, you don't know how many more trials are necessary to find the optimal solution, or if one even exists. The next approach we examine, the graphical method, offers more accurate solutions for simple problems such as this one.

The Graphical Method

With this approach the decision maker creates a graph that plots the problem's constraints. By examining the corners and extreme points of the graph, you can find the decision-variable values that maximize the objective function. Here is the graphical analysis of Custom Woodwork's production mix problem.

Plot the Constraints

Because we expressed the production constraints as linear combinations of the decision variables, we can plot the constraints easily. Figures 7–1 and 7–2 show the plots for the labor and wood constraints, respectively, with the number of chairs on the horizontal axis and chests on the vertical axis.

We combine the two plots in Figure 7–3, which shows the joint impact of the two constraints on possible production values.

For example, the number of labor hours limits chest production to 187.5 units (11,250/60) and chair production to 281.25 units (11,250/49). If that were the only constraint, those figures would be the true production maximums. The limited supply of wood imposes a second constraint, though: 142.9 chests (10,000/70) and 333.33 chairs (10,000/30). To find the combined constraint, we take the lower of the applicable values: 142.9 chests and 281.25 chairs. There is another important point to consider: the point where the constraints' plots meet. Solving the simultaneous equations for this point gives values of 187.5 chairs and 62.5 chests. These three points: (0, 142.9), (187.5, 62.5), and (281.25, 0) are plotted and linked in Figure 7–4.

In Figure 7–4, the area bounded by these three points and the (0, 0) origin forms the feasible region. The company can produce any combina-

FIGURE 7-1

Labor Constraint

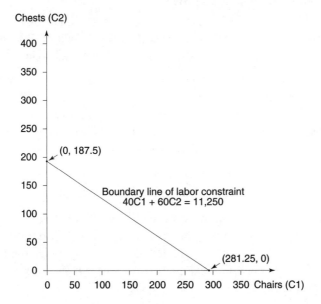

Chests (C2)

(0, 187.5)

Boundary line of labor constraint
40C1 + 60C2 = 11,250

(281.25, 0)

Chairs (C1)

FIGURE 7-2

Wood Constraint

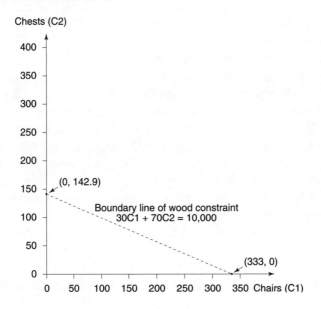

Chests (C2)

(0, 142.9)

Boundary line of wood constraint
30C1 + 70C2 = 10,000

(333, 0)

Chairs (C1)

FIGURE 7-3

Combined Boundary Lines

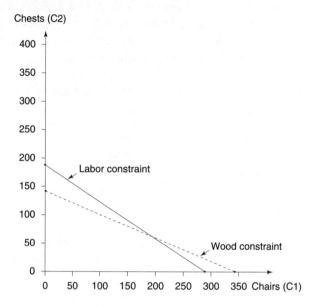

FIGURE 7-4

Feasible Region

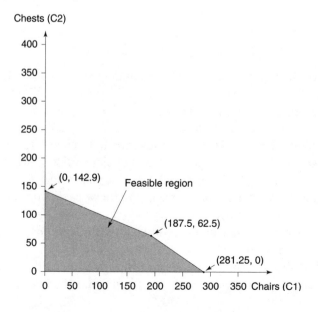

tion of chairs and chests that falls in this region or on the border. For example, 150 chairs and 50 chests is a feasible combination, while 150 chairs and 150 chests falls outside the region and is not feasible. Our goal is to find the profit-maximizing combination, and fortunately it is easy to identify here. LP theory has shown that in problems like this one, with an optimal solution and a finite objective function, the solution will occur at a corner or extreme point. Consequently, we need to compare profits at only four points: (0, 0), (0, 142.9), (187.5, 62.5), and (281.25, 0). Here are the results:

Point	Profit
(0, 0)	$0
(0, 142.9)	$171,480
(187.5, 62.5)	$215,625
(281.25, 0)	$210,938

The LP Solution

To maximize profits, Custom Woodwork, Inc., should produce 187.5 chairs and 62.5 chests. But how do you sell .5 of a chair or chest? Because customers want complete products, the owner must round off the numbers. As you'll see in the next section, rounding off the solutions is not always the right procedure because it can introduce a new set of problems.

As this example shows, graphical LP analysis works in the right circumstances. If you have more than two decision variables, though, you need a more powerful method: LP software.

Optimization Software: What'sBest! and Microsoft Excel Solver

Early LP software required extensive programming skills. As PCs became popular in the 1980s, LP programs like What'sBest! from LINDO Systems Inc. first appeared as Lotus 1-2-3 and Microsoft Excel spreadsheet add-ins. Today's spreadsheets include built-in LP and NLP routines, and this chapter uses both What'sBest! and the Solver function in Microsoft Excel 5.0 to demonstrate spreadsheet-based optimization techniques. Spreadsheets offer several advantages for optimization analysis. First, most financial analysts are comfortable working with spreadsheets. We know how to design effective worksheet layouts, enter functions, and manipulate data. Second, spreadsheets have integrated graphics modules, which reduces the time needed to develop graphical presentations of analytical results.

After describing the model and expressing it mathematically, you are ready to build the spreadsheet's optimization model. As you design your worksheet, emphasize the user's perspective. Specifically, ask yourself if a third party could look at your spreadsheet and understand it. If another user has difficulty interpreting your results, you need to redesign the spreadsheet so it is easier to follow. We illustrate this with the Custom Woodwork, Inc., analysis, which is an easy worksheet to design. We first present the problem using What'sBest! and then with Microsoft Excel 5.0's Solver function.

The usual layout in a spreadsheet LP places the decision variables at the top of the worksheet with constraints listed below. The Custom Woodwork product mix analysis uses this format, as shown in Figure 7–5.

Let's examine the key cells in the spreadsheet (Figure 7–5). We place our decision variables, the number of chairs and chests to make, in cells B5 and C5 and list the profit per unit for each product directly below in cells B7 and C7. The Total Profit cell, cell F7, has the formula =(B5 * B7) + (C5 * C7). In other words, the total profit equals the combined profit for chairs (B5 * B7) and chests (C5 * C7).

The lower part of the worksheet provides the component requirements and the constraints. Cells B11 and C11 give the labor requirements for chairs and chests, 40 and 60 hours, respectively; cells B12 and C12

FIGURE 7–5

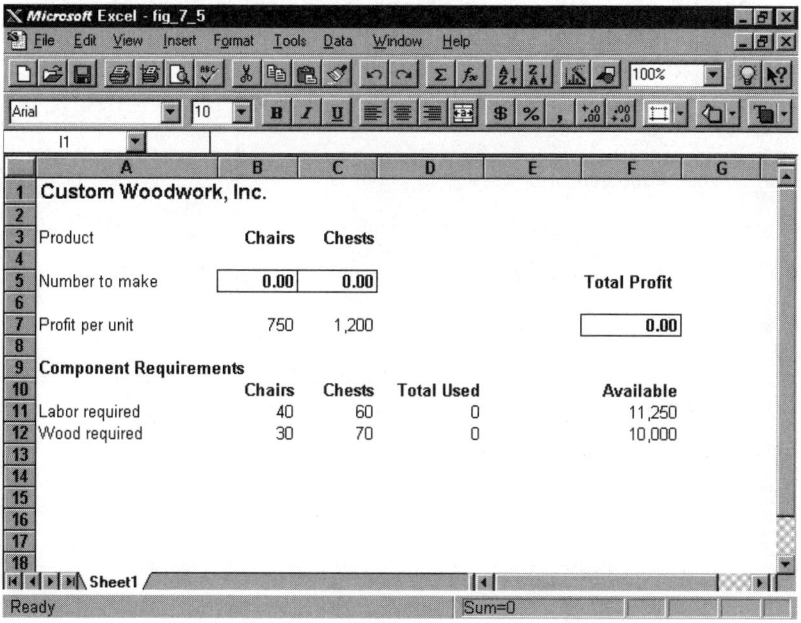

give the wood requirements for each product. Cell D11 shows the total labor required for a production mix by using the formula =(B5 * B11) + (C5 * C11). Cell D12 does the same for the wood used with the formula =(B5 * B12) + (C5 * C12). As we know, the maximum values in these cells are constrained: 11,250 hours of labor and 10,000 board feet of labor available. We list these constraints in cells F11 (labor) and F12 (wood).

After designing the spreadsheet's layout, we then identify the critical cells for the LP program being used. Figure 7–6 shows the What'sBest! (WB!) pull-down menu.

For our purposes, the first four items on the menu in Figure 7–6 are the most important. The Adjustable cells are the decision variables, cells B5 and C5. The Best cell identifies the objective function, which is the profit formula in cell F7. A submenu (not shown) lets us choose between minimizing or maximizing the Best cell's value. We want to maximize profit, so we choose that option. The Constraint selection identifies the constraint cells. Using a submenu (not shown), we identify cells D11 and D12 as the constrained cells and cells F11 and F12 as their respective maximums. The program places the <= sign in cells E11 and E12 to highlight the constraint, as seen in Figure 7–7. (We do not discuss the other

FIGURE 7–6

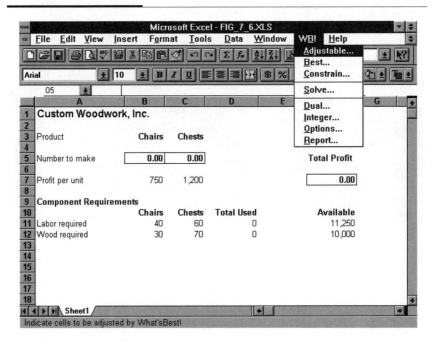

FIGURE 7–7

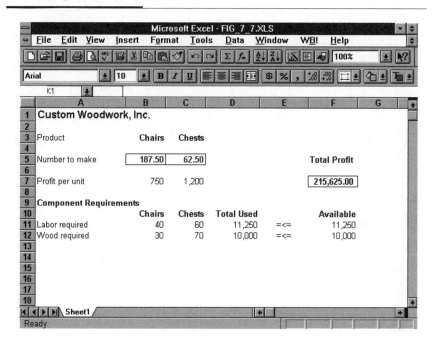

selections on the What'sBest! menu because those topics are covered in the review of the Microsoft Excel 5.0 Solver function.)

After providing this information about the model, we click on the Solve selection to learn if there is a solution. As expected, cells B5 and C5 in Figure 7–7 show that the business earns maximum profit by making 187.50 chairs and 62.50 chests, the same answer we found with the graphical approach.

The Microsoft Excel 5.0 Solver function works similarly to What'sBest! Using the same worksheet as the one in Figure 7–5, you select the Solver item from the Tools pull-down menu (Figure 7–8).

The Solver program is also easy to use. First, we choose the Target cell, which contains the value we wish to optimize. In this example, we set it to F7 (Total Profit) and select the Max (maximize) button. (The program uses absolute cell references: $F$7, etc., to identify the problem's parameters. We use relative references [F7] to make the text easier to read.) We enter the decision-variables location in the Changing Cells text box, and we list the constraints in the bottom box. The only difference between this example and the previous one that used What'sBest! is the additional nonnegativity constraint, B5:C5 >= 0. This constraint prevents

FIGURE 7-8

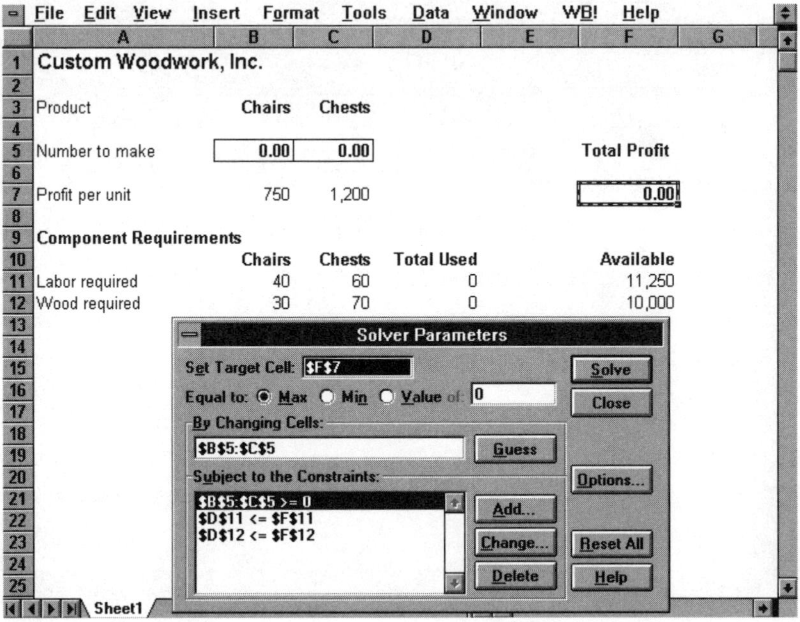

─	File	Edit	View	Insert	Format	Tools	Data	Window	WB!	Help	♦

	A	B	C	D	E	F	G	↑
1	Custom Woodwork, Inc.							
2								
3	Product	Chairs	Chests					
4								
5	Number to make	0.00	0.00			Total Profit		
6								
7	Profit per unit	750	1,200			0.00		
8								
9	Component Requirements							
10		Chairs	Chests	Total Used		Available		
11	Labor required	40	60	0		11,250		
12	Wood required	30	70	0		10,000		

Solver Parameters

Set Target Cell: $F$7 — [Solve]

Equal to: ● Max ○ Min ○ Value of: 0 — [Close]

By Changing Cells:
$B$5:$C$5 — [Guess]

Subject to the Constraints: — [Options...]

$B$5:$C$5 >= 0
$D$11 <= $F$11
$D$12 <= $F$12

[Add...] [Change...] [Reset All] [Delete] [Help]

Sheet1

the program from returning an optimal solution that has negative values for the number of chairs or chests. (We discuss the features available through Solver's Options... menu in the appendix. For this example we left the default selections intact and changed only the Assume Linear Model option by turning it on.) This screen arrangement should look familiar, because it duplicates the original statement of the problem:

Maximize (C1 * 750) + (C2 * 1,200)

Subject to

(C1 * 40) + (C2 * 60) <= 11,250

(C1 * 30) + (C2 * 70) <= 10,000

C1 >= 0

C2 >= 0

where C1 equals the number of chairs and C2 equals the number of chests.

After we enter the parameters, we click the Solve button and the program returns Figure 7–9. The target cells contain the same solutions we found earlier: 187.5 chairs and 62.5 chests for a maximized profit of $215,625. The Solver Results dialog box also allows you to generate three

FIGURE 7-9

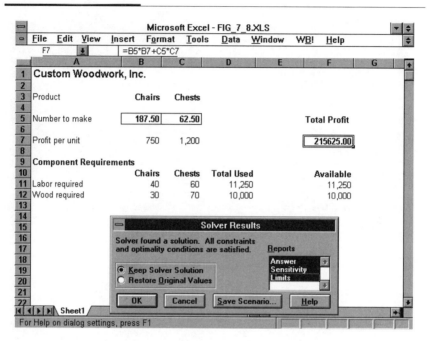

reports: answer, sensitivity, and limits. We select each report so we can examine the results in the next section.

INTERPRETING THE RESULTS

Software LP programs offer another benefit besides speed and ease of use: They generate additional information that is valuable to the decision maker. This information gives the decision maker insight into the nature and validity of the LP solution, which provides information beyond the basic decision-variables solution. The Microsoft Excel 5.0 Solver generates three reports that we examine in this section: the answer (Figure 7–10), sensitivity (Figure 7–11), and limits (Figure 7–12) reports.

The Answer Report

The first two parts of the answer report in Figure 7–10 are straightforward. The Target Cell section shows that we moved from an original value of zero in cell F7 to a maximum value of $215,625. The Adjustable Cells section contains the same type of information, showing the solution val-

FIGURE 7–10

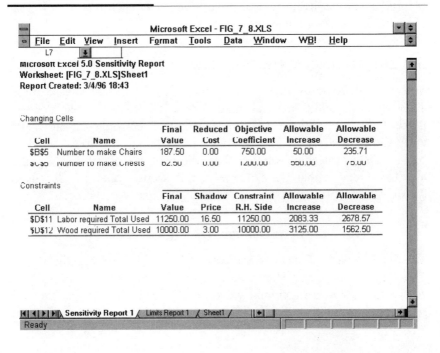

Microsoft Excel - FIG_7_8.XLS

File   Edit   View   Insert   Format   Tools   Data   Window   WB!   Help

J13

Microsoft Excel 5.0 Answer Report
Worksheet: [FIG_7_8.XLS]Sheet1
Report Created: 3/4/96 14:11

Target Cell (Max)

Cell	Name	Original Value	Final Value
$F$7	Total Profit	0.00	215625.00

Adjustable Cells

Cell	Name	Original Value	Final Value
$B$5	Number to make Chairs	0.00	187.50
$C$5	Number to make Chests	0.00	62.50

Constraints

Cell	Name	Cell Value	Formula	Status	Slack
$D$11	Labor required Total Used	11,250	$D$11<=$F$11	Binding	0
$D$12	Wood required Total Used	10,000	$D$12<=$F$12	Binding	0
$B$5	Number to make Chairs	187.50	$B$5>=0	Not Binding	187.50
$C$5	Number to make Chests	62.50	$C$5>=0	Not Binding	62.50

Answer Report 1 / Sensitivity Report 1 / Limits Report

Ready

FIGURE 7–11

Microsoft Excel - FIG_7_8.XLS

File   Edit   View   Insert   Format   Tools   Data   Window   WB!   Help

L7

Microsoft Excel 5.0 Sensitivity Report
Worksheet: [FIG_7_8.XLS]Sheet1
Report Created: 3/4/96 18:43

Changing Cells

Cell	Name	Final Value	Reduced Cost	Objective Coefficient	Allowable Increase	Allowable Decrease
$B$5	Number to make Chairs	187.50	0.00	750.00	50.00	235.71
$C$5	Number to make Chests	62.50	0.00	1200.00	550.00	75.00

Constraints

Cell	Name	Final Value	Shadow Price	Constraint R.H. Side	Allowable Increase	Allowable Decrease
$D$11	Labor required Total Used	11250.00	16.50	11250.00	2083.33	2678.57
$D$12	Wood required Total Used	10000.00	3.00	10000.00	3125.00	1562.50

Sensitivity Report 1 / Limits Report 1 / Sheet1 /

Ready

FIGURE 7-12

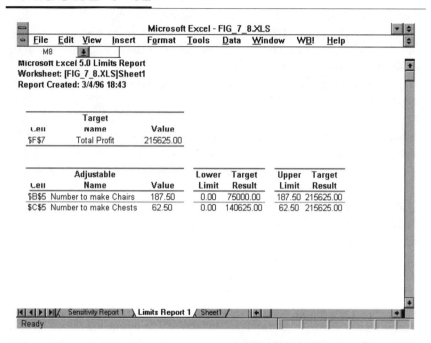

ues of 187.5 chairs and 62.5 chests. Part 3, Constraints, offers a summary of the optimization's constraints' formulas and information on how closely the variable approaches its constraint. For the labor and wood inputs, the constraints are binding—the solution uses all the available resources. Because there is no "slack," or excess capacity, the Slack column contains zeros for those constraints. The last two rows are for the nonnegativity constraints we imposed on the decision variables. The numbers in the Slack column, 187.5 (cell B5) and 62.5 (cell C5), show the difference between the cells' final values and their original constraint values of zero.

The Sensitivity Report

Our objective function for this profit-maximizing example takes the form:

Maximize (C1 * 750) + (C2 * 1,200)

where C1 is the number of chairs and C2 is the number of chests produced. When we stated the problem in this form, we assumed that the product profit margins of $750 and $1,200 were constant.

What happens to the product mix, though, if we must change that assumption? What if increased competition forces the company to lower prices (and profits) or decreased competition allows it to raise them? The firm's decision maker might have other questions about the LP's results, too. For example, how much would profits increase (or decrease) if more (or less) labor and material were available? You find these answers in the sensitivity report, shown in Figure 7–11.

The first part of the sensitivity report in Figure 7–11 describes the impact of changes to the objective function's coefficients ($750 and $1,200). In the row for cell B5, we see a value of 50 in the Allowable Increase column. Therefore, the firm could increase each chair's profit margin from $750 to $800, and the optimal product mix would not change. The value of 235.71 in the Allowable Decrease column has the opposite meaning. The profit margin for each chair could fall from $750 to $514.29 ($750 – $235.71), and the optimal product mix stays the same. (Try running the numbers with Solver to see the results.) These results assume that you keep the problem's other parameters, like the constraints, constant.

The Allowable Increase and Allowable Decrease values for chests have the same interpretation. The business could decrease profits on chests by $75 to $1,125 or increase them by $550 to $1,750 before requiring changes in the optimal product mix. (Don't confuse the objective function's result, which is the firm's profit, with the optimal product mix. If you increase [decrease] the profit contribution from a product, the firm's total profits will increase [decrease]. It is the optimal product mix that remains the same over the Allowable Increase/Decrease range, not the objective function's value.)

The Allowable Increase/Decrease results tell the decision maker how much flexibility he has with the objective function's coefficients before he must reoptimize the production mix. If he wants to increase the worker's wages, for example, he knows he can handle a $235 decrease in each chair's profit and a $75 decrease in each chest's profit. This information is valuable because it can be time-consuming and expensive to reorganize a production schedule, especially in a large multiproduct operation.

The fourth column, Reduced Cost, shows the difference between the product's marginal profit and the marginal value of the resources an additional unit consumes. The marginal cost for each additional unit is found in the lower section in the Shadow Price column. For example, the reduced cost for a chair is

$750 (profit contribution) – [40 * 16.50] (additional labor cost)
– [30 * 3] (additional wood cost) = 0

The reduced cost of zero has an interpretation you might recall from your economics courses: At the optimal production level, marginal cost equals marginal revenue. This formula is true for this example.

The lower part of the report provides sensitivity information for the problem's constraints. We specified two constraints here: labor (11,250 hours) and wood (10,000 board feet). The third column, Final Value, and fifth column, Constraint R.H. (right hand) Side, provide details on the solution's constraint values and the problem's constraints, respectively. In this example, our optimal product mix used all the available labor and wood. But what would happen to the objective function's value (the firm's profit) if we could relax those constraints? As an example, what if we could add another 1,000 labor hours or another 1,000 board feet?

We find that information in the remaining columns. Column four, Shadow Price, tells us the constrained resource's marginal value. We can also view this amount as the additional profit the firm would earn by loosening the original constraint by one unit. In other words, if the firm had one more hour of labor available (11,251 versus the original 11,250), profits would increase by $17. Similarly, if the firm had one more board foot of wood (10,001 versus 10,000), profits would increase by $3. This result also tells you the impact of reducing the constraint's value: If one less hour of labor is available, profits drop by $17 and there is a $3 loss for each less board foot.

These shadow prices are valid for a specified range, which is given in the Allowable Increase/Decrease columns. The $17 marginal profit contribution for labor holds for the range of 8,571 to 13,333 hours, while the range for wood's $3 shadow price is 8,438 to 13,125 board feet. The shadow price shown changes once the constraint moves outside its allowable range.

This information helps the decision maker to compare the marginal cost for additional resources with the increased production's marginal profit. If the marginal profit exceeds the marginal cost, using additional units of the resource will increase the firm's profits. If the marginal cost exceeds the marginal profit, using additional resources will reduce profits and the decision maker must justify the expenditure for other reasons.

The Limits Report

The limits report in Figure 7–12 shows the objective function's value at different feasible constraint levels. For example, if the firm produces 62.5 chests but no chairs, it will earn $75,000 profit. If it produces 187.5 chairs and no chests, it earns $140,625. The upper limit shows the objective function's maximum value at the constraint limits.

Integer Solutions

Programs such as What'sBest! and the Microsoft Excel 5.0 Solver produce mathematical solutions to LP problems. A mathematically correct solution, however, is not always a practical solution. In the Custom Woodwork example, the optimal solution is to produce and sell 187.5 chairs and 62.5 chests. Because most customers won't buy a half-chair or half-chest, the decision maker must round off the optimal solution to an integer value. This need for an integer solution is common because many items cannot be divided easily. (Imagine that you were optimizing the traffic patterns for an airline. How do you tell passengers that their flight has been optimized to terminate two-thirds of the way to their destination?) LP software handles this problem by allowing the user to force the decision variables to take integer values. Continuing with the Custom Woodwork example, we would add the following constraints as shown in the Microsoft Excel 5.0 Solver dialogue box in Figure 7–13.

The additional constraint in Figure 7–13 reads $B$5:$C$5 = Integer. This constraint forces the program to find the optimal integer solution values for the problem. You can see the results in Figure 7–14: The new optimal solution is to produce 188 chairs and 62 chests.

As Figure 7–14 shows, there is a cost for imposing an integer-solution constraint, though. First, the firm's total profit drops by $225 to $215,400. Second, the firm now has excess resources: 10 hours of labor

FIGURE 7–13

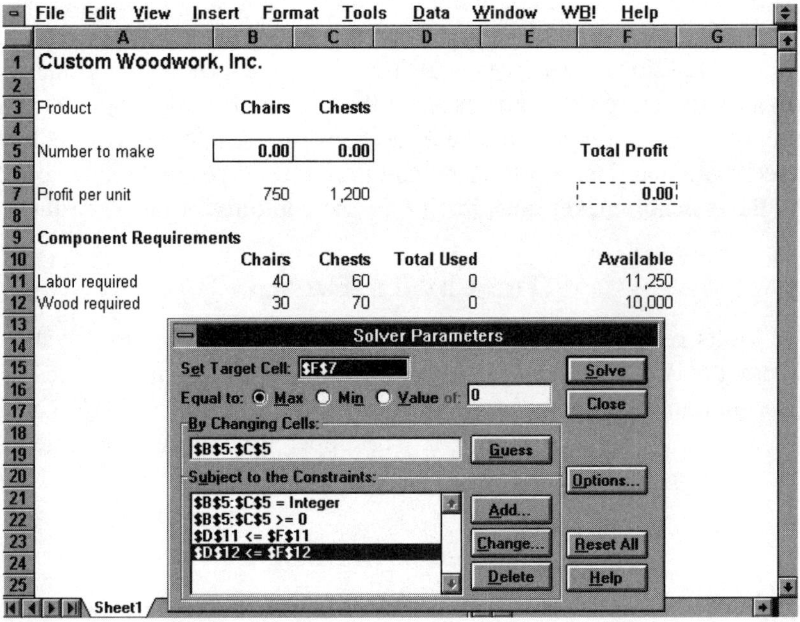

FIGURE 7–14

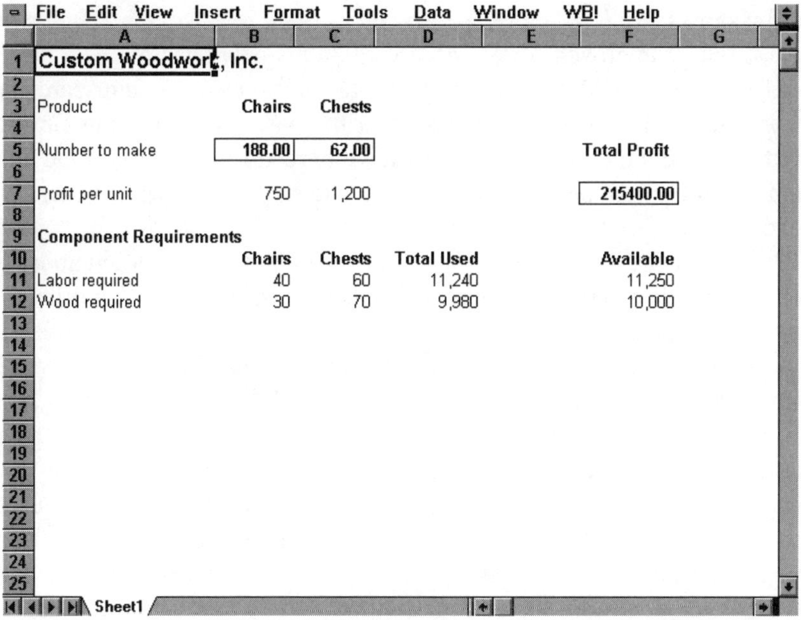

	A	B	C	D	E	F	G
	File Edit View Insert Format Tools Data Window WB! Help						
1	Custom Woodwork, Inc.						
2							
3	Product	Chairs	Chests				
4							
5	Number to make	188.00	62.00			Total Profit	
6							
7	Profit per unit	750	1,200			215400.00	
8							
9	Component Requirements						
10		Chairs	Chests	Total Used		Available	
11	Labor required	40	60	11,240		11,250	
12	Wood required	30	70	9,980		10,000	
13							
14							
15							
16							
17							
18							
19							
20							
21							
22							
23							
24							
25							

Sheet1

and 20 board feet of wood go unused. This illustrates a general theme for LP solutions: Imposing additional constraints, like requiring integer solutions, can never improve the objective function. At best, you will equal the objective function's previous value, but it is more likely you will see a weaker result.

APPLICATIONS

Linear programming has a wide range of potential applications to your clients' business problems and possibly to your own, as well. In these next sections we demonstrate potential applications to highlight the technique's versatility.

Example: Monitoring Cash Flow

Every business owner knows the importance of maintaining a healthy cash flow. Keeping an insufficient cash balance creates a risk of insolvency. It also reduces operating flexibility because the business can't take advantages of opportunities like pricing discounts on cash purchases. For these reasons, business owners watch their cash balances carefully. Linear programming can help a business manage its cash flow, as the example below shows.

A client approaches you for advice on his new business venture. He is a former research librarian, and he is starting a new on-line research and information retrieval firm. He has spent the past several months promoting his new company, and six firms have agreed to hire him. Some companies want him to perform specific short-term projects, while others will have ongoing needs.

The business looks promising, but your client is concerned about the firm's cash flow. He can invest $25,000 in start-up money, and he estimates his expenses will be $10,000 per month for the first six months. He will work full-time with one part-time staff member, and he believes he can bill out an average 60 hours per week, or 240 hours each month. He has received some projects with specific completion dates, while other clients have given him a range of hours that he can schedule flexibly. The billing rates for each customer vary, depending on the type and amount of the research required. His customers have different payment patterns, too—some pay within 30 days, while others take 60 days. Figure 7–15 provides the details on his current assignments.

FIGURE 7–15

Client No.	Assignment	Due Date	Total Hours	Hourly Rate	Payment Schedule (Days)
1	Project	5 mos.	300	25	60
2	Project	4 mos.	200	40	30
3	Project	3 mos.	100	50	30
4	Retainer		25-35/mo.	40	30
5	Retainer		30-40/mo.	35	60

As he projects the work and cash flows for the first six months, he has two main concerns. First, he wants to maximize his billings. Second, he does not want his cash balance to fall below zero. He knows that his cash balance will decrease at first, but he is confident that his marketing efforts will bring in new clients toward the end of the six-month period.

Using the information he has provided, we create a cash flow spreadsheet for the business. Working with the deadlines and other constraints, we create an initial work flow schedule in Figure 7–16.

The spreadsheet in Figure 7–16 has three sections: a monthly billing schedule, cash receipts, and cash balances. The number of hours entered in cells B5:G9 are your first efforts at scheduling within the constraints. The values in columns I, J, and K summarize the billing results, and total billings for the first six months are summed in cell K10. The key cell formulas for this section are

K5: = I5 * J5; Hours * Hourly rate = Billings for Client 1; repeated for cells J6:J9

K10: = Sum(K5:K9); sums total billings for period

The cash receipts section reflects the 30- and 60-day delays your client will experience in receiving payment for his services. For example, client 1

FIGURE 7–16

	File Edit View Insert Format Tools Data Window WB! Help										
	A	B	C	D	E	F	G	H	I	J	K
1	On-line Researchers, Inc.										
2	Cash Flow Worksheet: Initial Projections										
3											
4	Monthly Billings	1	2	3	4	5	6		Hours	Rate	Total Billings
5	Client 1	85	65	40	110	0	0		300	$ 25	$ 7,500
6	2	0	70	130	0	0	0		200	$ 40	$ 8,000
7	3	100	50	0	0	0	0		150	$ 50	$ 7,500
8	4	25	25	30	35	35	35		185	$ 40	$ 7,400
9	5	30	30	40	40	40	40		220	$ 35	$ 7,700
10	Total Hours	240	240	240	185	75	75		1055		$38,100
11	Hours Available	240	240	240	240	240	240		1440		
12											
13	Cash Receipts										
14	Client 1	0	0	2125	1625	1000	2750				
15	2	0	0	2800	5200	0	0				
16	3	0	5000	2500	0	0	0				
17	4	0	1000	1000	1200	1400	1400				
18	5	0	0	1050	1050	1400	1400				
19											
20	Cash Balances										
21	Beginning balance	25,000	15,000	11,000	10,475	9,550	3,350				
22	Income	-	6,000	9,475	9,075	3,800	5,550				
23	Expenses	10,000	10,000	10,000	10,000	10,000	10,000				
24	Ending balance	$15,000	$11,000	$10,475	$ 9,550	$ 3,350	$ (1,100)				
25											
26											
27											
28											
29											
30											

Assignments \ Initial Projections / Optimized Workflow

pays after 60 days. If your client bills for 85 hours work at $25/hour in the first month (cell B5), he will receive his payment of $2,125 in the third month. To reflect the 60-day delay, we record the cash receipt for that activity in cell E14, which is in the third month's column. (The cell formula for E14 is =B5 * J5.) Client 3 pays in 30 days, so payment for 100 hours service at $50/hour in the first month arrives in the second month.

The third section, Cash Balances, shows the business's cash flow. Your client deposits $25,000 to start the business (cell B21). His monthly cash income (cells B22:G22) is the sum of the cash payments he receives from clients, as detailed in the Cash Receipts section for each month. After paying his monthly expenses of $10,000 (cells B23:G23), he arrives at his ending cash balance for each month (cells B24:G24).

Our initial work schedule looks reasonable. It generates total billings of $38,100, but it does not fulfill one of the client's key conditions, because his cash balance goes below zero to negative $1,100 in the sixth month (cell G24). Instead of using a time-consuming trial-and-error method to resolve this, you set up the worksheet as a linear programming problem to see if you can find an optimal solution.

This model has multiple parameters so we list them here:

Target cell: Maximize cell K10 (total billings)

Decision variables: Cells B5:G9 (work schedule)

Constraints

   B5:G9 >= 0 (prevents negative hours in solution)

   G5 = 0 (imposes 5 month deadline for client 1's work)

   F6:G6 = 0 (imposes 4 month deadline for client 2's work)

   E7:G7 = 0 (imposes 3 month deadline for client 3's work)

   I5 = 300 (hours required for client 1)

   I6 = 200 (hours required for client 2)

   I7 = 150 (hours required for client 3)

   B8:G8 >= 10 (minimum monthly hours for client 4)

   B8:G8 <= 35 (maximum monthly hours for client 4)

   B9:G9 >= 10 (minimum monthly hours for client 5)

   B9:G9 <= 40 (maximum monthly hours for client 5)

   B10:G10 <= B11:G11 (maximum available hours = 240 per month)

   B24:G24 >= 0 (keep cash balance above zero)

Figure 7–17 shows the optimized worksheet using these parameters.

The solution in Figure 7–17 looks good. By optimizing the work schedule, we increased the period's total billings by $1,700 and that amount

FIGURE 7-17

	A	B	C	D	E	F	G	H	I	J	K
1	On-line Researchers, Inc.										
2	Cash Flow Worksheet: Initial Projections										
3											
4	Monthly Billings	1	2	3	4	5	6		Hours	Rate	Total Billings
5	Client 1	65.0	40.0	40.0	155.0	0.0	0.0		300	$ 25	$ 7,500
6	2	0.0	75.0	125.0	0.0	0.0	0.0		200	$ 40	$ 8,000
7	3	100.0	50.0	0.0	0.0	0.0	0.0		150	$ 50	$ 7,500
8	4	35.0	35.0	35.0	35.0	35.0	35.0		210	$ 40	$ 8,400
9	5	40.0	40.0	40.0	40.0	40.0	40.0		240	$ 35	$ 8,400
10	Total Hours	240.0	240.0	240.0	230.0	75.0	75.0		1100		$39,800
11	Hours Available	240.0	240.0	240.0	240.0	240.0	240.0		1440		
12											
13	Cash Receipts										
14	Client 1	0	0	1625	1000	1000	3875				
15	2	0	0	3000	5000	0	0				
16	3	0	5000	2500	0	0	0				
17	4	0	1400	1400	1400	1400	1400				
18	5	0	0	1400	1400	1400	1400				
19											
20	Cash Balances										
21	Beginning balance	25,000	15,000	11,400	11,325	10,125	3,925				
22	Income	-	6,400	9,925	8,800	3,800	6,675				
23	Expenses	10,000	10,000	10,000	10,000	10,000	10,000				
24	Ending balance	$15,000	$11,400	$11,325	$10,125	$ 3,925	$ 600				
25											
26											
27											
28											
29											
30											

Initial Projections \ Optimized Workflow

keeps the cash balance above zero in the sixth month. Although this new work schedule is an improvement, it doesn't change the risk of the new venture. If your client can't find new clients to generate more billable hours starting with the fifth month, he'll be out of business shortly afterward!

Example: Bond Portfolio Construction

Some business and personal financial commitments require a series of predictable payments. Examples include paying for a child's college expenses, and an investment with a phased-in payment program. The person paying the expense wants to reduce uncertainty about the payment amount while simultaneously incurring the lowest possible expense. For example, prudent parents start saving for their children's college expenses years in advance. They frequently invest the funds in growth-oriented investments like stock mutual funds to earn the highest possible returns. As the child approaches college age, though, the stock market's volatility can cause the parents to worry about the accumulated funds. Although the stock market has produced solid historical returns, it can be very volatile in the short term. To avoid the risk of unexpected losses when the money is needed, the parents can shift the funds to more conservative investments like government bonds. If the parents follow this strategy, they still will want to minimize their out-of-pocket expense even as they accept a lower rate of return on the more conservative investments.

This scenario sets the stage for our next LP example, which uses a sample model from the What'sBest! program. We assume that your clients' daughter starts college next year. They estimate the annual costs will be as follows: year 1: $22,000; year 2: $24,000; year 3: $26,000; year 4: $28,000. To avoid unpleasant surprises, they want to shift the funds from their current investments of growth stock mutual funds to government bonds while still minimizing their expense. This type of cash flow and funding analysis is ideal for linear programming, and you create the spreadsheets in Figures 7–18 and 7–19.

Figure 7–18 has two parts. The first part shows price and yield information on the available U.S. treasury bonds that meet your clients' required maturity dates. Here is a brief explanation of each column:

- Asking Price: The bond's usual quoted asking price divided by 100. For the example, the usual quote on the first bond (cell C6) is 101 19/32, or roughly $1,016 per bond.
- Interest Rate: The bond's stated (annual) coupon rate.

FIGURE 7–18

File Edit View Insert Format Tools Data Window WB! Help						
A	**B**	**C**	**D**	**E**	**F**	**G**
1 Meeting Funding Needs						
2						
3 AVAILABLE	Year of	Asking	Interest	Units	Investment/	
4 BOND OPTIONS:	Maturity	Price	Rate	Purchased	Bond Issue	
5						
6	1	1.0159	6.625	0.0	$0.00	
7		1.0184	6.875	0.0	$0.00	
8	2	1.0766	9.000	0.0	$0.00	
9		1.0016	5.375	0.0	$0.00	
10	3	0.9900	5.000	0.0	$0.00	
11		1.0934	8.875	0.0	$0.00	
12		1.0031	5.500	0.0	$0.00	
13	4	1.1044	8.500	0.0	$0.00	
14		1.0563	7.125	0.0	$0.00	
15						
16				TOTAL COST:	$0.00	
17						
18		Year 0	Year 1	Year 2	Year 3	Year 4
19 Amount Covered		$0.00	$0.00	$0.00	$0.00	$0.00
20						
21 Cash Flow Need		$0.00	$22.00	$24.00	$26.00	$28.00
22						
23 Note: All amounts in thousands						
24						
25						
26						
FUNDING						

FIGURE 7-19

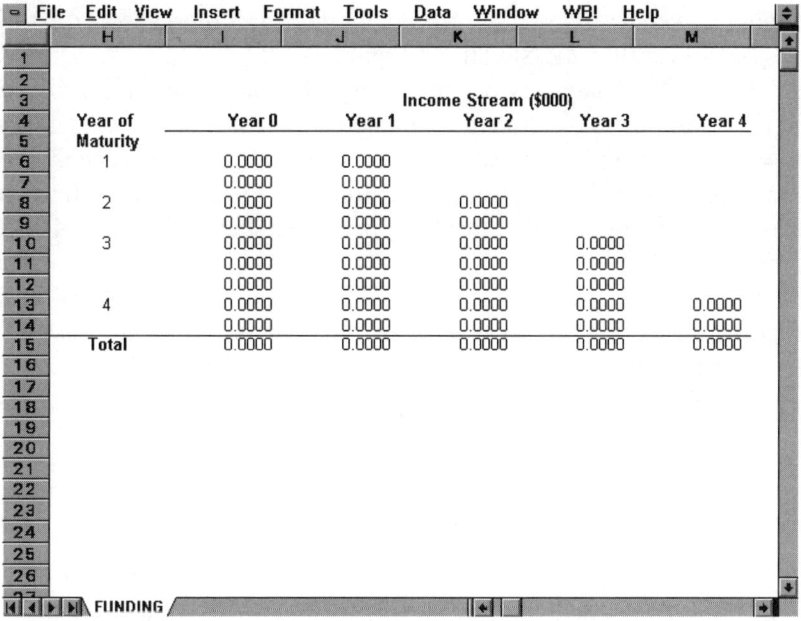

	H	I	J	K	L	M
1						
2						
3				Income Stream ($000)		
4	Year of	Year 0	Year 1	Year 2	Year 3	Year 4
5	Maturity					
6	1	0.0000	0.0000			
7		0.0000	0.0000			
8	2	0.0000	0.0000	0.0000		
9		0.0000	0.0000	0.0000		
10	3	0.0000	0.0000	0.0000	0.0000	
11		0.0000	0.0000	0.0000	0.0000	
12		0.0000	0.0000	0.0000	0.0000	
13	4	0.0000	0.0000	0.0000	0.0000	0.0000
14		0.0000	0.0000	0.0000	0.0000	0.0000
15	Total	0.0000	0.0000	0.0000	0.0000	0.0000

- Units Purchased: The problem's decision variable. Each unit represents a $1,000 investment in the bond described in that row.
- Investment/Bond Issue: Asking Price (column C) times number of Units Purchased (column E).
- Total Cost (cell F16): The target cell that we will attempt to minimize. It holds the sum of cells F6:F14 and shows the total amount the client must invest. Note: The amount in this cell is in thousands of dollars.

The purpose of the spreadsheet is to help you select the bonds that meet your clients' cash flow needs with the smallest possible outlay. Investment advisors will recognize this staggered maturity approach as a bond "ladder," where part of the portfolio matures each year. In this example we assume that the clients spend any principal or interest distributions they receive—they do not reinvest them.

Part 2 details the cash flow needs. Row 21 (cells B21:F21) lists the amount needed (Cash Flow Needed) for each year, and row 19 (cells B19:F21) shows the annual cash flow (Amount Covered) generated by the specific bond selections. (Amounts are in thousands of dollars.) The spreadsheet's main constraint is that the Amount Covered is greater than or equal to the Cash Flow Need. The values in this section come from two sources: Your clients provide the Cash Flow Need amounts, and the Amount Covered values come from cells I15:M15 in the second part of the spreadsheet, Income Stream, in Figure 7–19.

Figure 7–19 shows two sources of cash from the portfolio: interest and repaid principal. We assume one interest payment per bond each year, and we design the portfolio so that a single bond matures in each of years 1 through 4. The Income Stream section lists the cash flows from the bonds. We explain the cells' formulas in more detail after completing the optimization.

For this LP example we use LINDO Systems, Inc.'s What'sBest! Program. The optimization results are in Figures 7–20 and 7–21. The model's parameters are

Adjustable cells: Units Purchased (cells E6:E14).

Best cell: Minimize Total Cost (cell F16).

Constraints: Amount Covered greater than or equal to "Cash Flow Need" (cells B17:F17 >= B19:F19).

Using Figure 7–20, to minimize the projected college costs of $100,000, your client should invest $87,350 (cell F16) in the proportions

FIGURE 7–20

	File	Edit	View	Insert	Format	Tools	Data	Window	WB!	Help		

	A	B	C	D	E	F	G
1	Meeting Funding Needs						
2							
3	AVAILABLE	Year of	Asking	Interest	Units	Investment/	
4	BOND OPTIONS:	Maturity	Price	Rate	Purchased	Bond Issue	
5							
6		1	1.0159	6.625	15.8	$16.06	
7			1.0184	6.875	0.0	$0.00	
8		2	1.0766	9.000	0.0	$0.00	
9			1.0016	5.375	18.9	$18.88	
10		3	0.9900	5.000	0.0	$0.00	
11			1.0934	8.875	21.9	$23.91	
12			1.0031	5.500	0.0	$0.00	
13		4	1.1044	8.500	25.8	$28.50	
14			1.0563	7.125	0.0	$0.00	
15							
16					TOTAL COST:	$87.35	
17							
18		Year 0	Year 1	Year 2	Year 3	Year 4	
19	Amount Covered	$6.19	$22.00	$24.00	$26.00	$28.00	
20		>=	=>=	=>=	=>=	=>=	
21	Cash Flow Need	$0.00	$22.00	$24.00	$26.00	$28.00	
22							
23	Note: All amounts in thousands						
24							
25							
26							

FUNDING

FIGURE 7-21

	File	Edit	View	Insert	Format	Tools	Data	Window	WB!	Help		

	H	I	J	K	L	M
1						
2						
3				Income Stream ($000)		
4	Year of	Year 0	Year 1	Year 2	Year 3	Year 4
5	Maturity					
6	1	1.0471	16.8525			
7		0.0000	0.0000			
8	2	0.0000	0.0000	0.0000		
9		1.0133	1.0133	19.8659		
10	3	0.0000	0.0000	0.0000	0.0000	
11		1.9406	1.9406	1.9406	23.8065	
12		0.0000	0.0000	0.0000	0.0000	
13	4	2.1935	2.1935	2.1935	2.1935	28.0000
14		0.0000	0.0000	0.0000	0.0000	0.0000
15	Total	6.1946	22.0000	24.0000	26.0000	28.0000
16						
17						
18						
19						
20						
21						
22						
23						
24						
25						
26						

FUNDING

indicated in the Units Purchased column. This portfolio will provide $6,190 in the first year, followed by distributions of $22,000, $24,000, $26,000, and $28,000 during the next four years (cells C19 to F19). These distributions meet your clients' cash flow requirements for their daughter's college costs.

It is easier to explain the income streams now that we have portfolio values to work with in Figure 7–21. We examine the formulas in the uppermost left corner, cells I6:J7, which are representative of the remaining cells.

We assume that the bonds pay annual interest. Since the client is concerned with annual cash flow, this assumption does not change the results. Cells I6 and I7 calculate the annual interest received (in thousands of dollars) from the amounts invested in 1-year maturity bonds. Here are their formulas:

I6: = E6 * D6/100

I7: = E7 * D7/100

The LP solution calls for the purchase of 15.8 units of the first bond (cell E6). Using the formula for I6 and ignoring the rounding error gives us (15.8 * 6.625/100) = 1.0471. This particular bond generated $1,047 in interest for your clients for the first year (year 0). Cell I7 has a zero value because the optimal solution does not call for an investment in the second 1-year maturity bond. The remaining formulas in the column use the same (relative) formula to calculate the interest payments on the portfolio's other bonds.

Cells J6 and J7 calculate the combined value of the bonds' next interest payment and the repaid principal with the formula:

J6: = E6 * (1 + D6/100)

J7 = E7 * (1 + D7/100)

For example, with cell J6 this formula produces $15.8 * (1 + 6.625/100) = 16.85$ (rounded). This amount represents the bond's interest payment of 1.0471, which is the same as year 0 plus the repaid principal of 15.8. We repeat this principal and interest formula in the top two cells for each column, while the remaining cells calculate the nonmaturing bonds' annual interest payments. Cells I5:M15 total each year's cash flows, and those values are transferred to the Amount Covered cells in B19:F19.

Although the program provides a solution, there is a potential problem. The optimal Units Purchased solution calls for fractional purchases of bonds: 15.8 units, 18.9 units, and so on. Government bonds trade in integer units ($1,000 face value per unit), however, making fractional purchases impossible. Your first thought might be to impose an integer constraint on the adjustable cells. Depending on the software you are using, that constraint might prevent the program from finding a solution. (Both What'sBest! and the Microsoft Excel 5.0 Solver function failed to optimize the problem with the integer constraint.) The simplest solution here appears to be rounding up the numbers to the next integer value, although it increases your clients' outlay. You also might consider alternative conservative investments such as certificates of deposit that offer the same rates and maturities as the bonds originally considered but allow "fractional" purchases.

NONLINEAR PROBLEMS

The problems we have examined so far have linear objective functions and constraints. That condition does not apply to every problem you are likely to encounter, though. Some have nonlinear objective functions, others have nonlinear constraints, and some combine both. These nonlinear relationships change the nature of the optimization problem. When we used the graphical approach to the Custom Woodwork problem earlier, we saw that the optimal solution to an LP problem is always found at a corner point, or extreme point, of the feasible region. That information allows the LP software to greatly reduce the possible solution points because the program does not need to examine the many possible solutions in the feasible region. It checks the corners (extreme points), calculates the objective function, and the point that produces the highest (lowest) objective function value represents the solution.

Unfortunately, nonlinear problems aren't as cooperative. Some NLP problems' solutions occur at an extreme point, others are elsewhere on the feasible region's boundary, while others occur in the interior. Because the solution is not limited to the extreme points, the simplex corner-checking method we used with our LP examples doesn't work with NLP problems. The good news is that the LP software can recognize NLP problems and use the correct analytical technique automatically.

The software shields the user from the analytical details, but you should be aware of a potential problem with NLP programs: local versus global optimal solutions. The easiest way to demonstrate this problem is with a physical example. Imagine that you are hiking toward a range of mountains and your goal is to climb the highest peak in the range. A heavy fog sets in, and when you reach the range, you can see only the mountain you are about to climb. You climb it to the summit (a local maximum), but you still don't know if you have reached the highest peak in the range (the global maximum). NLP programs face a similar problem: If they start in the wrong part of the feasible solution, they will find a local optimal solution, but it might not be the global solution. As we demonstrate, one way to work around this problem is to run several searches that use different starting points.

Example: Resource Allocation

In this section we modify the Custom Woodwork example to introduce a basic NLP problem. We previously assumed constant profit margins for each chair and chest. We modify that assumption here by recognizing that profits are a function of selling price and costs. The usual economic relationship between price and demand is that a higher price for a product leads to less demand. We recognize that trade-off here and allow the model to reflect the impact of changing prices. Figure 7–22 shows the initial worksheet.

In Figure 7–22 we retain the earlier worksheet's format but with several important changes. First, we assume constant marginal costs (cells B6

FIGURE 7-22

File Edit View Insert Format Tools Data Window WB! Help	

C9 `=(360-0.08*C5)`

	A	B	C	D	E	F	G
1	Custom Woodwork, Inc.						
2							
3	Product (per unit)	Chairs	Chests				
4							
5	Price	1800	3500			Total Profit	
6	Cost	1,100	1,900				
7	Profit	700	1,600			223200.00	
8							
9	Demand	136.00	80.00				
10							
11	Component Requirements						
12		Chairs	Chests	Total Used		Available	
13	Labor required	40	60	10,240		11,250	
14	Wood required	30	70	9,680		10,000	
15							
16							
17							
18							
19							
20							
21							
22							
23							
24							

Sheet2 \ Woodwork II - Initial Estimate

and C6) but allow unit profits to vary as prices change. (Formula: Cells B7:C7 [Profit] equal B5:C5 [Price] minus B6:C6 [Cost].) Second, we asked the business owner to give us a history of his sales over the past few years. We ran a regression analysis to determine the relationship between product demand and price. The regression results confirmed that demand varies negatively with price: higher prices lead to lower demand. We recognize that relationship in cells B9:C9 with these formulas from the regression output:

Demand for chairs (cell B9): $= 280 - .08 * B5$ (B5: chair price)

Demand for chests (cell C9): $= 360 - .08 * C5$ (C5: chest price)

The model's objective function (total profit formula, cell F7) is straightforward: Maximize Total Profit, which consists of profit per unit (cells B5:C5) times demand (cells B9:C9). You might not realize at first that this is a nonlinear function, but if we express it mathematically you can see why it violates the linearity requirement. Let P1 and C1 equal price and demand for chairs, and P2 and C2 represent price and demand for chests. We can then rewrite the objective function as

Total Profit $= (P1 - 1100) * C1 + (P2 - 1900) * C2$

Our demand functions for C1 and C2 are

C1 = 280 – .08 * P1

C2 = 360 – .08 * P2

If we substitute these equations for C1 and C2 into the Total Profit function, we have

Total Profit = (P1 – 1100) * (280 – .08 * P1) + (P2 – 1900) * (360 – .08 * P2)

We won't simplify the equation here, but you can see that the profit function will include squared P1 and P2 terms, which makes it a nonlinear formula.

After building the spreadsheet, you make initial price estimates of $1,800 for chairs and $3,500 for chests. You can see the results in Figure 7–22. Total profits equal $223,200, and there are unused labor hours and board feet. To find an optimal solution, you develop the following parameters:

Target cell	Maximize F7 (Total Profit)
Variable cells	B5:C5 (Prices)
Constraints	B5 >= 1,500; <= 2,500 (chair price range: $1,500 to $2,500)
	C5 >= 2,200; <= 4,000 (chest price range: $2,200 to $4,000)
	Labor and wood constraints same as earlier example (cells F13:F14)

For this example we used the Microsoft Excel 5.0 Solver function with the default options. You can change the program's NLP solution-method options, and we discuss those features in the appendix. The optimized results are shown in Figure 7–23. Total Profits have increased by more than $27,000 to $250,344.83, with the optimal prices set at $2,310.34 for chairs and $3,224.14 for chests. Of course, we are assuming that the demand function we derived from historical results will remain applicable for the upcoming period. An unexpected event, such as the emergence of a new competitor, could force the owner to reevaluate his pricing strategy.

We mentioned earlier the issue of local versus global optimal solutions. This example demonstrates the potential problem. We started the optimization with initial prices of $1,800 for chairs and $3,500 for chests (refer to Figure 7–22). This solution was feasible because it did not violate the problem's constraints. If you rerun the problem with initial starting prices of zero, the program gives you a different set of optimal prices that generate less profit than the previous solution. You won't know that you have found a local optimal solution, though, because the program stops searching once it finds a solution, local or global. Because a nonlinear problem can have several local optimal solutions, plan to solve your

FIGURE 7–23

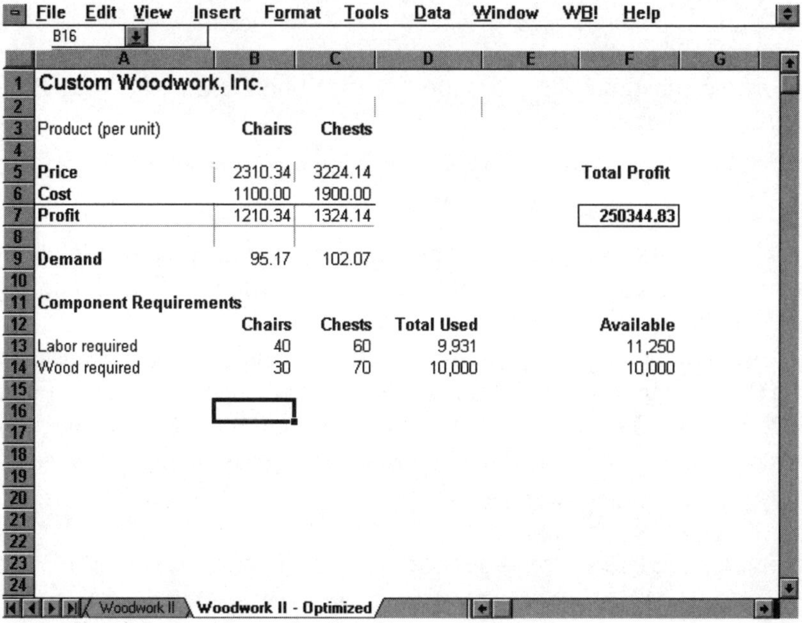

	A	B	C	D	E	F	G
	File Edit View Insert Format Tools Data Window WB! Help						
	B16						
1	Custom Woodwork, Inc.						
2							
3	Product (per unit)	Chairs	Chests				
4							
5	Price	2310.34	3224.14			Total Profit	
6	Cost	1100.00	1900.00				
7	Profit	1210.34	1324.14			250344.83	
8							
9	Demand	95.17	102.07				
10							
11	Component Requirements						
12		Chairs	Chests	Total Used		Available	
13	Labor required	40	60	9,931		11,250	
14	Wood required	30	70	10,000		10,000	
15							
16							

Woodwork II \ Woodwork II - Optimized

models again with different starting points to verify that you have found the global solution.

Example: Efficient Investment Portfolios

The typical investor faces a classic optimization problem. His ideal portfolio would earn a high return with very little volatility, but because the investor can't find that ideal risk/return tradeoff in the markets, he must settle for a constrained optimization. This tradeoff involves trying to find the highest (expected) return possible for a given level of risk, or conversely, the least amount of risk for a given (expected) return. Portfolios that offer the highest expected return for a given level of risk (or lowest risk for a given return) are called "efficient portfolios," and this section demonstrates the NLP method for constructing such a portfolio. (Readers will recognize the following material as the Markowitz model, named after Professor Harry M. Markowitz.)

This method of portfolio formation requires knowledge of the securities' expected returns and covariance matrix. The usual technique for calculating these values is to use the securities' historical returns. The investor then specifies a target return, and the optimization creates a portfolio mix to meet that expected return with the lowest possible risk. Figure 7–24 shows a standard spreadsheet portfolio optimization model.

Here is an explanation of the key cells in Figure 7–24's worksheet.

- A5:C5: User input; based on historical (or expected) security returns.
- B10:D10: Covariance matrix calculated from the historical returns.
- B17:D17: Variable cells; initially set at current portfolio weights.
- E17: Formula: =SUM(B17:D17); set as a constraint (E17 = 1) so that portfolio weights sum to one.
- B20: Formula: =SUMPRODUCT(A5:C5, B17:D17); gives the portfolio's weighted return.
- B21: Constraint cell; used as minimum required return for the portfolio.
- B23: Portfolio variance; used as target cell for minimization. Formula: =SUMPRODUCT(MMULT(B17:D17, B10:D12), B17:D17).

FIGURE 7–24

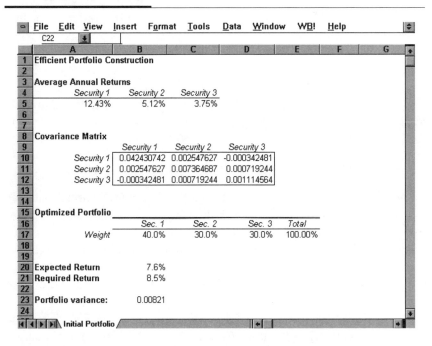

A note on the formula in cell B23 might be helpful. A portfolio's variance has two components: the contribution from the individual securities' variances and the securities' covariances. For example, with a two-security portfolio, the variance formula is

$$\text{Variance} = W1^2 * V1 + W2^2 * V2 + 2 * W1 * W2 * \text{Covariance}(V1, V2)$$

where

W1 = portfolio weight in security 1

W2 = portfolio weight in security 2

V1 = variance of security 1

V2 = variance of security 2

Entering this equation in a spreadsheet for a two-security problem is easy, but as you add securities, the formula becomes unwieldy. Cell B23 uses the Microsoft Excel 5.0 matrix manipulation functions to simplify the formula. (If you are familiar with matrix multiplication, the cell's formula is the equivalent of W^TEW, where E represents the covariance matrix.)

In this original scenario, the investor has allocated 40 percent to security 1 and 30 percent each to securities 2 and 3. The resulting portfolio's expected return is 7.6 percent (cell B20) with a variance of 0.00821 (cell B23). The investor wants to increase his portfolio's expected return to 8.5 percent (cell B21), but he wants to minimize the variance for that target return. He uses the Solver parameters described above plus an additional nonnegativity constraint, cells B17:D17 >= 0. This prevents the program from selling any securities short as it seeks a solution. These parameters produce the portfolio shown in Figure 7–25.

The portfolio in Figure 7–25 has the following weights: security 1: 49.9%; security 2: 30.6%; security 3: 19.5%; and the portfolio variance is .01210.

Example: Multiple Portfolio Risk Criteria

Some advisors (and investors) point to a problem with using variance as the standard measure of portfolio risk. Variance is a statistical measure that includes fluctuations above the mean (expected value) as well as fluctuations below the mean. Most investors aren't concerned about the risk that their portfolio will perform above its expected return, though—they are concerned primarily with the risk of losing money from a poorer than expected performance.

The statistical measures of semivariance and downside risk focus exclusively on the risk that the portfolio's return will fall below its target

FIGURE 7-25

	A	B	C	D	E	F	G
	File Edit View Insert Format Tools Data Window WB! Help						
	A32						
1	Efficient Portfolio Construction						
2							
3	Average Annual Returns						
4	Security 1	Security 2	Security 3				
5	12.43%	5.12%	3.75%				
6							
7							
8	Covariance Matrix						
9		Security 1	Security 2	Security 3			
10	Security 1	0.042430742	0.002547627	-0.000342481			
11	Security 2	0.002547627	0.007364687	0.000719244			
12	Security 3	-0.000342481	0.000719244	0.001114564			
13							
14							
15	Optimized Portfolio						
16		Sec. 1	Sec. 2	Sec. 3	Total		
17	Weight	49.9%	30.6%	19.5%	100.00%		
18							
19							
20	Expected Return	8.5%					
21	Required Return	8.5%					
22							
23	Portfolio variance:	0.01210					
24							
	Optimal Portfolio / Initial Portfolio /						

value. Downside-risk optimization focuses on minimizing the difference between the target and returns below the target. Semivariance modifies that calculation by minimizing the difference between the target and the square of the returns below the target. The model shown in Figure 7–26 calculates all three risk measures, giving the investor a selection of results from which to choose. (The original version of this model was developed for What'sBest! but the following material uses the Microsoft Excel 5.0 Solver function. Both programs solve the problem equally well, but it is easier to explain some of the model's features using Solver.)

The model in Figure 7–26 is more complex than the previous example, and we explain the cell entries and optimization parameters in detail. Cells B3:D3 are the target cells—they represent the portfolio's asset allocation among the three securities. The model has 12 scenarios, and cells B4:D15 show the assets' returns in each of the scenarios. (The user provides this information.) Each scenario has a 1 in 12 (8.3%) probability of occurring, and this likelihood is reflected in cells E4:E15. Cells F4:F15 give the weighted returns for each scenario. For example, cell F4 has the formula

=$B$3 * B4 + $C$3 * C4 + $D$3 * D4

F I G U R E   7–26

	File Edit View Insert Format Tools Data Window WB! Help								‡

| | A51 | ↓ | | | | | | | |

	A	B	C	D	E	F	G	H	I	J	↑
1	PORTFOLIO SCENARIO MODEL										
2		Asset 1	Asset 2	Asset 3	Prob.	Return	Difference				
3	Scenario	40.0%	30.0%	30.0%			Over	Under			
4	1	130.0%	122.5%	114.9%	8.3%	123.2%	8.2%	0.0%			
5	2	110.3%	129.0%	126.0%	8.3%	120.6%	5.6%	0.0%			
6	3	121.6%	121.6%	141.9%	8.3%	127.7%	12.7%	0.0%			
7	4	95.4%	72.8%	92.2%	8.3%	87.7%	0.0%	27.3%			
8	5	92.9%	114.4%	116.9%	8.3%	106.6%	0.0%	8.4%			
9	6	105.6%	107.0%	96.5%	8.3%	103.3%	0.0%	11.7%			
10	7	103.8%	132.1%	113.3%	8.3%	115.1%	0.1%	0.0%			
11	8	108.9%	130.5%	173.2%	8.3%	134.7%	19.7%	0.0%			
12	9	109.0%	119.5%	102.1%	8.3%	110.1%	0.0%	4.9%			
13	10	108.3%	139.0%	113.1%	8.3%	119.0%	4.0%	0.0%			
14	11	103.5%	92.8%	100.6%	8.3%	99.4%	0.0%	15.6%			
15	12	117.6%	171.5%	190.8%	8.3%	155.7%	40.7%	0.0%			
16											
17	Expected Return =		116.9%								
18	Target Return		115.0%			Variance =		0.0295			
19						Semi-Variance =		0.0102			
20	Invest Total 100%		100.0%			Downside Risk =		0.0567			
21											
22											
23											
24											
25											
26											↓

◄ ◄ ► ►\ Portfolio Risk /		←		→

(We include the dollar signs to stress that these cells, the asset's weights, are used as constants in calculating cells F4:F15.) We use the Over (G4:G15) and Under (H4:H15) differences as adjustable cells, and they are explained shortly.

Moving to the lower half of the worksheet, cell C17 is the portfolio's expected (probability-weighted) return, and it has the formula

=SUMPRODUCT(E4:E15, F4:F15)

Cell B18 has the portfolio's target return, which serves as a constraint for the expected return. The values for the three portfolio-risk measures are given in cells H18:H20 with these formulas:

Variance (H18): = E4 * (G4+H4)^2 +E5 * (G5+H5)^2 + ... + E15 * (G15+H15)^2

Semivariance (H19): = E4 * H4^2 + E5 * H5^2 + ... + E15 * H15^2

Downside risk (H20): = SUMPRODUCT(E4:E15, H4:H15)

As we mentioned earlier, each formula treats variations around the expected returns differently. The variance formula treats the Over and Under differences (columns G and H) equally. The semivariance calculation squares the Under difference, magnifying its impact, while downside risk uses the Under value without modification.

The model has the following additional constraints:

B3:D3 >= 0 (A nonnegativity constraint that prevents short selling.)

C17 >= C18 (Specifies minimum required portfolio return.)

C20 = 1 (Portfolio weights must sum to one.)

We illustrate the model's minimized solution for the variance (cell H18) risk measure in Figure 7–27. The portfolio's allocation (cells B3:E3) becomes 52.5% in asset 1, 33.9% in asset 2, and 13.6% in asset 3. The portfolio's expected return (cell C17) meets the target return of 15% (cell C18), and the variance is minimized in cell H18 at 0.0211.

Now that the Over and Under Difference cells (G4:H15) in Figure 7–27 have values, we can explain their purpose more easily. If you look again at the cell formulas for the three risk measures, you see that each measure uses the values cells G4:H15. In mathematical terms, the risk measures are functions of the values in G4:H15. Our goal in each optimization is to minimize the relevant risk measure.

We want positive values (>= 0) in cells G4:I15, so we use a formula in each cell that forces it to produce a positive number or zero. (We

FIGURE 7–27

File Edit View Insert Format Tools Data Window WB! Help										
A32										
	A	B	C	D	E	F	G	H	I	J
1	PORTFOLIO SCENARIO MODEL									
2		Asset 1	Asset 2	Asset 3	Prob.	Return	Difference			
3	Scenario	52.5%	33.9%	13.6%			Over	Under		
4	1	130.0%	122.5%	114.9%	8.3%	125.4%	10.4%	0.0%		
5	2	110.3%	129.0%	126.0%	8.3%	118.8%	3.8%	0.0%		
6	3	121.6%	121.6%	141.9%	8.3%	124.4%	9.4%	0.0%		
7	4	95.4%	72.8%	92.2%	8.3%	87.3%	0.0%	27.7%		
8	5	92.9%	114.4%	116.9%	8.3%	103.4%	0.0%	11.6%		
9	6	105.6%	107.0%	96.5%	8.3%	104.8%	0.0%	10.2%		
10	7	103.8%	132.1%	113.3%	8.3%	114.7%	0.0%	0.3%		
11	8	108.9%	130.5%	173.2%	8.3%	125.0%	10.0%	0.0%		
12	9	109.0%	119.5%	102.1%	8.3%	111.6%	0.0%	3.4%		
13	10	108.3%	139.0%	113.1%	8.3%	119.3%	4.3%	0.0%		
14	11	103.5%	92.8%	100.6%	8.3%	99.5%	0.0%	15.5%		
15	12	117.6%	171.5%	190.8%	8.3%	145.8%	30.8%	0.0%		
16										
17	Expected Return =		115.0%							
18	Target Return		115.0%			Variance =		0.0211		
19						Semi-Variance =		0.0105		
20	Invest Total 100%		100.0%			Downside Risk =		0.0572		
21										
22										
23										
24										
25										
26										

Portfolio Risk

want positive numbers because financial models don't use "negative" variance.) As we move across the row with scenario 1 in Figure 7–27 (row 4), we see that the portfolio's expected return is 125.4% (F4). Our target return (C18) is 115.0%, which means that the scenario 1 return is 10.4% over the target return. We want that value to appear in G4, but it should not appear in H4 because it is an "over" result, not an "under." We accomplish this identification of results by using an IF function, as in the following formula for cell G4:

= IF(F4 − $C$18 > 0, F4 − C18, 0)

This formula translates as follows: "If the value of cell F4 minus cell $C$18 exceeds zero, use that positive value; otherwise, return a value of zero." Cell H4 uses the same approach but with the cell order reversed:

H4 = IF($C$18 − F4 > 0, $C$18 − F4, 0)

Using the relative G and H cell address with the constant $C$18 value produces the greater-than-zero values for G4: H15 you will find in Figure 7–27.

Once you build the worksheet, it is easy to calculate values for the other risk measures. Simply recall the Solver menu and set the target cell to minimize the desired cell. By comparing results you can determine which measure is most appropriate for your needs.

LINEAR PROGRAMMING IN ACTION

The optimization problems we developed in this chapter are not particularly complicated because they are intended to explain and demonstrate the LP and NLP methods. In actual practice, though, a variety of users rely on these tools to analyze extremely complex problems. Large manufacturing firms traditionally have used mainframe LP and NLP programs for optimization problems like scheduling, product input cost minimization, and factory and warehouse location analyses. In March 1987, *The Wall Street Journal* reported that PC-based optimization programs were being used in a variety of situations: Grant Hospital (Chicago) saved over $80,000 per month in overtime and temporary staff expenses using What'sBest! to create schedules for 300 nurses; Newfoundland Energy Ltd. moved its LP program for crude-oil mixing from the mainframe to the PC, saving thousands in mainframe access charges; and Hawley Fuel Corp. (New York) minimized its coal purchase costs by optimizing a spreadsheet-based LP program.

Numerous financial applications of LP and NLP programs also exist. In a monograph published by LINDO Systems, Inc., "Financial Optimization Problems," Professor Linus Schrage describes several models:

Bond portfolio construction.

The Markowitz mean/variance portfolio model.

Municipal bond bidding.

Foreign exchange cash transfer.

Location of regional processing centers.

SOURCES AND SUGGESTED READING

Bulkely, W. M. "The Right Mix: New Software Makes the Choice Much Easier." *The Wall Street Journal,* March 27, 1987, p. 17.

Microsoft Excel User's Guide. Redmond, WA: Microsoft Corporation, 1993.

Ragsdale, C. T. *Spreadsheet Modeling and Decision Analysis: A Practical Introduction to Management Science.* Cambridge, MA: Course Technology, Inc., 1995.

Schrage, L. *Financial Optimization Problems.* Chicago: LINDO Systems, Inc., 1995.

Schrage, L. *LINDO: An Optimization Modeling System.* 4th ed. Danvers, MA: Boyd & Fraser Publishing Co., 1991.

What'sBest! User's Guide. Chicago: LINDO Systems, Inc., 1994.

SOFTWARE RESOURCES

Microsoft Excel Solver
Microsoft Corporation
One Microsoft Way
Redmond, WA 98052-6399

What'sBest!
LINDO Systems, Inc.
1415 North Dayton Street
Chicago, IL 60622
Tel. 800-441-2378 or 312-871-2524
Fax 312-871-1777
E-mail: info@lindo.com
Web: http://www.lindo.com
Suggested retail price: $149 – $4,995 (varies with capacity)
Educational pricing also available

CHAPTER 8

Spreadsheet Tools

INTRODUCTION

In surveys of PC users, spreadsheet programs always rank as one of the most widely used software categories. The first spreadsheets, such as VisiCalc and Lotus 1-2-3, played an important role in helping the PC gain acceptance among business users in the early 1980s. Of course, today's Windows-environment spreadsheet programs bear only a faint resemblance to their DOS predecessors. They still use a row-by-column grid system for cell identification and data entry, but modern spreadsheets have so many additional features that the traditional numerical operations are only part of their repertoire. Today's spreadsheets combine database, graphics, and user-defined functions in one environment. You can link spreadsheets to other programs and develop customized features with their built-in programming languages.

Despite this increase in the spreadsheet's capabilities, many users tap into just a fraction of their program's power. They use their new spreadsheet software in the same way they used their old program: Crunch a few numbers, create basic graphs, and if they are feeling adventurous, they might try building a macro to automate some routine task. This chapter presents techniques to help you get more out of your spreadsheet. The focus, as in the rest of the book, is on analytical tools for financial applications, but the techniques we develop can be applied to all your spreadsheet tasks. With a modest investment of time and effort, we believe you can improve your spreadsheet productivity tremendously.

The material in this chapter uses Microsoft Excel for Windows (versions 5.0 and 7.0). We decided to work with Excel exclusively for several reasons. The first reason is the growing acceptance of Microsoft's programming language, Visual Basic for Applications (VBA). As we show later, this language, which is included in Excel, gives the user increased control of the spreadsheet. VBA can also be used with other Microsoft applications, extending the user's skill to other programs she might use. The second reason is a practical one. Not too long ago, a user could maintain a reasonable level of expertise with several spreadsheet programs simultaneously. As the programs became more powerful, though, it became more difficult (at least for this author!) to stay current with multiple spreadsheets, leading to a decision to focus exclusively on Microsoft Excel. Readers who use other spreadsheets will still find the chapter's material valuable, though, because the leading programs share many common features. You might have to locate your program's equivalent function or command sequence, but you should be able to use most of the chapter's material.

The chapter has three parts. The first part examines components that are a standard part of Excel, which includes functions, analytical tools, and other useful features like audit tools and pivot tables. The second part looks at add-ins, which are third-party programs that extend Excel's analytical capabilities. We saw examples of add-ins earlier in the book with @RISK (Chapter 3) and What'sBest! (Chapter 7). The final part discusses user-developed tools, including customized functions, macros, and VBA programs.

STANDARD FEATURES

Functions

Functions are the engines that drive the spreadsheet's calculations. Microsoft Excel comes with several hundred built-in functions that are grouped by category: mathematical, statistical, financial, and so. These functions act as mini-programs that calculate a value for the cell based on the arguments (inputs) that the user provides. To place a function in a cell, the user can type the required input or access it by pull-down menu: Insert, Function, Function Category. Using the menus invokes the Function Wizard, which prompts the user for the required input and offers help documentation in many cases.

Financial Functions

Tables 8–1, 8–2, and 8–3 list the financial functions available in Excel 7.0. For convenience, we grouped them into debt securities, accounting, and time value of money categories.

TABLE 8-1

Debt Securities Functions

Function Name	Purpose
ACCRINT	Returns the accrued interest for a security that pays periodic interest.
ACCRINTM	Returns the accrued interest for a security that pays interest at maturity.
COUPDAYBS	Returns the number of days from the beginning of the coupon period to the settlement date.
COUPDAYS	Returns the number of days in the coupon period that contains the settlement date.
COUPDAYSNC	Returns the number of days from the settlement date to the next coupon date.
COUPNCD	Returns the next coupon date after the settlement date.
COUPNUM	Returns the number of coupons payable between the settlement date and maturity date.
COUPPCD	Returns the previous coupon date before the settlement date.
CUMIPMT	Returns the cumulative interest paid between two periods.
CUMPRINC	Returns the cumulative principal paid on a loan between two periods.
DISC	Returns the discount rate for a security.
DOLLARDE	Converts a dollar price, expressed as a fraction, into a dollar price, expressed as a decimal number.
DOLLARFR	Converts a dollar price, expressed as a decimal number, into a dollar price, expressed as a fraction.
DURATION	Returns the annual duration of a security with periodic interest payments.
EFFECT	Returns the effective annual interest rate.
INTRATE	Returns the interest rate for a fully invested security.
MDURATION	Returns the Macauley modified duration for a security with an assumed par value of $100.
ODDFPRICE	Returns the price per $100 face value of a security with an odd first period.
ODDFYIELD	Returns the yield of a security with an odd first period.
ODDLPRICE	Returns the price per $100 face value of a security with an odd last period.
ODDLYIELD	Returns the yield of a security with an odd last period.
PRICE	Returns the price per $100 face value of a security that pays periodic interest.
PRICEDISC	Returns the price per $100 face value of a discounted security.
PRICEMAT	Returns the price per $100 face value of a security that pays interest at maturity.

(continued)

T A B L E   8–1 (concluded)

Function Name	Purpose
RECEIVED	Returns the amount received at maturity for a fully invested security.
TBILLEQ	Returns the bond-equivalent yield for a Treasury bill.
TBILLPRICE	Returns the price per $100 face value for a Treasury bill.
TBILLYIELD	Returns the yield for a Treasury bill.
YIELD	Returns the yield on a security that pays periodic interest.
YIELDDISC	Returns the annual yield for a discounted security, for example, a Treasury bill.
YIELDMAT	Returns the annual yield of a security that pays interest at maturity.

We assume the reader is familiar with the mechanics of inserting functions into cells, so we do not elaborate on that topic here. Instead, we focus on the function's construction. As an example, we use the future value function, which takes the following form: =FV(rate, nper, pmt, pv, type). The function has two parts: its name (FV), which appears after the equal sign, and its arguments (rate, nper, pmt, pv, type), which appear in the parentheses. Depending on the function's purpose, the required arguments can be numbers, text, logical values like TRUE or FALSE, or cell references. The result you get from using a function is called a value. The FV functions takes numerical arguments and returns a numerical value. The first three arguments are required:

rate: interest rate per period.

nper: number of payment periods in an annuity.

pmt: payment made each period.

The remaining two arguments are optional. If you do not include values, the program assumes a default value of zero.

pv: present value of any lump sum.

type: set to 0 if payments are due at end of period (default); set to 1 if payments are due at beginning of period.

Example You want to calculate the future value of a one-time deposit of $100. It will earn 5 percent for two years. If you deposit the $100 at the beginning of the first year, what will it be worth after two years? Using the FV function, you enter the function: =FV(0.05,2,0,–100) and receive the value $110.25. (We use a negative sign for the $100 deposit to signify a cash outflow.)

TABLE 8–2

Accounting Functions

Function Name	Purpose
AMORDEGRC	Returns the depreciation for each accounting period.
AMORLINC	Returns the depreciation for each accounting period.
DB	Returns the depreciation of an asset for a specified period using the fixed-declining balance method.
DDB	Returns the depreciation of an asset for a specified period using the double-declining balance method or some other method you specify.
SLN	Returns the straight-line depreciation of an asset for one period.
SYD	Returns the sum-of-the-year's digits depreciation of an asset for a specified period.
VDB	Returns the depreciation of an asset for a specified or partial period using a declining balance method.

TABLE 8–3

Time Value of Money Functions

Function Name	Purpose
FV	Returns the future value of an investment.
FVSCHEDULE	Returns the future value of an initial principal after applying a series of compound interest rates.
IPMT	Returns the interest payment for an investment for a given period.
IRR	Returns the internal rate of return for a series of cash flows.
MIRR	Returns the internal rate of return where positive and negative cash flows are financed at different rates.
NOMINAL	Returns the annual nominal interest rate.
NPER	Returns the number of periods for an investment.
NPV	Returns the net present value of an investment based on a series of periodic cash flows and a discount rate.
PMT	Returns the periodic payment for an annuity.
PPMT	Returns the payment on the principal for an investment for a given period.
PV	Returns the present value of an investment.
RATE	Returns the interest rate per period of an annuity.
XIRR	Returns the internal rate of return for a schedule of cash flows that is not necessarily periodic.
XNPV	Returns the net present value for a schedule of cash flows that is not necessarily periodic.

The value of built-in functions is obvious: They save the user time in locating and typing formulas, and they reduce the chance for typing errors while composing the formula. But what happens if you cannot find a function that performs the calculation you need? The obvious solution is to write the formula needed, but another solution is to build the function yourself. User-defined functions are an easy way to customize your spreadsheets so you don't have to recreate a function each time you need it. As we show later in the chapter, Excel allows users to create their own customized functions, which then become available in the same way as built-in functions.

Statistical Functions

Table 8–4 lists several of Excel 7.0's built-in statistical functions. We will use several of these functions in the chapter to demonstrate their potential applications.

Mathematical Functions

Excel provides an extensive list of built-in mathematical functions. Because many of them are specialized, Table 8–5 lists only the functions that a user working in finance is likely to encounter.

Spreadsheet Simulations

In Chapter 3 we examined the use of a third-party add-in, @RISK, to develop and run spreadsheet simulations. As we show in the next section, you can create spreadsheet simulations by using Excel's built-in mathematical functions.

Random Numbers

The key to creating simulations for modeling uncertainty in a worksheet is the proper use of the program's random number generating functions. Two are listed in Table 8–5: RAND, which returns a number between 0 and 1, and RANDBETWEEN, which returns a number between the endpoints you specify. Both functions are based on uniform distributions, which makes every value between the endpoints equally likely. Table 8–6 shows a list of random values generated by the RAND() and RANDBETWEEN(0, 5) functions.

Using these random number functions with their uniform distribution is straightforward. Simply enter the appropriate random number function in the cell's formula, and the formula's results will include the random element. For example, assume that you are modeling a firm's pro-

TABLE 8-4

Statistical Functions

Function Name	Purpose
AVERAGE	Returns the average of its arguments.
BINOMDIST	Returns the individual term binomial distribution probability.
CHIDIST	Returns the one-tailed probability of the chi-square distribution.
CHITEST	Returns the test for independence.
CONFIDENCE	Returns the confidence interval for a population mean.
CORREL	Returns the correlation coefficient between two data sets.
COUNT	Counts how many numbers are in the list of arguments.
COUNTA	Counts how many values are in the list of arguments.
COVAR	Returns covariance, the average of the products of paired deviations.
DEVSQ	Returns the sum of squares of deviations.
EXPONDIST	Returns the exponential distribution.
FDIST	Returns the F probability distribution.
FORECAST	Returns a value along a linear trend.
FREQUENCY	Returns a frequency distribution as a vertical array.
FTEST	Returns the result of an F-test.
GEOMEAN	Returns the geometric mean.
GROWTH	Returns values along an exponential trend.
HARMEAN	Returns the harmonic mean.
INTERCEPT	Returns the intercept of the linear regression line.
KURT	Returns the kurtosis of a data set.
LARGE	Returns the k-th largest value in a data set.
LINEST	Returns the parameters of a linear trend.
LOGEST	Returns the parameters of an exponential trend.
LOGINV	Returns the inverse of the lognormal distribution.
LOGNORMDIST	Returns the cumulative lognormal distribution.
MAX	Returns the maximum value in a list of arguments.
MEDIAN	Returns the median of the given numbers.
MIN	Returns the minimum value in a list of arguments.
MODE	Returns the most common value in a data set.
NORMDIST	Returns the normal cumulative distribution.
NORMINV	Returns the inverse of the normal cumulative distribution.
NORMSDIST	Returns the standard normal cumulative distribution.
NORMSINV	Returns the inverse of the standard normal cumulative distribution.
PEARSON	Returns the Pearson product moment correlation coefficient.
PERCENTILE	Returns the k-th percentile of values in a range.
PERCENTRANK	Returns the percentage rank of a value in a data set.

(continued)

T A B L E 8–4 (concluded)

Function Name	Purpose
PERMUT	Returns the number of permutations for a given number of objects.
POISSON	Returns the Poisson distribution.
PROB	Returns the probability that values in a range are between two limits.
QUARTILE	Returns the quartile of a data set.
RANK	Returns the rank of a number in a list of numbers.
SKEW	Returns the skewness of a distribution.
SLOPE	Returns the slope of the linear regression line.
SMALL	Returns the k-th smallest value in a data set.
STANDARDIZE	Returns a normalized value.
STDEV	Estimates standard deviation based on a sample.
STDEVP	Calculates standard deviation based on the entire population.
STEYX	Returns the standard error of the predicted y-value for each x in the regression.
TDIST	Returns the student's t-distribution.
TREND	Returns values along a linear trend.
TTEST	Returns the probability associated with a student's t-test.
VAR	Estimates variance based on a sample.
VARP	Calculates variance based on the entire population.
ZTEST	Returns the two-tailed P-value of a z-test.

duction costs. Each unit costs $5 to make, and you believe demand will be between 10,000 and 15,000 units. If you create a cell formula with the entry =5 * RANDBETWEEN(10000, 15000), you will be sampling from a uniform distribution with endpoints at $50,000 and $75,000. Table 8–7 shows a few sample iterations from a worksheet using this formula.

The uniform distribution can serve as the foundation for other distributions. Ragsdale (1995) provides the following formulas, listed here in Table 8–8, with μ, σ, and λ representing the particular distribution's parameters.

A drawback to using user-defined cell formulas in a spreadsheet simulation, instead of an add-in like @RISK, is the effort required to design and run multiple iterations. Also, after running the simulation, the user who lacks VBA programming skills must "manually" perform the statistical analysis and create any graphs he desires. While a spreadsheet user with modest experience certainly can do these tasks, a frequent simulation user probably would find the add-in's efficiency attractive.

TABLE 8–5

Mathematical Functions

Function Name	Purpose
EXP	Returns e raised to the power of a given number.
INT	Returns the integer portion of a number.
LN	Returns the natural logarithm of a number.
LOG	Returns the logarithm of a number to a specified base.
MDETERM	Returns the matrix determinant of an array.
MINVERSE	Returns the matrix inverse of an array.
MMULT	Returns the matrix product of two arrays.
MOD	Returns the remainder from division.
POWER	Returns the result of a number raised to a power.
PRODUCT	Multiplies its arguments.
QUOTIENT	Returns the integer portion of a division.
RAND	Returns a random number between 0 and 1.
RANDBETWEEN	Returns a random number between the numbers you specify.
SERIESSUM	Returns the sum of a power series based on the formula.
SQRT	Returns a positive square root.
SUM	Adds its arguments.
SUMIF	Adds the cells specified by a given criteria.
SUMPRODUCT	Returns the sum of the products of corresponding array components.
SUMSQ	Returns the sum of the squares of the arguments.
SUMX2MY2	Returns the sum of the difference of squares of corresponding values in two arrays.
SUMX2PY2	Returns the sum of the sum of squares of corresponding values in two arrays.
SUMXMY2	Returns the sum of squares of differences of corresponding values in two arrays.

Analytical Tools

In this section we examine several of Excel's built-in analytical tools that are available through the Tools menu. These tools automate the steps required to set up and run an analytical procedure, saving the user considerable time and reducing the chance of error.

Solver

Do you ever use your spreadsheet to develop what-if scenarios? In a what-if scenario, you change the value of a key variable to see how the critical

TABLE 8-6

Random Values

RAND()	RANDBETWEEN(0,5)
0.3278	2
0.0637	1
0.0193	5
0.7715	0
0.5534	4
0.0658	3
0.7302	4
0.6996	4

TABLE 8-7

Random Production Costs

Iteration	Value
1	57,350
2	70,720
3	52,700
4	69,600
5	66,765

TABLE 8-8

Distribution Formulas

Desired Distribution	Formula
Symmetric Triangular	a+(b–a) * (RAND() +RAND()) / 2
Normal	NORMINV(RAND(), μ, σ)
Exponential	$-1 / \lambda$ * LN(RAND())

cells in the spreadsheet change. Typical what-if questions are, What happens if inflation averages 5 percent instead of 3 percent? What will happen to the level of required funding if the investment earns 6 percent instead of 12 percent? The usual approach to questions like this is to play with the spreadsheet's variables to examine the resulting changes in the outcome. That method works with simple problems, but it is time-consuming and inefficient with more complex cases.

A better way to approach what-if problems is to use the Solver, one of Excel's analytical routines. Chapter 7 discussed the Solver in detail so we won't repeat that material here. Instead, we show how you can use the Solver to build more efficient what-if scenarios based on adjustable and constraint cells.

We create the spreadsheet model shown in Figure 8–1. We need to know the annual funding needed for a client to accumulate $100,000 in 10 years, assuming yearly deposits and an annual return of 10 percent. In the first two years, your client can save only $5,000 per year. After that, he can save more, and in years 4 through 10 he can increase his yearly savings by 5 percent each year. Figure 8–1 shows one approach to solving this problem.

Cells F3 and F4 in Figure 8–1 show the $5,000 annual limit. The figures in column H, Account Value, total the deposits plus the interest they have earned. The goal is to find a deposit amount for year 3 (cell F5) that will cause the ending balance in cell H12 to equal the target value of $100,000 in cell C3. For your first estimate of the annual funding needed,

FIGURE 8–1

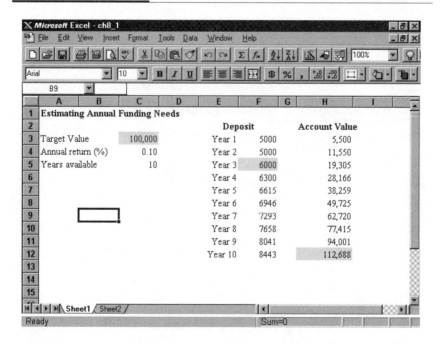

you enter $6,000 in cell F5. The result in cell H12: $112,688—too much.
If you have time to spare, you can keep trying new values for cell F5 until
you come close to the $100,000 target.

A more efficient approach is to use the Solver so you avoid this type
of search altogether. Invoke the Solver input screen (Menu: Tools, Solver)
and enter the following values:

Target cell: $H$12

Equal to Value: $100,000

By changing cells: $F$5

Hit the Solve button and the program generates the solution shown
in Figure 8–2. Your client should deposit $5,134 in year 3 and increase the
amount by 5 percent each year.

Goal Seek

The example in Figures 8–1 and 8–2 does not utilize much of the Solver's
power, but it will find a solution to this type of problem. The Solver's real
strength is finding solutions to problems with multiple objectives and constraints. In problems like this, when you know the answer you want but

FIGURE 8–2

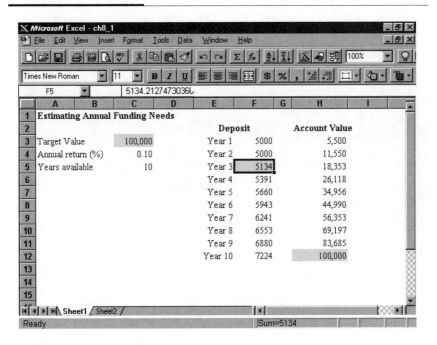

need to calculate the single variable your formula needs to return that answer, use the Goal Seek method (Menu: Tools, Goal Seek) as an alternative to Solver. As you can see in Figure 8–3, the Goal Seek's dialogue box is much simpler than the Solver's.

As Figure 8–3 shows, to use Goal Seek you identify the goal cell (Set cell), assign it a target value (To value), and identify the variable cell (By changing cell). After you provide this input, Goal Seek calculates the value necessary to produce the specific goal you provided. If the goal is an amount returned by a formula, it calculates a value that, when supplied to your formula, causes the formula to return the number you want. We do not show the solved problem here because the result is identical to that in Figure 8–2.

Scenario Manager

The scenario manager (Menu: Tools, Scenarios…) is not an analytical function, but it is a useful tool for managing your what-if scenarios. It allows you to create, view, and save multiple scenarios with up to 32 sets of changing cells for each scenario. You also can generate summary reports, merge scenarios from a group into a single model, and protect your scenarios so that they cannot be modified.

FIGURE 8–3

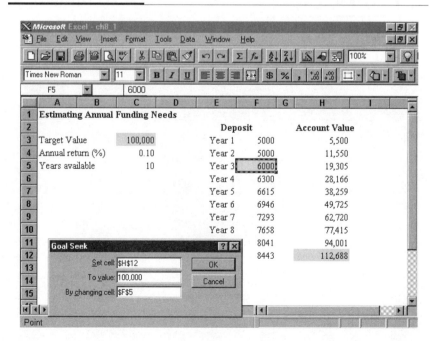

Figure 8–4 shows the setup for a simple investment portfolio worksheet. The portfolio contains two types of securities: stocks and bonds. Our initial assumption is that the stock portfolio will earn an average 10 percent annual total return, while the bonds will have an average 7 percent total return. (We aggregate the total return components for the illustration, but it would be straightforward to show income and capital gains separately.)

The worksheet in Figure 8–4 assumes the initial investment in year 0 is $10,000 each in both stocks and bonds (cells B6 and B7). The formulas in cell C6..E7 for years 1, 2, and 3 take the previous year's asset value and multiply it by the assumed return for the assets (cells B2 and B3). We assigned the names stocks_return and bonds_return to cells B2 and B3, respectively, for convenience. For example, cell C6 has the formula: =B6 * (1 + stocks_return) and cell C7 reads = B7 * (1 + bonds_return). The Portfolio total cells B8..E8 simply sum the separate asset values.

We assume the returns described above will be the normal scenario, but we know that investment returns vary unpredictably. To account for that variation in return, we want to create two other scenarios: a high and low return. Table 8–9 lists the three scenarios' returns.

To create the scenarios, we use the WorkGroup toolbar. (If you are not familiar with this toolbar, the fastest way to bring it up is to place your

FIGURE 8–4

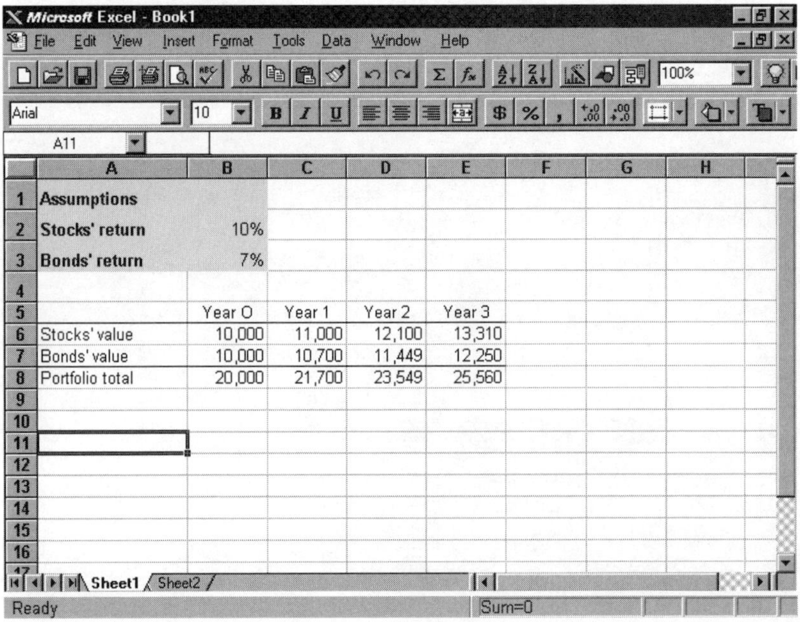

TABLE 8–9

Scenario Returns

Scenario	Returns
Normal	Stocks: +10%
	Bonds: +7
Low	Stocks: –5
	Bonds: –3
High	Stocks: +30
	Bonds: +20

cursor over any of the toolbars currently displayed on your screen. Click on the right mouse button, and a toolbar menu will pop up. Click on the WorkGroup selection to display the toolbar.) Follow these steps to create the scenarios.

1. Select cells B2:B3, the stock and bond return cells.
2. Leave those cells selected and type Normal in the WorkGroup selection box, as shown in Figure 8–5.
3. Repeat the process, entering the new values for the high scenario (stocks +30%, bonds +20%) and entering the name High in the dialogue box. Do the same for the low scenario (stocks –5%, bonds –3%).

To check your input, go to the scroll down arrow on the right side of the WorkGroup toolbar dialogue box. When you click on the arrow, a list with the three scenarios should appear. After you select a scenario, the appropriate values for the scenario's returns will appear in cells B2 and B3, and the values in cells C6:E8 should reflect the changes in cells B2 and B3. Figure 8–6 shows the dialogue box selections and the high-returns scenario.

Creating scenarios can save you considerable time because you don't have to create a new worksheet for each set of assumptions. The approach we've taken so far is still somewhat limited, though, because it assumes that stock and bond returns move in unison. What happens if stocks earn a normal return but bonds earn a high return during the same period? It is easy to create this kind of flexibility in the scenarios. The first step is to select a single variable cell, either stock or bond returns in this example. Next, go to the WorkGroup dialogue box and enter a new name for the scenario, based on the variable cell's value. Repeat this step of creating a new name for each

FIGURE 8–5

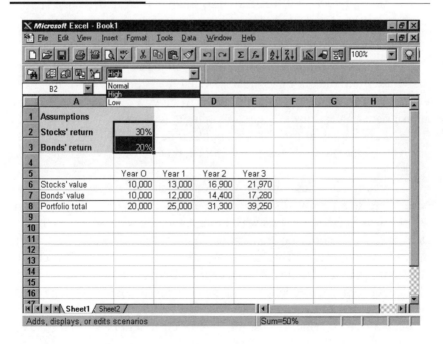

FIGURE 8–6

value in the variable cell. As you can see in Figure 8–7, we used Bonds Low, Bonds Normal, and Bonds High for the three bond returns, with equivalent names for the stock returns. As the dialogue box menu shows, we have a total of nine scenarios: the original three in which the values move in unison and the six new ones in which we can mix-and-match returns. Figure 8–7 shows a normal stock return (10%) and a high bond return (20%) in the same scenario. We can now change the scenario for either stocks or bonds without changing the other's value in the worksheet.

As an alternative to the WorkGroup toolbar, you can work with the scenarios through the Scenario Manager (Menu: Tools, Scenarios). This method will list the worksheet's scenarios, and it will let you generate a Scenario Summary Report that provides details on the variable and results cells in your model (not shown here).

Analysis Toolpak

Excel provides a wide range of data analysis tools, located under the Tools, Data Analysis menus. In the following sections we examine several of those tools and demonstrate their use. Our data set consists of roughly 21 years of monthly returns from two securities. (Data not shown.)

FIGURE 8–7

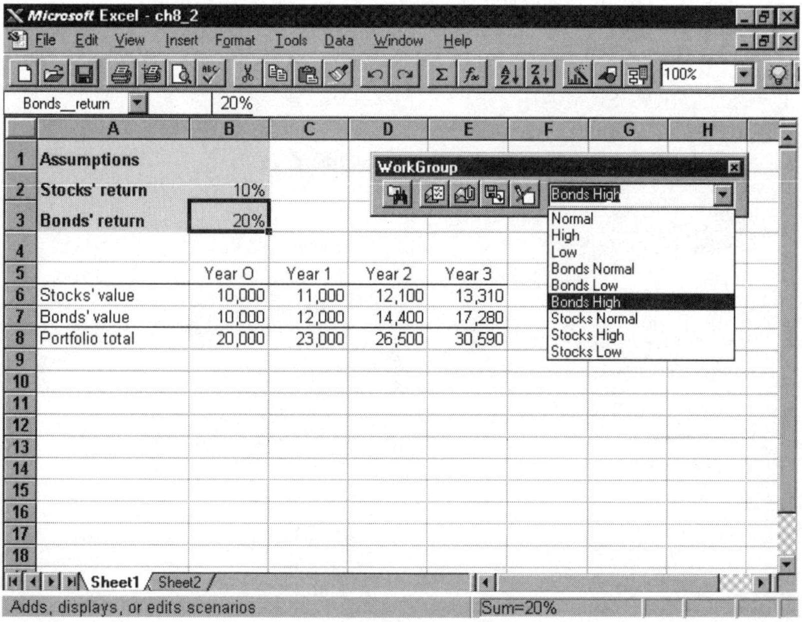

Data Analysis: Descriptive Statistics

The descriptive statistics analysis provides a summary of the data's key statistics. Table 8–10 lists the results of analyzing the securities' monthly returns. Most of the statistics listed in Table 8–10 are also available as individual functions.

We assume that the reader is familiar with most of the descriptive statistics so we do not provide explanations for the entire list. Here are brief explanations for the less frequently used terms.

Kurtosis Describes the relative steepness or flatness of a distribution compared to the normal distribution. Positive kurtosis indicates a relatively peaked distribution, while negative kurtosis indicates a relatively flat distribution.

Skewness Characterizes the degree of asymmetry of a distribution around its mean. Positive skewness indicates a distribution with an asymmetric tail extending toward more positive values. Negative skewness indicates a distribution with an asymmetric tail extending toward more negative values. In contrast, a normal distribution (the "bell curve") has a symmetric distribution around the mean value.

Confidence Level (95%) Indicates the range around the mean in which the population mean is likely to be found. Using the results for the first security, you can be 95% confident that the mean is in the range of 1.296 ± 0.534, or .762 to 1.830.

TABLE 8–10

Descriptive Statistics

Name	Security 1	Security 2
Mean	1.296	0.790
Standard Error	0.271	0.108
Median	1.350	0.730
Mode	2.600	−0.090
Standard Deviation	4.279	1.710
Sample Variance	18.313	2.923
Kurtosis	3.193	3.303
Skewness	−0.426	0.557
Range	34.950	14.710
Minimum	−21.520	−5.130
Maximum	13.430	9.580
Sum	322.790	196.780
Count	249.000	249.000
Confidence Level (95.0%)	0.534	0.213

Data Analysis: Covariance

In constructing a portfolio, investors usually look for diversification by choosing securities whose patterns of returns differ from one another. The covariance statistic measures how closely two returns, or any two data ranges, track each other. The formula for the covariance of two data sets (x, y) is

$$cov(x, y) = \frac{1}{n} \sum (x_i - \bar{x})(y_i - \bar{y})$$

where $\bar{x}$ and $\bar{y}$ represent the sample means for the two data sets. A positive covariance means that large values of one data set are associated with large values of the other set, and vice versa for negative covariance. Covariance near zero means the values in the data sets are unrelated. Table 8–11 shows the variances and covariance (2.4825) for the two securities.

Data Analysis: Correlation

One problem with the covariance measure is the difficulty in comparing results. In Table 8–11, for example, is a covariance of 2.4825 large or small? To circumvent this scale problem, it is easier to use the correlation measure when comparing the relationship between two data sets because the correlation measure ranges from –1 to 1. A value near 1 implies a strong positive relationship between the two variables, while a value near –1 implies a strong negative relationship. As with the covariance measure, a value near zero means the variables are unrelated. We use the Greek letter ρ (pronounced "row") to denote the correlation measure, whose formula is

$$\rho(x, y) = \frac{cov(x, y)}{\sigma_x \sigma_y}$$

where $\sigma_x \sigma_y$ is the product of the x and y variables' standard deviations. The correlation between the two securities is .339, indicating that their relationship is weakly positive.

TABLE 8–11

Variance/Covariance Matrix

	Security 1	Security 2
Security 1	18.3131	
Security 2	2.4825	2.9232

Data Analysis: Histograms

Histograms are a useful tool for visualizing a data set's frequency distribution. We discussed these distributions in depth in Chapter 3, and readers who need more background on histograms should review that material. If you decide to create a histogram, we recommend you examine your data to develop appropriate bin ranges (x-axis intervals). If you do not use the program's option to specify your own bins, the program applies its defaults, which are based on the data's minimum and maximum values. If those values fail to produce an acceptable graph, you will need to specify your own bins.

Data Analysis: Moving Averages

We illustrated moving averages in Chapter 7, where we discussed their use as a forecasting tool. Excel provides a moving average calculator that spares you the effort of setting up the formulas. You specify the data range and the interval (length of averaging period), and the program creates the moving average using the formula

$$F_{(t+1)} = \frac{1}{N} \sum_{j=1}^{N} A_{t-j+1}$$

where F_j is the forecasted value at time j, N equals the length of the averaging period, and A_j is the actual value at time j. Table 8–12 shows the results of calculating a moving average using two periods, MA(2), and four periods, MA(4).

TABLE 8–12

Moving Averages

Value	MA(2)	MA(4)
100.00	N/A	N/A
105.00	102.50	N/A
112.00	108.50	N/A
107.00	109.50	106.00
111.00	109.00	108.75
119.76	115.38	112.44
122.86	121.31	115.16
126.95	124.90	120.14
139.29	133.12	127.21
146.50	142.89	133.90
155.16	150.83	141.97

Data Analysis: Rank and Percentile

The rank and percentile tool sorts a data range and assigns each value a rank and percentile. This tool is useful if you need to rank your data and estimate the percentile breakdown. Table 8–13 shows the procedure's output using the stock return data (Security 1) for input. (We show only the top 10 returns here.)

Data Analysis: Regression

Regression is a useful tool for both data analysis and forecasting. Because we covered it in detail in Chapter 5, we will not review the concepts behind the method here. Instead, we focus on Excel's regression capabilities, using the same housing price data (Table 8–14) that we worked with in Chapter 5.

We want to explore the relationship between the dependent variable (price), and the independent variables of house size, number of bedrooms, and number of bathrooms. Figure 8–8 shows the Excel dialogue box that we fill in to set up the regression. We checked all the available options in this example. Depending on the nature of your work, you might not need as much analytical detail as we provide here.

As Tables 8–15 to 8–18 show, the regression output contains a wealth of results. In fact, Excel's regression tool provides more analytical and graphical detail than some statistics program. (We do not include the graphical results here.)

TABLE 8–13

Ranked Returns

Point	Return	Rank	Percentage
145	13.43	1	100.00
92	12.67	2	99.50
1	12.51	3	99.10
13	11.99	4	98.70
204	11.43	5	98.30
94	11.26	6	97.90
116	11.25	7	97.50
71	10.95	8	97.10
185	9.75	9	96.70
175	8.98	10	96.30

TABLE 8-14

Housing Price Data

Price ($)	Square Feet	Bedrooms	Bathrooms
200	1065	3	1.5
228	1254	3	2
235	1300	3	2
285	1577	4	2.5
239	1600	3	2
293	1750	4	2
285	1800	4	2.5
365	1870	4	2
295	1935	4	2.5
290	1948	4	2
385	2254	4	3
505	2600	3	2.5
425	2800	4	3
415	3000	4	3

FIGURE 8-8

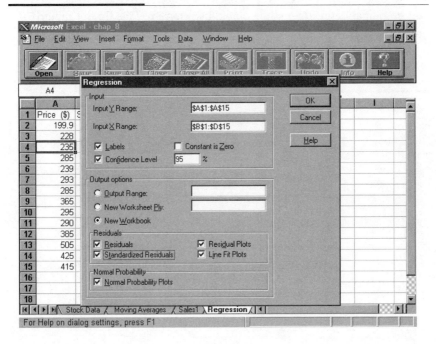

TABLE 8-15

Regression Statistics

Multiple R	**0.914**
R Square	0.835
Adjusted R Square	0.786
Standard Error	40.951
Observations	14.000

TABLE 8-16

ANOVA (Analysis of Variance)

	df	SS	MS	F	Significance F
Regression	3.000	85044.916	28348.305	16.904	0.000
Residual	10.000	16770.093	1677.009		
Total	13.000	101815.009			

TABLE 8-17

Other Regression Statistics

	Coefficients	Standard Error	t Stat	P-value	Lower 95%	Upper 95%
Intercept	125.864	87.362	1.441	0.180	−68.791	320.519
Square feet	0.154	0.035	4.405	0.001	0.076	0.231
Bedrooms	−22.321	27.075	−0.824	0.429	−82.648	38.006
Bathrooms	−8.788	45.447	−0.193	0.851	−110.051	92.476

Data Analysis: Sampling

Much statistical analysis is based on the technique of sampling. A good example of this is political polling done through voter surveys. If the poll is structured properly and the sample of voters is large enough, the survey can provide an accurate representation of the total population's opinion. Some degree of uncertainty exists always, of course—that is why survey results are reported with a "plus or minus x degree of error," where x is usually 3 to 5 percent.

TABLE 8-18

Residual Output

Observation	Predicted Price ($)	Residuals	Standard Residuals
1.000	209.205	−9.305	−0.227
2.000	233.824	−5.824	−0.142
3.000	240.885	−5.885	−0.144
4.000	256.692	28.308	0.691
5.000	286.937	−47.937	−1.171
6.000	287.642	5.358	0.131
7.000	290.924	−5.924	−0.145
8.000	306.063	58.937	1.439
9.000	311.647	−16.647	−0.407
10.000	318.036	−28.036	−0.685
11.000	356.222	28.778	0.703
12.000	436.050	68.950	1.684
13.000	440.037	−15.037	−0.367
14.000	470.738	−55.738	−1.361

Businesses, especially manufacturing firms, also use sampling extensively. For example, how can a light-bulb manufacturer predict that the average life of a bulb is 3,000 hours, when the only way to test a bulb is to burn it out? Once again, by taking a sufficiently large sample, the manufacturer can make that prediction with a fairly high degree of confidence.

When the population is too large to process or chart, you can use a representative sample to estimate the population statistics. Excel's sampling tool creates a sample from a population by treating the input range as a population. In the sampling dialogue box, you specify the population as the input range and tell the program how many random samples it should withdraw from the population. You can also create a sample that contains only values from a particular part of a cycle if you believe that the input data is periodic. For example, if the input range contains quarterly sales figures, sampling with a periodic rate of four places values from the same quarter in the output range.

The next two subjects we discuss, auditing tools and pivot tables, are not conventional analytical tools—they do not perform a particular analysis or generate any statistics. They are two of Excel's most useful features, though, and they can make the spreadsheet designer's and user's jobs much easier.

Auditing Tools

Have you ever spent hours building a spreadsheet, only to get inaccurate results because a bug lies somewhere in your cell references? It happens all too frequently, especially when your model contains multiple dependencies among the cells. If you type a single cell address incorrectly, you can spend hours searching for the error.

Excel provides the auditing tools (Menu: Tools: Auditing) to help track down spreadsheet design errors. If you pull down the Auditing menu, you will find the following selections:

- Trace Precedents: Draws tracer arrows to the cells directly referred to by the selected formula.
- Trace Dependents: Draws tracer arrows to the formulas that refer directly to the active cell.
- Trace Error: Draws tracer arrows to the source of an active cell containing an error value.
- Remove All Arrows: Clears all arrows from worksheet.
- Show Auditing Toolbar: Displays specialized auditing toolbar.

Earlier in the chapter we developed an annual funding-needs worksheet (see Figure 8–1). We redisplay that worksheet in Figure 8–9 using the auditing tools, but with one important change. In the original model, the formula for cell H12, the ending account value, is =(H11+F12)*(1+$C$4). Let's assume we accidentally typed C5 instead of C4 in cell H12. Naturally, the results are very strange: Our final account value is now over $1,000,000. We know there is an error somewhere, so we use the Trace Precedents tool to find the worksheet cells that influence cell H12. As the arrows indicate, those cells are H11, F12, and C5, not C4. The incorrect formula in cell H12 refers to the Years available cell instead of the Annual return (%) cell.

This example demonstrates the potential value of the auditing tools. Even when we look directly at an obvious error in a formula, it is surprisingly easy to overlook it. The precedent and dependent arrows add a visual accuracy check to the worksheet, and we suggest you use them before you run your worksheet models. Double checking your model before you rely on its results might save aggravation and embarrassment later!

Pivot Tables

There is a difference between business data and business information. Although data in the form of raw numbers have value, their usefulness to

FIGURE 8-9

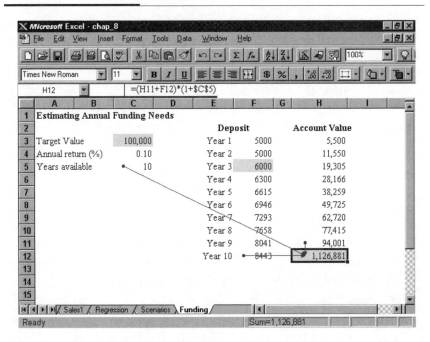

us depends on our ability to process them into information. One of Excel's features, the pivot table, can help transform data into information. Using this tool in Excel could help your clients and you manage business data more effectively.

We assume that your client owns several retail sporting stores. Each time an item is sold in one of the stores, the following data gets entered into a centralized database: date, store number, sales representative, merchandise line (golf, baseball, etc.), item number, and amount of sale. Thousands of transactions occur each month, and Table 8–19 shows a sample of the database. Your client wants to access the data in a user-friendly format that she can control so she doesn't have to tie up her accountant's time generating reports.

Each entry in the company's database in Table 8–19 is an example of multidimensional data. Ideally, a manager would like a flexible view of the data: month by line, store by rep, and so on. Unless the manager is skilled with the database program, though, she is often forced to rely on reports generated by others in the company. Because those employees probably have other responsibilities besides generating reports, the manager might be hesitant to take up too much of their time with requests for customized reports.

TABLE 8-19

Sales Database Entries

Month	Store	Rep	Line	Item	Amount
Jan	1	11	1	111	75
Jan	2	22	2	222	44
Jan	2	23	3	325	90
Feb	1	11	1	111	105
Feb	1	12	3	302	22
Feb	1	13	2	255	280

Many PC users are more comfortable with spreadsheets than with database programs, so Excel's pivot tables can be the ideal solution for accessing that data. In this section we demonstrate the basics of creating and working with pivot tables. It is not a difficult technology to master, but providing in-depth instruction is beyond the scope of this text. Readers who want additional material should consider the references listed at the end of the chapter.

Step 1 The first step to creating a pivot table is to invoke the Pivot-Table Wizard, which you access through Excel's Data pull-down menu. The PivotTable Wizard automates the data import and table creation process, and its introductory screen lets you specify your data source as described in Table 8–20. (We used Excel 7.0 in this example and do not show all the input screens.)

In this example, our data are stored in a database file that is a larger version of the records in Table 8–19. We select External Data Source as our option, which leads us to step 2.

Step 2 In step 2, the Wizard prompts us to invoke Microsoft Query, an add-in program that lets us access files created by database programs. We launch Query with the Get Data command. We select dBASE files from the available options and specify the source file by its name and location. This selection brings up Figure 8–10, a Query screen that lists the database's field names in the scroll box Sales1. We drag each field's name tile to the open box directly below the Sales1 scroll box. (If you did not want to include a field in your pivot table, you would not drag it to the box. This example has only six fields so we include all of them.) You see the result

TABLE 8-20

Pivot Table Data Sources

Source	Description
Microsoft Excel list or database	Data from a multicolumn list created in Excel that contains labeled columns.
External data source	Data created by database programs.
Multiple consolidation ranges	Data stored in Excel worksheet ranges that have row and column labels.
Another pivot table	Data in an existing pivot table in the same workbook.

FIGURE 8-10

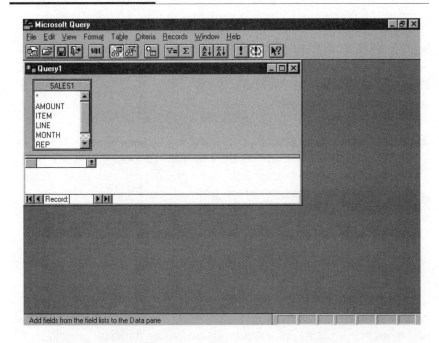

in Figure 8–11, which lists the field names in the top row with the individual data items below them.

A note on the database terminology we are using might be helpful here. By *field* we mean the categories used in the database: month, rep, and so on. A *data field* contains a specific value: January, Rep 1, $11, for example. A *record* is a collection of fields (containing data fields) that identifies a complete database entry. In this example, it would be all the pieces of information entered to record a transaction.

FIGURE 8–11

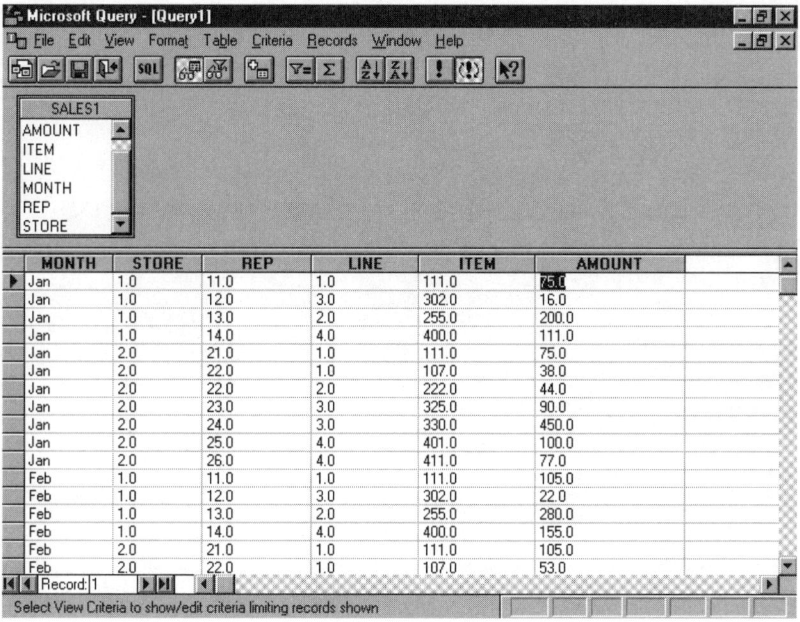

Step 3 We instruct the program to return to Excel, and we see the screen in Figure 8–12. This is the initial pivot table creation screen. The fields we selected are shown as tiles on the far right, and the table layout screen is in the center of the dialogue box. It has sections marked Row, Column, and Data.

To create the pivot table, we drag and drop the field tiles with the mouse into the desired location on the table layout. We want to use sales (dollars) as the data, so we move the Amount tile into the Data area. We assume your client wants to start with a breakdown of sales by store and line, so we move those tiles to the Row and Column areas, respectively. Figure 8–13 shows the results of our drag-and-drop operations.

Step 4 The PivotTable Wizard's remaining input screens offer several data summary and display options (not shown here). The final result is the pivot table shown in Figure 8–14, which shows sales broken out by store (rows) and product lines (columns), with grand totals provided for each row and column.

The reader should note the cells in Figure 8–14 that contain the field tiles for LINE and STORE. Those tiles are "live": the user can switch

FIGURE 8-12

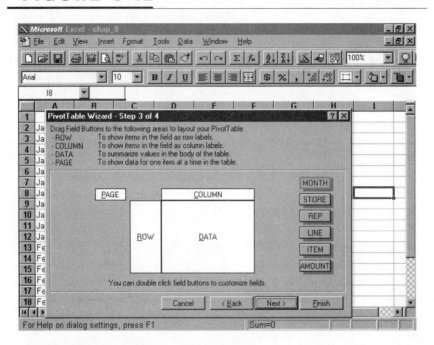

FIGURE 8-13

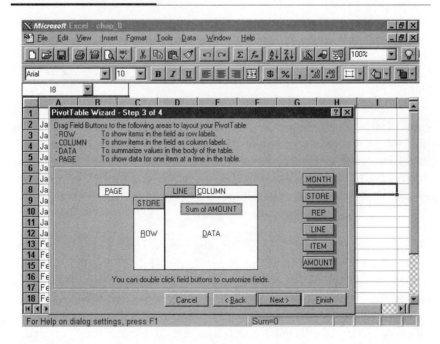

FIGURE 8-14

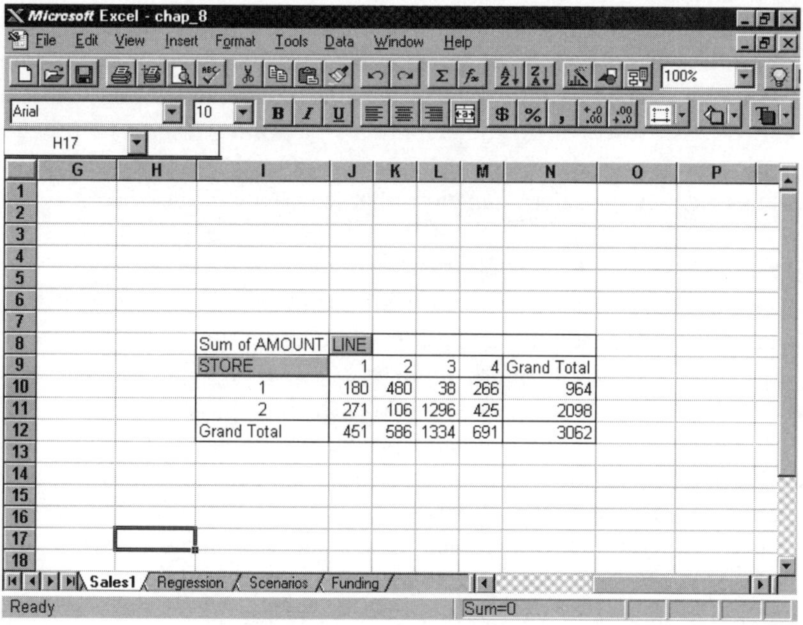

them between column and row location to change the view of the data. Also, by clicking on a cell in the table, the user can bring in new data to include the underlying data in the table

Using Pivot Tables

Our example demonstrates the problem of working with multidimensional data and a pivot table's value in converting that raw data to useful information. As you begin to work with pivot tables in client or internal applications, you will find that they work best on unprocessed data of the type used in this example. If the data are aggregated and summarized in a worksheet, consider using Excel's Auto Filter feature (Menu: Data: Filter). This feature works well with data already organized in a worksheet.

ADD-INS

@nalyst

Add-ins extend a spreadsheet's analytical capabilities while allowing the user to work within the spreadsheet's familiar environment. Tech Hackers Inc. produces a group of useful financial add-ins under the *@nalyst* line.

The add-ins include general financial analysis functions, with other packages available for bond, option, and mortgage-backed securities. You use the *@nalyst* functions as you would a built-in function by entering the function's formula in the cell. The function format is the same: function name followed by required and optional arguments in parentheses. The next section reviews two sets of functions found in the *financial @nalyst* program: amortization (annuity) and finance (cash flow) functions. (The program also contains calendar and math functions that we do not discuss here.)

Amortization Functions

Excel provides a basic set of amortization and annuity programs (refer to Table 8–3), but these are not designed for more complicated problems. The *financial @nalyst* amortization add-in has eight functions that are based on the same fundamental set of cash flow equations. These equations relate the present value (initial principal) of an amortized loan to the sum of discounted values of level periodic payments in the future. Each function solves one of the equations for a particular variable. Four basic variables are common to the cash flow equations: initial principal, periodic interest rate, term (number of periods), and periodic payment. Given any three of these four variables, we can solve for the fourth. If the problem differs from this straightforward setup, though, it becomes more difficult to solve. Possible complications include advance and residual payments and fractional periods.

To allow computation of these more complicated problems, the amortization functions use required and optional parameters, which are listed in Table 8–21.

As you can see from the examples in the table, the optional parameters considerably expand the range of amortization calculations you can perform. The required and optional parameters are combined in the functions listed in Table 8–22.

Finance (Cash Flow) Functions

The *financial @nalyst* cash flow add-in provides increased flexibility for analyzing complex cash flows. Table 8–23 lists the functions and their descriptions.

It is difficult to gauge the functions' flexibility from their descriptions. More specifically, they can handle the following complications:

Arbitrary initial cash flow.

Arbitrary delay between the initial and the first cash flow.

Arbitrarily long time periods between adjacent cash flows.

TABLE 8-21

@*nalyst* Amortization Parameters

Required Parameters	Description	Example
PRINCIPAL	Initial loan principal	25000
INT	Periodic interest rate	0.0113
TERM	Term of loan (number of payments)	84
PAYMENT	Periodic payment	492.86

Optional Parameters	Description	Default	Example
RESIDUAL	Remaining balance on l oan at end of loan period	0.00	5000
RES_OFF	Number of periods after last periodic payment that residual is to be paid	0	1.5484
ADV	Number of advance payments made at loan inception	0	2
ODD	Number of periods between loan inception and date of first payment (not including advance payments)	1.0	0.5
SIMP	Flag specifying whether simple or compound interest is used for fractional period components of odd and res_off	0 (comp)	1 (simple)

Source: *@nalyst* Reference Manual.

Distinct discount and interest rates associated with each cash flow.

Compound or simple discounting over fractional portions of time periods.

Compound or simple interest over fractional portions of time periods.

Simple discounting or interest over entire time periods.

Path-dependent discounting and interest accumulation for floating discount rates.

If you have ever tried to modify an add-in's functions, you are familiar with one of their key features: Users cannot modify an add-in unless the developer provides the underlying code. As we show later in the chapter, you can develop your own add-ins for Excel, even if you do not have extensive programming experience. With their built-in security features,

T A B L E   8–22

@*nalyst* Amortization Functions

Function	Description
AMAINT	Calculates the accumulated interest paid on an amortized loan after n payments
AMINT	Calculates the periodic interest rate for an amortized loan
AMPMT	Calculates the periodic payment for an amortized loan
AMPMTI	Calculates the interest portion of the n-th periodic payment of an amortized loan
AMPRN	Calculates the initial principal of an amortized loan
AMRES	Calculates the end value of an amortized loan (balloon payment or residual) or the future value of an annuity
AMRPRN	Calculates the remaining balance of an amortized loan after n payments
AMTERM	Calculates time length of an amortized loan, expressed as number of payments

Source: @*nalyst* Reference Manual.

you can distribute your add-ins without concern that other users might tamper with them.

USER-DEVELOPED TOOLS

We begin this section with a review of spreadsheet macros, which serves as an introduction to spreadsheet customization for many users. On the surface, a macro is just a recorded series of keystrokes. But as we show shortly, when you create an Excel macro, you actually work with the underlying programming language, Microsoft's Visual Basic for Applications (VBA). Although a macro's flexibility is limited, we start with macros to introduce VBA and the concepts of spreadsheet customization.

Example: An Introductory Macro

Our first macro is very simple. Let's assume that you prefer to use a standardized numerical format in your spreadsheets with the numbers in a comma format with no decimals (example: 10,000). Currently, you highlight the range you want to reformat, go to the Format pull-down menu, and work your way through the formatting input screens. A macro can automate the process for you so you don't have to repeat the keystrokes

T A B L E   8–23

financial **@nalyst** Finance Functions

Function	Description
DURAT	Calculates duration of a given cash flow structure
FUTY	Calculates future value of a given cash flow
IRATE	Calculates the internal rate of return of a given cash flow structure
NETPY	Calculates net present value of a given cash flow structure
SCMARG	Calculates the discount scenario margin (the margin to add to each discount rate in order to arrive at a given net present value)

Source: *@nalyst* Reference Manual.

each time. To build the macro, move your cursor so the first cell of the range you wish to format is highlighted, as shown in Figure 8–15.

Next, go to the Tools pull-down menu; select Record Macro and Use Relative References. After checking this item, you go back to the main menu. Select Tools, Record Macro, Record New Macro. This brings up the dialogue box prompting you for a name and description. In the name box, enter MyFormat and in the description box, type Test Formatting Macro. Click on the Options>> button, and you should see a screen that looks like Figure 8–16.

As in Figure 8–16, your input screen should show the macro name and description in the top two boxes. Click on the Shortcut Key and accept the default key (Ctrl + h in this case). Leave the Store in and Language defaults as is. Click on the OK button, and the program returns you to the worksheet, where you will notice a STOP button has popped up. (When you finish recording the macro, click on that button to turn off the macro recorder.)

Now you are ready to record your macro. Follow these steps to create the formatting macro.

1. Select the range with the mouse or by pressing the Ctrl + Shift + Down Arrow keys simultaneously.
2. Select the Format menu, Cells, Number tab, Number menu item. Once in the Number menu, set the number of decimal places to zero and select the comma format you want. Excel 5.0 and 7.0 input screens are different here, so you need to follow your version's prompts.

FIGURE 8–15

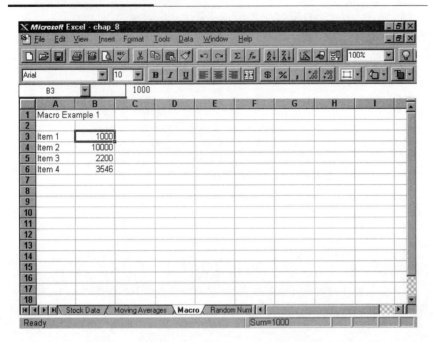

3. Click on OK and then select the first number in the range.

4. Click on the STOP button to turn off the macro recorder.

Congratulations—you just created a macro. To test it, enter a new column of numbers, at least some of which are greater than 1,000. Highlight the first number in the range, press the Ctrl + h keys together, and your macro will change the cells to the desired comma/ no decimal format. If it doesn't work, you probably entered something incorrectly, so open a new worksheet and try repeating the steps described above again.

Admittedly, this macro doesn't do very much. But it gave you an introduction to VBA programming, even if you didn't realize it. To see the program you just created, move through your workbook's open worksheets until you find the tab with the title Module1. Go to it, and you will see something like Code Sample 8–1.

Code Sample 8–1
```
'

' MyFormat Macro
' Test formatting macro
'
```

FIGURE 8–16

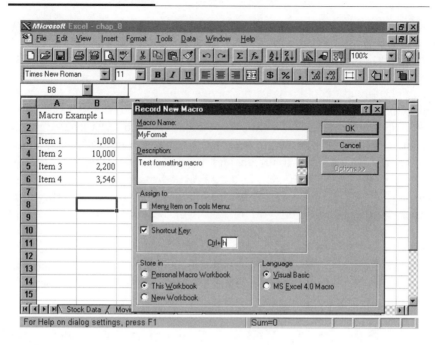

```
' Keyboard Shortcut: Ctrl+h
'
Sub MyFormat()
    ActiveCell.Range("A1:A4").Select
    Selection.NumberFormat = "#,##0"
    ActiveCell.Select
End Sub
```

This sample is your macro translated into VBA. As you entered keystrokes in Excel's macro recorder, it "translated" those keystrokes into the corresponding VBA language. This feature relieves you from the chores of learning the VBA language and remembering the statements needed to run your macro. We do not interpret the individual lines in the MyFormat macro, but you probably can derive their meanings from the macro's context. This does not imply that you should not learn more about VBA—we simply cannot cover the subject adequately in the space allotted to it here. We strongly recommend that readers who work extensively with Excel learn more about the language, and we suggest several books for that purpose at the end of the chapter. Our goal here is to introduce the language while giving the reader a sense of its power and versatility.

Macro Design Process

Before we develop a more complex macro, we first review the macro design process and suggest steps to make your macro efforts go more smoothly. The first step is to check if Excel already provides the feature you need. The program includes such a wide range of built-in features that it might already contain your problem's solution. The second step is to plan the macro and its desired results before recording your keystrokes. With a complex macro, we suggest you examine the tasks needed to see if you can break any large tasks into smaller, simpler tasks. This approach makes the macro easier to create, and it simplifies the testing and debugging process. Third, you should do a practice run of your macro before turning on the recorder. Write down your steps as you walk through the macro—this step will help you remember the sequence later, and it might point out potential problem areas. Finally, test your macro thoroughly before using it in a situation where its performance really counts. That advice may sound obvious, but most of us are very good at overlooking our errors. If possible, have another person test the macro before you begin using it.

Example: A More Complex Macro

In this example your client owns and manages a financial services firm that provides financial consulting (business and personal), insurance, and investments. The firm operates in New England and New York. Part of its income comes from salaried staff (Direct revenues) with the balance generated by independent contractor affiliates (Agent revenues). An area manager in each state reports sales each month, using the format shown in Table 8–24.

Your client wants an easy-to-use management information system that she can access on her PC to track company sales. In this section, we use Excel macros to build worksheets that will provide this information. We approach the job in two stages. First we automate the data retrieval and pivot table creation process. Then we build point-and-click menus to make the macro even easier to use. If you decide to work with this model, remember to try it on a practice run before turning on the macro recorder.

Step 1. Create the Pivot Table

The company's data are stored in a database file named sales.dbf. We will use the PivotTable Wizard to access the data. Before creating the pivot table, though, we use Microsoft's Open Database Connectivity (ODBC) drivers so we can connect to the sales file as an external data source. When Excel opens a database file like this one as a worksheet, it loads the

TABLE 8–24

Sales Report Sample

Date	State	Channel	Category	Sales
3/1/95	MA	Direct	Consulting	1100.00
3/1/95	MA	Direct	Consulting	687.50
3/1/95	MA	Agent	Consulting	165.00
3/1/95	MA	Agent	Investment	1750.00

entire file into the PC's memory. As the database grows larger with thousands or even millions of records, its size can begin to strain the system's resources. We avoid that problem with the following steps:

1. Go to the Windows Control panel and click on the ODBC icon.
2. Select dBASE files and click the Add button.
3. Select Microsoft dBASE driver and click the OK button.
4. Enter a source name and select the file you want added as a data source (sales.dbf in this example).
5. Close the screens and back out of ODBC.

After identifying the file as a data source, we can start the macro recorder, name the macro, and take the following steps:

1. Select Pivot Table from the Data menu, and choose External Data Source.
2. Click on the Get Data button, select Other, and choose the new data source you created in the steps above. Click on OK and USE.
3. Select the data file (sales.dbf) in the Add Tables screen and click on ADD and CLOSE.
4. Move the field tiles (Date, State, etc.) to the selection box (refer to Figure 8–13 for an example).
5. Move down the first row to the State column. Highlight a single state like MA and click on the Criteria Equals button in the toolbar. In the Files menu, click on the Return Data selection.
6. Drag and drop the tiles onto the pivot table, as we show in Figure 8–17.
7. Select your table display options, click on the Finish button, and you get the result in Figure 8–18.

FIGURE 8-17

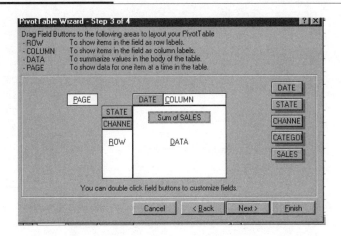

If you want to see the VBA code used in building your pivot table, click on the Module1 worksheet tab. Your code should resemble the listing in Code Sample 8–2.

Code Sample 8–2

```
'

' Retrieve_FinCon_data Macro
' Retrieve Fin Con data and create pivot table
'

'

Sub Retrieve_FinCon_data()
  ActiveSheet.PivotTableWizard SourceType:=xlExternal,
SourceData:= _
    Array( _
    "DSN=Financial Consultants Sales; CollatingSequence=ASCII;
DefaultDir=c:\books\irwin\ch8;Deleted=1;DriverId=277;FIL=dBase
IV;PageTimeout=600;Statistics=0;UID=admin;" _
    , _
    "SELECT SALES.DATE, SALES.STATE, SALES.CHANNEL,
SALES.CATEGORY, SALES.SALES
FROM `c:\books\irwin\ch8`\SALES.DBF SALES
WHERE (SALES.STATE='MA')" _
    ), TableDestination:="R5C1", TableName:="PivotTable1",
RowGrand _
```

FIGURE 8-18

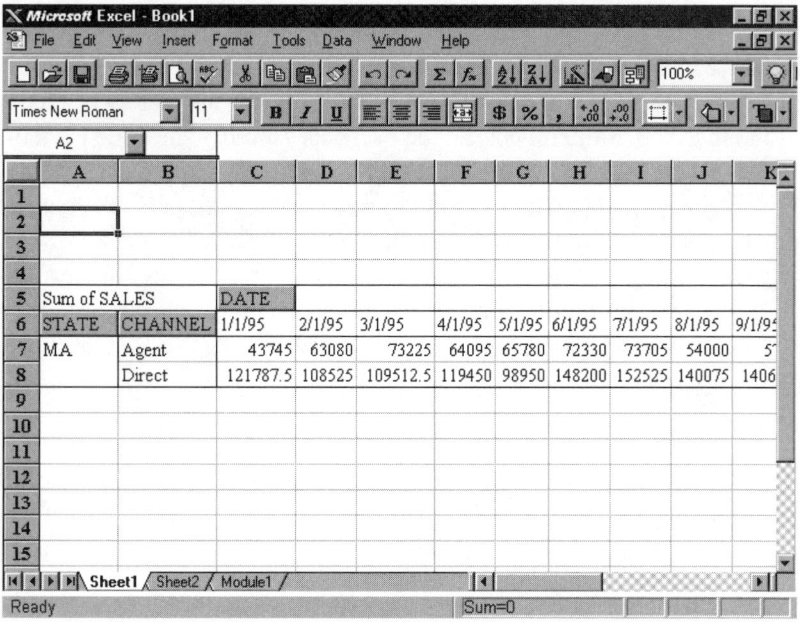

```
:=False, ColumnGrand:=False
ActiveSheet.PivotTables("PivotTable1").PivotFields("STATE").
Subtotals _
   = Array(False, False, False, False, False, False, False, False,
False, False, _
   False, False)
ActiveSheet.PivotTables("PivotTable1").AddFields
RowFields:=Array( _
   "STATE", "CHANNEL"), ColumnFields:="DATE"
ActiveSheet.PivotTables("PivotTable1").PivotFields("SALES").
Orientation _
   = xlDataField
Range("A2").Select
End Sub
```

When you see code like this, you appreciate Excel's macro feature
even more! Don't worry if the code doesn't make sense at this point—you
need a decent background in VBA programming to interpret it. We

include it to show how macros can perform complex tasks and relieve the user from entering lines of code.

Step 2. Adding User Controls

The code in Sample 8–2 creates the pivot table for the state we selected. But the macro is limited because the user must modify the code each time to select a new state for review. The easiest solution is to create buttons in the worksheet that launch macros to retrieve the desired data. To spare you from reams of additional VBA code, we include the code for the full macro, including buttons and an automated graphing feature, in the appendix. Because macro buttons and pull-down menus are easy to create, we list the steps for making them. Figure 8–19 shows the button-creation process up to step 3.

Making Macro Buttons

1. Activate the Drawing toolbar, select the Button icon, and use the cursor to create a button.
2. Select Macro Name menu; select an appropriate macro from list.
3. Type a new name on the macro button.
4. Click on an adjacent cell to deactivate button.
5. Click on the macro button to test it.

Adding an Application's Macro to a Menu

If you prefer to place your macro on a pull-down menu, follow these steps:

1. Activate the Module sheet where the macro code is located. Click on the Menu Editor button in the VBA toolbar.
2. Select the End of Menu item in the Menus list and click on Insert.
3. Type &MIS in the Captions box. The ampersand tells Excel where to place the character underline so you can have faster access to menu items.
4. Go to the Menu Items list, select End of Menu, and click Insert.
5. Type &Access Sales in the caption box, enter the name of your macro in the Macro box, and click OK.

When you return to the main worksheet, you should see a new menu item MIS on the top menu bar. Select MIS, and the menu item Access Sales should appear. Clicking on Access Sales will launch the macro.

FIGURE 8–19

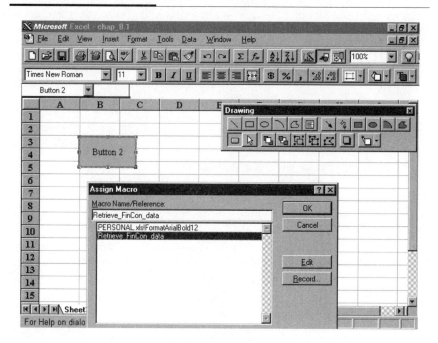

USER-DEFINED FUNCTIONS

The last topic we cover is user-defined spreadsheet functions. Excel allows users to create customized functions using VBA. If these functions are designed properly, the user can access them through the Insert Function menus and through the Function Wizard. You cannot write a function through the macro recorder, but as we show, creating basic functions with VBA is straightforward.

User-defined functions must use the following general syntax:

Function name [(argument list)]
   VBA statements
End Function

For example, to create a user-defined function that calculates a firm's current ratio, you could use the following syntax in a Module worksheet:

Function CurrentRatio(Curr_Assets, Curr_Liabilities)
   CurrentRatio = Curr_Assets / Curr_Liabilities
End Function

The function name is CurrentRatio, and its arguments are Curr_Assets (current assets) and Curr_Liabilities (current liabilities). The statement needed to make the calculation appeared in line 2: Current ratio equals current assets divided by current liabilities. Line 3 signals the end of the function's code. As with any programming language, VBA has certain syntax rules you must honor: no blank spaces in function names and arguments, certain keywords are reserved, and so on. In addition, a user-defined function cannot:

Insert, delete, or format cells.

Change cell values.

Move, rename, delete, or add sheets.

Change the calculation mode or screen view.

You can find the details on these syntax rules in Excel's on-line help section or the programming books listed at the end of the chapter.

After you create the function, Excel makes it accessible through the User Defined section of the Functions menu. The program will prompt you for input, and you can add comments to the input screen for user guidance. Figure 8–20 shows Excel's Function Wizard prompting the user for the CurrentRatio function's arguments.

There is no firm rule on when you should create a function. If you find that you need to use a formula more than two or three times in a workbook, it makes sense to create a function. A function will save you time, and it reduces the chance of typing errors. Table 8–25 lists some common functions used in financial analysis (Mayes and Shank, 1995) that you might want to incorporate in your work. We do not claim that these functions are the best way to analyze financial data, but we hope they will serve as guides to creating usable functions. (The code "As Double" at the end of each function's second line declares the variable type. This expression helps with memory conservation, but you don't have to include this line in your functions.)

FIGURE 8–20

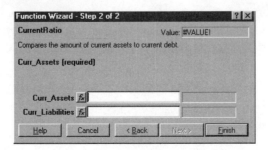

TABLE 8–25

Sample Financial Analysis Functions

1. Liquidity Ratios

'Current Ratio
Function CurrentRatio(Curr_Assets, Curr_Liabilities) As Double
   CurrentRatio = Curr_Assets / Curr_Liabilities
End Function

'Quick Ratio
Function QuickRatio(Curr_Assets, Inventory, Curr_Liabilities) As Double
   QuickRatio = (Curr_Assets − Inventory) / Curr_Liabilities
End Function

2. Efficiency Ratios

'Inventory Turnover
Function InventoryTurnover(CostGoodsSold, Inventory) As Double
   InventoryTurnover = CostGoodsSold / Inventory
End Function

'Accounts Receivable Turnover
Function AR_Turnover(CreditSales, Acct_Rec) As Double
   AR_Turnover = CreditSales / Acct_Rec
End Function

'Average Collection Period
Function AvgCollPeriod(Acct_Rec, AnnCredSales) As Double
   AvgCollPeriod = Acct_Rec / (AnnCredSales / 360)
End Function

'Fixed Asset Turnover
Function FA_Turnover(Sales, NetFixedAssets) As Double
   FA_Turnover = Sales / NetFixedAssets
End Function

'Total Asset Turnover
Function TA_Turnover(Sales, TotalAssets) As Double
   TA_Turnover = Sales / TotalAssets
End Function

3. Leverage Ratios

'Total Debt Ratio
Function TotDebtRatio(TotalDebt, TotalAssets) As Double
   TotDebtRatio = TotalDebt / TotalAssets
End Function   *(continued)*

T A B L E   8-25 (concluded)

```
'Long Term Debt Ratio
Function LT_DebtRatio(LT_Debt, TotalAssets) As Double
   LT_DebtRatio = LT_Debt / TotalAssets
End Function

'Long Term Debt to Total Capitalization
Function LTD_TotalCap(LT_Debt, PrefEquity, CommEquity) As Double
   LTD_TotalCap = LT_Debt / (LT_Debt + PrefEquity + CommEquity)
End Function

'Debt to Equity
Function Debt_Equity(TotalDebt, TotalEquity) As Double
   Debt_Equity = TotalDebt / TotalEquity
End Function

'Long Term Debt to Equity
Function LTD_Equity(LT_Debt, PrefEquity, CommEquity) As Double
   LTD_Equity = LT_Debt / (PrefEquity + CommEquity)
End Function
```

After you create a function, you have several ways to store it for future use. If you wish to use it in only one worksheet, store it with that worksheet. If you wish to make the functions available to other worksheets, you can use either of the following methods:

1. Save only the Module worksheet (delete any other pages in the file). When you want to use your user-defined functions, open the file where they are stored. The functions will be accessible to any other open workbooks.

2. Create an add-in. This method has the advantage of hiding your functions' source code from users, which prevents unauthorized changes to your work. To create an add-in, open the functions file and unhide it if necessary. Use the Tools, Make Add-In command to save the workbook with an .XLA filename extension. To add it to Excel's Add-Ins dialogue box, select the Tools, Add-Ins menu and click on the Browse button. Locate your add-in file and click on OK. Excel will add the program to the Add-Ins pull-down menu, allowing users to access your functions when needed.

SOURCES AND SUGGESTED READING

Harris, M. *Teach Yourself Excel Programming with Visual Basic for Applications in 21 Days.* Indianapolis, IN: SAMS Publishing, 1996.

Jacobson, R. *Microsoft Excel Basic for Applications Step by Step: Version 5 for Windows.* Redmond, WA: Microsoft Press, 1994.

Mayes, T. R. and T. M. Shank. *Financial Analysis with Microsoft Excel.* Orlando, FL: Harcourt Brace & Company, 1995.

Ragsdale, C. T. *Spreadsheet Modeling and Decision Analysis: A Practical Introduction to Management Science.* Cambridge, MA: Course Technology, Inc., 1995.

Soucie, R., ed. *Excel Professional Techniques.* Indianapolis, IN: Que Corporation, 1994.

Visual Basic User's Guide. Redmond, WA: Microsoft Press, 1993.

SOFTWARE RESOURCES

Microsoft Excel
Microsoft Corporation
One Microsoft Way
Redmond, WA 98052-6399

Tech Hackers Inc.
50 Broad Street
New York, NY 10004
Tel. 212-344-9500
Fax 212-344-9519
Software prices (PC/UNIX):
financial @nalyst: $295/395
bond @nalyst: $795/995
options @nalyst: $595/795
mbs @nalyst: $595/795

CHAPTER 9

Modeling Tools

INTRODUCTION

During the past 30 years, the field of finance has transformed itself dramatically, especially in the use of quantitative analytical methods. In the first half of the century, finance was arguably a subset of accounting. In the 1950s and 60s, economics had a strong influence on the field, with financial researchers drawing heavily on utility theory to develop models of resource allocation. Examples from that period include the Markowitz mean variance theory of portfolio selection and the Sharpe and Lintner Capital Asset Pricing Model (CAPM).

For finance practitioners, particularly those working in the investments markets, the 1970s ushered in an era of radical change. With the publication of the Black-Scholes option pricing model in 1973, finance research moved from academia to Wall Street, and the two have been closely linked ever since. Financial research is no longer relegated to obscure academic journals with readership limited to a small number of the author's fellow academics. Today, investment firms actively develop, adopt, and extend pricing models, and many highly regarded academics work for these investment firms as consultants or full-time employees. In many areas like derivatives models and financial risk management, the division between finance theory and practice has been eliminated, and the lag time between conceptualization and implementation has been shortened considerably.

A concurrent development since the early 1970s has been the inclusion of higher-level mathematics in financial models: Continuous time mathematics, stochastic differential equations, and partial differential equations now appear frequently. Financial models have begun to resemble those used in engineering and the physical sciences, leading the news media to label some branches of finance as "rocket science." Several universities now offer graduate degree programs in financial engineering in which students combine math, statistics, and computer science with current finance theory.

These rapid advances in finance can create a technology gap for advisors, especially those who do not work for large investment firms. Even if the advisor understands the mechanics of a financial model, she may encounter problems working with that model when using traditional personal computer software. Modern finance models frequently require skill in numerical analysis and knowledge of a computer programming language like C. In contrast, many advisors rely on spreadsheets for their quantitative work, but a spreadsheet's built-in functions are often inadequate for the new models.

An advisor can resolve this problem in several ways. The first is to develop the skills needed from mathematics, statistics, numerical analysis, and programming. The second option is to purchase stand-alone programs or spreadsheet add-ins that expand your PC's analytical and modeling capabilities. As we showed in previous chapters, these programs and add-ins are available for applications like Monte Carlo simulations and financial asset valuation. The final option, which is the subject of this chapter, is to use PC-based mathematical software. These programs give the user access to mathematical and statistical functions, graphics, and user-defined functions and programs. They may require more time and effort to master than an add-in, but in return they provide powerful analytical and modeling tools. Although these programs were designed initially for math and engineering applications, they are gaining increasing acceptance among finance users. We believe that the material in the following sections, which focuses on financial applications, will demonstrate some of the reasons for that growing acceptance.

SOFTWARE: GENERAL FEATURES

We work with three Windows-based mathematical programs in this chapter: Mathcad, Mathematica, and MATLAB. The programs share several key features:

- The ability to perform numerical and symbolic calculations.
- The ability to generate graphs to assist in data and function visualization.
- A built-in programming language that allows users to create programs and functions.

Numeric calculations in these programs are straightforward: $2 + 2 = 4$, for example. These are frequently the types of calculations you would perform on a spreadsheet, although the math programs can work with a wider variety of numbers and numerical operations (complex numbers, numerical integration, and so on). Symbolic calculations use symbols, instead of numeric values: $x^2 * x^3 = x^5$. The ability to work with symbolic computations makes the math programs very flexible, especially in creating user-defined functions. The programs' graphics features include two- and three-dimensional representations of functions and data. Since most of us lack the ability to visualize complex functions, the graphics feature helps us understand problems more clearly. Finally, the programming languages increase the user's control of the program. The user can create loops, if-then statements, customized graphs, and user-defined functions to perform specific tasks.

The three programs also use a roughly similar approach to problem solving. Each provides hundreds of built-in functions with the base package. These include widely used mathematical, statistical, and data manipulation functions. Add-on packages provide more specialized routines for finance and other disciplines. (We will let you know when we use an add-on package with a program.) Because each program has a unique user interface, we will work with each program separately for the rest of the chapter. We use overlapping material when possible, though, to permit comparisons among the programs. We should also mention that many of the programs' graphs were originally generated in color, although they are reproduced here in black and white.

MATHCAD

Figure 9–1 introduces the main Mathcad screen (version PLUS 6.0; from MathSoft, Inc.) with several calculations used as examples. The first section, Basic math calculations, illustrates the format for simple calculations; the user types in the equation, enters the equals sign, and the program generates the result. The next section, "Basic symbolic calculations," contains no numbers, only variables. The results for each calculation are shown directly below the equation.

FIGURE 9-1

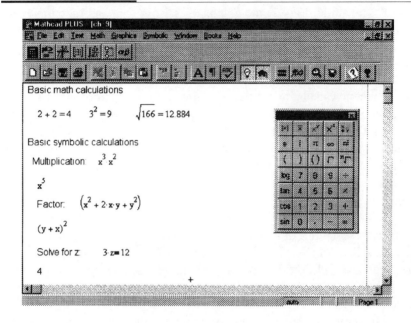

The right side of Figure 9–1 shows Mathcad's pop-up arithmetic palette. The palettes gives the user point-and-click access to the program's most commonly used functions. The other palettes (not shown) are

Evaluation and Boolean

Graphing

Vectors and matrix

Calculus

Programming

Greek letters

Figure 9–2 shows several additional basic calculations, including matrix multiplication, differentiation, and integration. Although we do not show the explicit steps for solving each, the technique usually involves entering an equal sign or using a specific selection from the Symbolic pull-down menu.

Our final introductory example demonstrates an elementary two-dimensional graph. We have a dependent variable v, which is a function of t: $v = t^2$. We assign t the values 0, 1, 2, 3 and calculate the corresponding values for v. The left half of Figure 9–3 shows the range of allowed

FIGURE 9–2

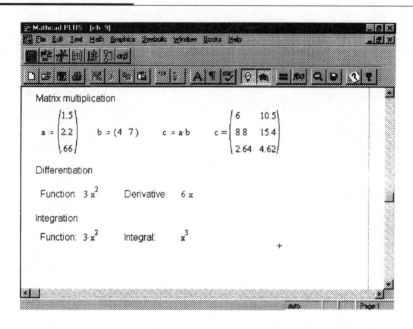

values for *t,* the function's definition, $v(t) := t^2$, and the table of resulting values for *v* (0, 1, 4, 9). (The user is not required to calculate the table of values manually. If the user follows the input structure shown on the left side of Figure 9–3, Mathcad will calculate the table's values and create the graph's data points automatically.) The graph plots the values for *t* on the x-axis and the corresponding values for *v* on the y-axis.

User-Defined Functions

The equation in Figure 9–3 also serves as an introduction to Mathcad's user-defined functions. The expression $v(t) := t^2$ must follow a particular syntax. The name of the function, *v*, comes first on the left side of the equation, followed by the function's argument list, which must be within parentheses. The list may include more than one argument. The argument list is followed by the combination of the colon and equal sign, (:=), which serves as Mathcad's definition symbol. The right side of the equation contains an expression that defines the function, t^2. In this example, the expression involves only the name (*t*) found in the argument list. The expression can contain also any previously defined variables.

FIGURE 9–3

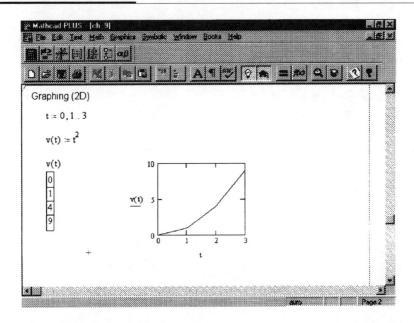

When you place a function in an equation, Mathcad follows a series of steps:

1. Evaluates the arguments in parentheses.
2. Replaces the dummy arguments in the function definition with the actual arguments you place between the parentheses.
3. Performs any arithmetic the function has specified.
4. Returns the result as a value of the function.

Example: Pricing Bond Cash Flows

Figure 9–4 shows examples of building a standard financial equation in a problem that demonstrates the present value calculation of a series of cash flows. The first and second year-end cash flows are $100, and at the end of year 3 the final cash flow is $1,100. Cash flows like this could be generated by a $1,000 face value bond with a 10 percent coupon that matures in three years.

In Figure 9–4 we list the cash flows in C, a column vector. The variable n takes its value by measuring the length of C, which has three elements in this example. We assign the variable i, which stands for the dis-

FIGURE 9-4

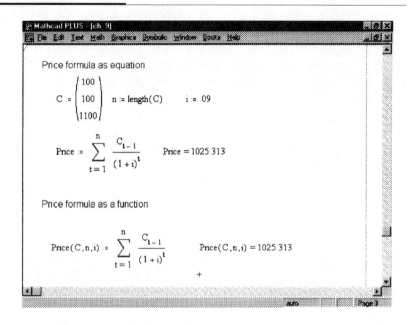

count rate we are using, a value of 9 percent. We create the equation for price using the standard discounted cash flow formula.[1] Because Mathcad initializes the C vector with a first value of zero, we set the first cash flow subscript to $t - 1$. (In other words, Mathcad by default identifies the cash flows in C as C_0, C_1, and C_2. You can change that initialization to C_1, C_2, and C_3 if desired, but we use the default here.)

After we define the equation for price, we enter Price = to the equation's right and it produces the result Price = 1025.313. This value is the result of the following calculations:

$$\frac{C_0}{(1+.09)^1} + \frac{C_1}{(1+.09)^2} + \frac{C_2}{(1+.09)^3}, \text{ or } \frac{100}{(1+.09)^1} + \frac{100}{(1+.09)^2} + \frac{1100}{(1+.09)^3}$$

In the bottom half of Figure 9-4, we create a Price function. Following the syntax rules outlined above, we enter the arguments (C, n, i) in the parentheses following the function's name. We define the function's operations on the right side of the equals sign. To calculate a price now, we must

---

1 Readers can find details on the financial formulas used in this section in any investments textbook. We recommend Taggart (1996) for in-depth explanations of the formulas.

call the function with its arguments. Because those arguments already have values, we can use the variable names when we call the function and get the same result, 1025.313.

We can modify the calculation easily to allow for interest rates that change over time. Assuming the usual upward-sloping yield curve, in Figure 9–5 we change our discount rate (i) from a single value to a vector with increasing rates: year 1: 8 percent; year 2: 8.5 percent; and year 3: 9 percent. We also change the variable i in both equations to i_{t-1} so that the corresponding discount rates and cash flows match up properly. The result is a new price of $1015.357, which is calculated by

$$\frac{100}{(1+.08)^1} + \frac{100}{(1+.085)^2} + \frac{1100}{(1+.09)^3}$$

Our final modification to this example is to allow for semiannual interest payments and a separate payment of the bond's face value at maturity. We modify the vector of cash flows C to include six coupon payments of $50 and one $1,000 payoff at maturity, designated by M. We also change the vector of interest payments to reflect semiannual discount rates. The value for n changes automatically with changes to C, so it does not require any modification. As shown in Figure 9–6, we modify the for-

FIGURE 9–5

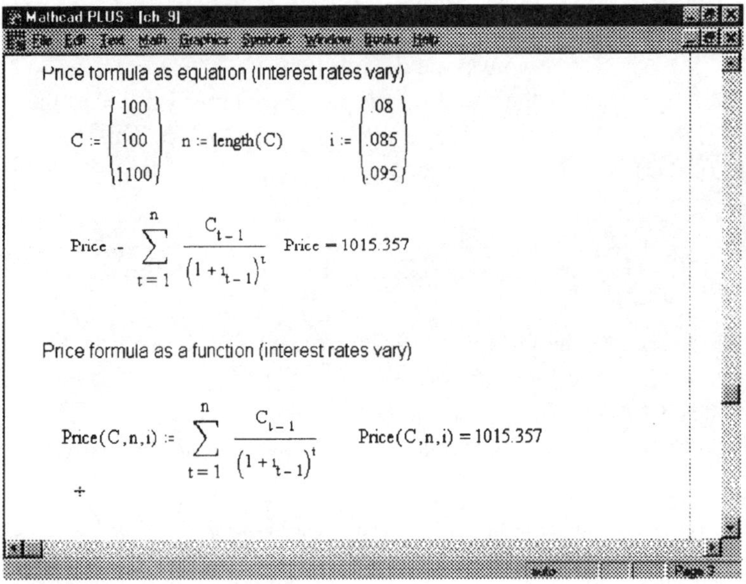

FIGURE 9-6

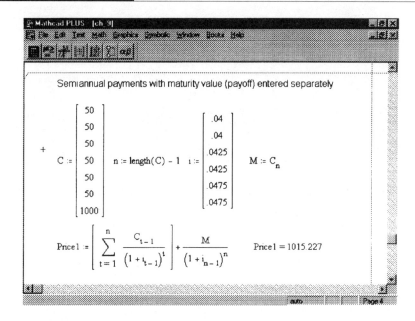

mula to reflect these changes, showing the equation in its traditional form with coupon and maturity payoff values separated.

Example: Bond Price Sensitivity

Two of the most important factors that influence a bond's price are current yields in the market and the bond's coupon rate. In this example we use Mathcad to calculate several measures of interest rate sensitivity. We compare two bonds that mature in 10 years. The first is a zero-coupon bond, and the second pays a 7 percent annual coupon (3.5 percent semiannual). Both bonds have a maturity value of $1,000, and we assume level interest rates for the period.

In Figure 9–7 we build a pricing function Price2 to calculate the bonds' prices under various market yields. The function's arguments include the bond's semiannual coupon (C), its face value (M), the number of periods (n = 20 semiannual periods), and the semiannual interest rate (i). We calculate the bonds' prices for three semiannual market yields: 6 percent (i = .03), the current market yield of 7 percent (i = .035), and 8 percent (i = .04). Table 9–1 summarizes the results.

Because the bonds have different cash flows, it is difficult to compare their relative sensitivity to changes in interest rates. The Macaulay

FIGURE 9-7

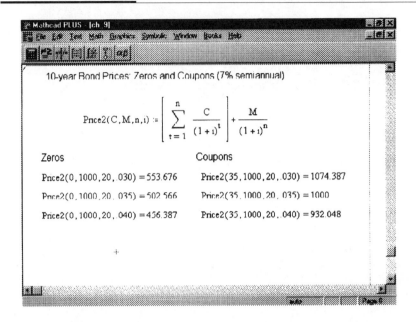

```
Mathcad PLUS - [ch_9]
File  Edit  Text  Math  Graphics  Symbolic  Window  Books  Help
```

10-year Bond Prices: Zeros and Coupons (7% semiannual)

$$\text{Price2}(C,M,n,i) := \left[\sum_{t=1}^{n} \frac{C}{(1+i)^t} \right] + \frac{M}{(1+i)^n}$$

Zeros

Price2(0,1000,20,.030) = 553.676

Price2(0,1000,20,.035) = 502.556

Price2(0,1000,20,.040) = 456.387

Coupons

Price2(35,1000,20,.030) = 1074.387

Price2(35,1000,20,.035) = 1000

Price2(35,1000,20,.040) = 932.048

TABLE 9-1

Bond Prices

	Zero-Coupon Bond	7% Coupon Bond
6%	553.676	1074.387
7	502.556	1000.00
8	456.387	932.048

duration formula measures the percentage change in a bond's price for a given change in market interest rates. A higher Macaulay duration indicates a greater sensitivity to changes in interest rates. The formula is usually stated as

$$\text{Macaulay duration} = \frac{\sum_{t-1}^{n} \frac{tC}{(1+i)^t} + \frac{nM}{(1+i)^n}}{P}$$

where P is the bond's price at the current market yield (7 percent in this example). We use this formula in Mathcad and calculate the bonds' durations as shown in Figure 9–8.

FIGURE 9-8

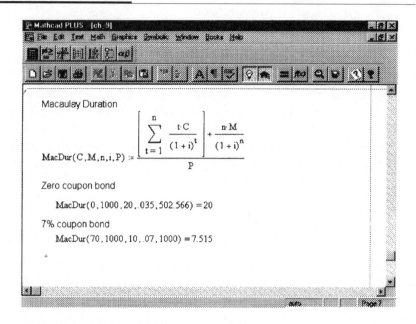

The functions take the same arguments as shown in Figure 9–7 with the addition of price P. The results show that the zero-coupon bond's duration equals its maturity with a Macaulay duration of 20, while the 7 percent coupon bond has a duration of 7.52. This result indicates that the zero-coupon bond will be more sensitive than the coupon bond to changes in interest rates, as expected.

Another measure of bond price sensitivity is the modified duration measure, which relates percentage changes in the bond's price to percentage changes in yield. We calculate modified duration by dividing the Macaulay duration by $(1 + i)$. Using the Macaulay durations we just calculated gives us the results in Table 9–2.

If you examine the bond prices in Table 9–1, you will notice that the changes in bond prices are not completely symmetrical for increases and decreases in market yields. For example, when rates fall from 7 percent to 6 percent, the zero-coupon bond's price increases by $51.11 ($502.566 to $553.676). In contrast, when rates increase from 7 to 8 percent, the bond's price falls by only $46.179 ($502.566 to $456.387). The same relationship holds for the coupon bond over the same rate changes: price increases by $74.387 but falls by only $67.952.

TABLE 9-2

Duration Estimates

	Macaulay Duration	Modified Duration
Zero-coupon bond	20	20 / (1.07) = 18.69
7% coupon bond	7.515	7.515 / (1.07) = 7.02

This asymmetry occurs because the bond price-yield relationship is not linear. To estimate the degree of curvature, we calculate a convexity measure using the following formula:[2]

$$\frac{1}{P}\left\{\frac{2C}{i^3}\left[1-\frac{1}{(1+i)^n}\right]-\frac{2Cn}{i^2(1+i)^{n+1}}+\frac{n(n+1)\left(M-\frac{C}{i}\right)}{(1+i)^{n+2}}\right\}$$

This formula produces the results seen in Figure 9–9.

Our emphasis in this chapter is on using mathematical software for financial analysis, so we do not discuss the financial assumptions required for using duration and convexity measures. We assume that the reader will refer to an investments text for that background material.

Example: Option Pricing

As we mentioned earlier in the chapter, the development of the Black-Scholes option pricing model was an important event in modern finance. We use the following notation in discussing the model:

C: European call price.

P: European put price.

S: price of the underlying stock (does not pay dividend).

X: option's exercise price.

T: time remaining to option's expiration.

r: (instantaneous) risk-free interest rate.

$N(d_1)$: cumulative probability for a standard normal random variable.

$N(d_2)$: cumulative probability for a standard normal random variable.

σ: annualized standard deviation of the stock's price.

---

2 Taggart (1966) provides details of the convexity formula's derivation.

FIGURE 9–9

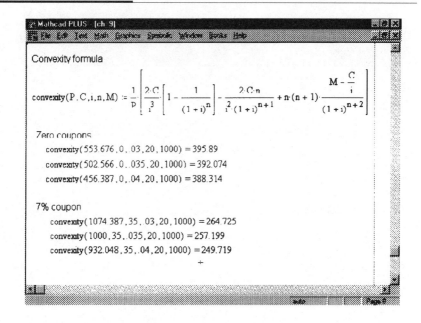

The Black-Scholes formula for a European call is

$$C = SN(d_1) - Xe^{-rT}N(d_2)$$

where

$$d_1 = \frac{\ln(S/X) + rT}{\sigma\sqrt{T}} + \frac{1}{2}\sigma\sqrt{T}$$

and

$$d_2 = d_1 - \sigma\sqrt{T}$$

Although it looks formidable, the option pricing formula is straightforward to build in Mathcad, as we show in Figure 9–10.

We call your attention to the formula in Figure 9–10

$$\text{EuroCall} := S * \text{cnorm}(d1) - X * e^{-rT} * \text{cnorm}(d2)$$

Mathcad's cnorm(x) function returns the cumulative standard normal distribution function, which we designated as N( ) in the option pricing formula. Including the built-in function in the equation saves the user from looking up the values in a table and entering them manually.

FIGURE 9–10

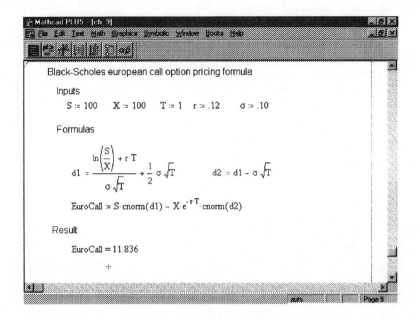

Example: Portfolio Selection

The usual assumption in portfolio analysis is that an investor wants to maximize the expected return for a given level of risk, or conversely, wants to minimize the risk for a given expected return. Portfolios that meet either of these conditions are considered mean-variance efficient, and a plot of these portfolios with risk/return axes forms the well-known efficient frontier.

In this section we use Mathcad to calculate the optimized weights of a mean-variance efficient portfolio. The section's matrix notation follows that used in Ingersoll (1987). We use more mathematics here than elsewhere in the book, but we believe most readers will be able to follow the material with no problems. This section focuses on the portfolio computations, and we provide details of the derivations in the appendix.

To use this method, we need three pieces of information: the securities' expected returns, the returns' covariance matrix, and a target (desired) portfolio return. Table 9–3 provides the required information. (The covariance matrix is shown in Figure 9–11.)

Our desired portfolio return in this example is 14 percent, and our goal is to find the least risky combination of securities that will earn that

TABLE 9-3

Details on Securities

	Security 1	Security 2	Security 3
Expected return	.12	.16	.10
Variance	.45	.54	.30

expected return based on the information in Table 9–3. We will need to calculate several commonly used portfolio statistics, which we present in both summation and matrix notation.

Expected Return

$$E(r_p) = \sum_{i=1}^{n} w_i E(r_i) \tag{9.1}$$

E is the expectations operator, r_p is the portfolio return, r_i represents the return on security i, and w_i is the weight of security i in the portfolio.

$$E(r_p) = w'Z \tag{9.1a}$$

where w' represents a transposed vector of securites' weights. For example, if we let w_1, w_2, and w_3 each equal .33, the w vector would be

$$\begin{bmatrix} .33 \\ .33 \\ .33 \end{bmatrix}$$

and the transposed vector w' would be [.33 .33 .33]. Z is the column vector that contains the securities' expected returns:

$$\begin{bmatrix} .12 \\ .16 \\ .10 \end{bmatrix}$$

Portfolio Variance

$$\sigma_p^2 = \sum_{i=1}^{n} w_i^2 \sigma_i^2 + \sum \sum_{i \neq j} w_i w_j \, \text{cov}(r_i, r_j) \tag{9.2}$$

where cov is the covariance between securities in the portfolio. In matrix form, we use Equation 9.2a

$$\sigma_p^2 = w' \sum w \tag{9.2a}$$

FIGURE 9–11

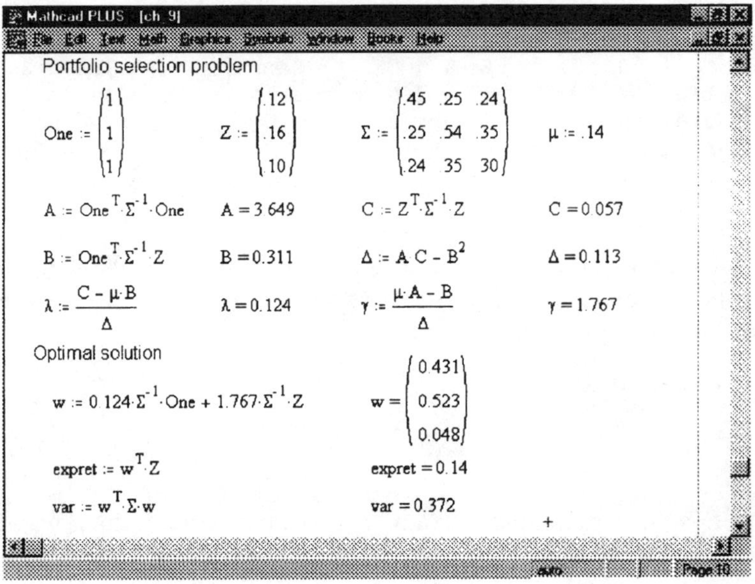

Mathcad PLUS - [ch 9]

File Edit Text Math Graphics Symbolic Window Books Help

Portfolio selection problem

$$\text{One} := \begin{pmatrix} 1 \\ 1 \\ 1 \end{pmatrix} \qquad Z := \begin{pmatrix} 12 \\ 16 \\ 10 \end{pmatrix} \qquad \Sigma := \begin{pmatrix} .45 & .25 & .24 \\ .25 & .54 & .35 \\ .24 & .35 & .30 \end{pmatrix} \qquad \mu := .14$$

$A := \text{One}^T \cdot \Sigma^{-1} \cdot \text{One} \qquad A = 3.649 \qquad C := Z^T \cdot \Sigma^{-1} \cdot Z \qquad C = 0.057$

$B := \text{One}^T \cdot \Sigma^{-1} \cdot Z \qquad B = 0.311 \qquad \Delta := A \cdot C - B^2 \qquad \Delta = 0.113$

$\lambda := \dfrac{C - \mu \cdot B}{\Delta} \qquad \lambda = 0.124 \qquad \gamma := \dfrac{\mu \cdot A - B}{\Delta} \qquad \gamma = 1.767$

Optimal solution

$w := 0.124 \cdot \Sigma^{-1} \cdot \text{One} + 1.767 \cdot \Sigma^{-1} \cdot Z \qquad w = \begin{pmatrix} 0.431 \\ 0.523 \\ 0.048 \end{pmatrix}$

$\text{expret} := w^T \cdot Z \qquad \qquad \text{expret} = 0.14$

$\text{var} := w^T \cdot \Sigma \cdot w \qquad \qquad \text{var} = 0.372$

with Σ representing the variance-covariance matrix of the securities' returns.

Ingersoll also provides the following method for calculating a portfolio's optimal weights, given an expected return of μ. Letting w equal the solution vector, the formulas are

$$w = \lambda \Sigma^{-1} 1 + \gamma \Sigma^{-1} \bar{z} \qquad (9.3)$$

where Σ^{-1} is the inverse of the variance-covariance matrix, λ and γ are described below, and $\bar{z}$ represents the elements of the Z vector or each security's expected return. Next, we define the components of Equation 9.3.

$$\lambda = \frac{C - \mu B}{\Delta}$$

$$\gamma = \frac{\mu A - B}{\Delta}$$

$$A \equiv 1' \Sigma^{-1} 1 \qquad (9.3a)$$

$$B \equiv 1' \Sigma^{-1} \bar{z}$$

$$C \equiv \bar{z} \Sigma^{-1} \bar{z}$$

$$\Delta \equiv A C - B^2 > 0$$

Once again, we can use Mathcad to solve the problem, relieving us of the tedious calculations. Figure 9–11 shows the problem's setup and solution.

In the top line of Figure 9–11, we create the vectors and matrices needed for the problem. Lines 2 through 4 show the intermediate calculations and their values. In the bottom half of the screen, we use Equation 9.3 with the numeric values for λ and γ. This equation gives us the optimal weights in the w vector to achieve a target return of 14 percent: 43.1 percent in security 1, 52.3 percent in security 2, and 4.8 percent in security 3. Those weights produce a portfolio return of 14 percent with a variance of 37.2 percent. These formulas allow short selling, which could result in negative portfolio weights. If we wished to prohibit short selling, we would need an additional constraint requiring each security's weight to be nonnegative.

Example: Programming

Although we do not describe the details of Mathcad's programming language, we can provide an investment portfolio simulation to demonstrate its use. In this example the program reads in a data file that contains 60 monthly returns for 400 securities. The program's purpose is to create simulated portfolios of various sizes by selecting random stock combinations from the portfolio. We realize that programming code is always cryptic to a nonuser, so we describe the purpose of each line in the program.

1. M:= READPRN(stocks)
Reads the returns data file and stores the values in a matrix M. The matrix holds each stock's returns in a separate row.

2. months := cols(M)
   stocks := rows(M)
Examines the matrix's size and assigns the number of columns (60) to the variable months and the number of rows (400) to stocks.

3. $T := M^T$

   $i := 0..\text{cols}(T) - 1$

   $C_i := i$

   $R(x) := \text{rnd}(1)$
Transposes the matrix and creates a variable R(x) that will take on random values.

4. $f(T,k): A \leftarrow csort(augmentC, \overrightarrow{R(C)}),1)$

   $B \leftarrow submatrix(A,0,k-1,0,0)$

   for $\in 0..k-1$

   $S^{(n)} \leftarrow T^{\langle\langle(B_n)\rangle\rangle}$

   S

Despite its odd appearance, the code in line 4 performs a very useful function. It takes the returns data, "shuffles" it like a deck of cards, and selects the first k cards as the sample portfolio. To visualize the process, imagine that you want to create a random hand of five cards. You shuffle the deck and take the top five cards. The program treats each security's returns as a single card in a deck of 400 cards. It shuffles by randomizing their location in the data set and takes k returns, with the number k specified by the user. This action creates a random portfolio. By repeating the process (reshuffling the deck), we can estimate statistics for portfolios of size k. This next function, for example, calculates the average variance for a portfolio with k securities.

5. $V(Q,k):= $ for $m \in k-1..0$

   $A^{\langle m\rangle} \leftarrow Q^{\langle m\rangle} - mean(Q^{\langle m\rangle})$

   $\dfrac{mean(A^T \cdot A)}{months}$

Calculates the average portfolio variance for the simulated portfolios of size k.

Mathcad Add-Ons

MathSoft offers several add-on packages for Mathcad in the form of electronic books and function packs that include specialized features. Applications of particular interest to financial users include McGraw-Hill's Financial Analyst, the Personal Finance Electronic Book, and the Mathcad Selections from Numerical Recipes Function Pack. We describe each briefly.

McGraw-Hill's Financial Analyst can be used as a stand-alone program or as a Mathcad electronic book. The software includes 201 commonly used financial tools from the book *The McGraw-Hill Pocket Guide to Business*

Finance by Siegel, Shim, and Hartman. Topics covered include corporate finance, investment management, budgeting, inventory control, and more.

The program is interactive: users can modify values in the electronic book or copy formulas to personal worksheets as needed. Detailed worksheets are provided for examples that involve more complicated calculations. Each worksheet has an input variables section near the top of the document followed by a calculations and output section. By changing the input variables and tables in these worksheets, users can gain intuition about the effects of each variable or adapt the problem to suit their own needs. Figures 9–12, 9–13, and 9–14 show the worksheets for internal rate of return calculations.

The Personal Finance Electronic Book by Marc Vanderplas contains useful formulas for analyzing personal finance problems. Selected topics include

Real estate analysis: the lease-purchase-borrow decision; rental property cash flow.

Mortgage refinancing: fixed versus adjustable rate.

Comparison of IRA versus non-IRA investment plans.

Whole life versus term insurance.

FIGURE 9-12

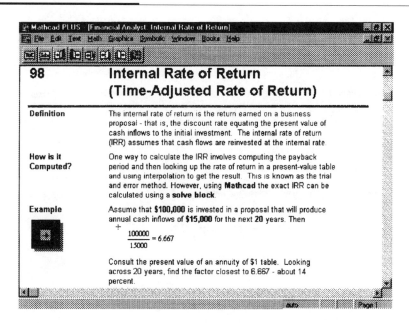

Mathcad PLUS - [Financial Analyst: Internal Rate of Return]

File   Edit   Text   Math   Graphics   Symbolic   Window   Books   Help

98   Internal Rate of Return (Time-Adjusted Rate of Return)

Definition
The internal rate of return is the return earned on a business proposal - that is, the discount rate equating the present value of cash inflows to the initial investment. The internal rate of return (IRR) assumes that cash flows are reinvested at the internal rate.

How is it Computed?
One way to calculate the IRR involves computing the payback period and then looking up the rate of return in a present-value table and using interpolation to get the result. This is known as the trial and error method. However, using **Mathcad** the exact IRR can be calculated using a **solve block**.

Example
Assume that **$100,000** is invested in a proposal that will produce annual cash inflows of **$15,000** for the next 20 years. Then

$$\frac{100000}{15000} = 6.667$$

Consult the present value of an annuity of $1 table. Looking across 20 years, find the factor closest to 6.667 - about 14 percent.

FIGURE 9-13

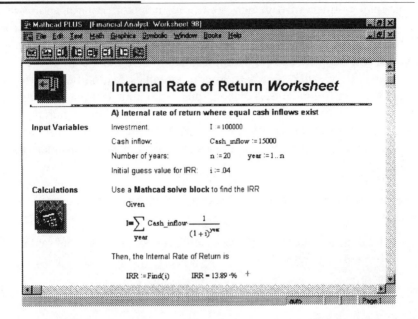

FIGURE 9-14

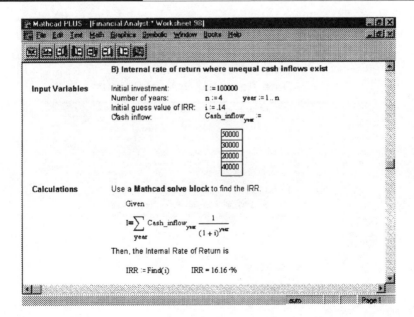

The Mathcad Selections from Numerical Recipes Function Pack contains formulas from the second edition of the book, *Numerical Recipes* by Press, Vetterling, Teukolsky, and Flannery. *Numerical Recipes* is widely used as a reference in applied mathematics, and it contains both analytical methods and program code for many numerical analysis procedures. The Mathcad function pack provides over 140 of the book's functions in a format similar to that shown in Figures 9–12 through 9–14.

MATHEMATICA

In this section, we work with Mathematica for Windows from Wolfram Research, Inc. The examples in this section use version 2.2.3. We introduce the program by showing a typical dialogue screen in Figure 9–15. The key elements to note in Figure 9–15 are the sequentially numbered *In[#]* and *Out[#]* lines. This version of Mathematica creates an in-out dialogue with the user: The user gives commands in response to an *In[#]:=* prompt and the program provides its output following an *Out[#]:=* prompt.

The first calculation in Figure 9–15, *In[1]:=* 100/2.5, is a standard numerical calculation. The user enters the values and the desired operation, and the program generates a response in *Out[1]:=* 40. The second

FIGURE 9–15

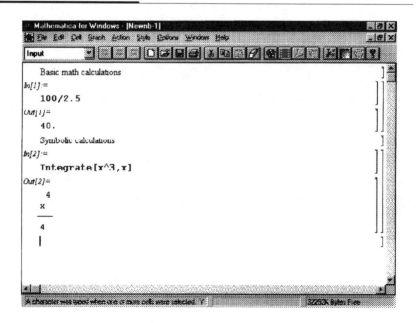

calculation, *In[2]:* = Integrate[x^3,x], shows a symbolic integration that is the equivalent of

$$\int x^3 dx$$

with the response given in *Out[2]*.

To avoid excessive duplication, we do not repeat all the introductory examples developed earlier in the chapter. Suffice it to say that Mathematica has over 750 built-in mathematical operations that the user can access, ranging from general to specialized functions. Because this material focuses on financial applications, we work with only a small fraction of the program in this section. The first topics we discuss in-depth are user-defined functions and formulas, one of Mathematica's most powerful features.

User-Defined Functions and Formulas

Mathematica allows the user to create customized functions and formulas. These can perform a wide variety of tasks, and they can call on Mathematica's built-in functions during their operation. By combining customized and built-in functions, the user can extend the program's versatility significantly. In this section we provide several basic examples of user-defined functions and formulas. We use the italicized *In[#]* and *Out[#]* to represent user-program dialogue.

The functions we work with follow a standard syntax: function name and argument(s) on the left side with the function's definition on the right side. For example, the following function cubes the arguments presented to it:

In[1]: = f[x_]:= x^3
In[2]: = f[3]
Out[2]: = 27

The blank in the argument brackets [x_] allows the user to specify the function's arguments. Of course, user-defined functions can take multiple arguments. The capital asset pricing model is usually stated as:

$$E\left(r_j\right) = r_f + \beta_j \times \left[E\left(r_m\right) - r_f\right]$$

where $E(r_j)$ is the expected return on security j, r_f is the risk-free rate, β_j is the beta of security j, and $E(r_m)$ is the expected market return. This can be stated as a Mathematica function:

In[3]:= CAPM[rf_,beta_,retm_]:=rf + beta*(retm − rf)

In this example, rf represents the risk free rate, beta stands for β, and retm is the expected market return. We use the corresponding arguments in line *In[4]* and get the result in line *Out[4]*:

In[4]:= CAPM[.05,1.2,.12]
Out[4]:= 0.134

Example: Pricing Bond Cash Flows

For this section we use the same scenario that we developed earlier in the chapter. We start with a bond that pays $100 annual interest (10 percent coupon) and matures in three years at its face value of $1,000. Our discount rate is a level 9 percent. We enter the cash flows as a sequential list, followed by a value for the discount rate and the present value formula:

In[5]:= cflow = {100,100,1100}
In[6]:= discrate = .09
In[7]:= Sum[cflow[[t]] / ((1 + discrate)^t), {t, 1, 3}]
Out[7]:= 1025.30

The entries in lines *In[5]* and *In[6]* are straightforward: cflow identifies the sequential cash flows and discrate is the constant discount rate we will use. Line *In[7]* is the Mathematica equivalent of the formula:

$$\sum_{t=1}^{3} \frac{cflow_t}{(1+discrate)^t}$$

The key to matching the cash flow with the proper exponent for the discount rate is the information in brackets: {t, 1, 3}, which tells the Sum function that the value for *t* ranges from 1 to 3, and the program automatically increments the value of *t* with each calculation. The notation, cflow[[t]], assigns the *t*-th item in the cflow list to the cflow variable, producing the following formula:

$$\sum \left[\frac{cflow[[t=1]]}{(1+discrate)^{t=1}} + \frac{cflow[[t=2]]}{(1+discrate)^{t=2}} + \frac{cflow[[t=3]]}{(1+discrate)^{t=3}} \right]$$

We can include different interest rates for different periods by placing the rates in a list whose positions correspond with the appropriate cash flows.

In[8]:= cflow = {100,100,1100}

In[9]:= discrates = {.08, .085, .095}

In[10]:= Sum[cflow[[t]] / ((1 + discrates[[t]])^t), {t, 1, 3}]

Out[10]:= 1015.36

By adding the [[*t*]] to discrate in the denominator, we instruct the formula to use the *t*-th value in the discrates list. The full version of the formula then becomes

$$\sum\left[\frac{cflow[[t=1]]}{\left(1+discrates[[t=1]]\right)^{t=1}}+\frac{cflow[[t=2]]}{\left(1+discrates[[t=2]]\right)^{t=2}}+\frac{cflow[[t=3]]}{\left(1+discrates[[t=3]]\right)^{t=3}}\right]$$

Example: Modeling Stock Prices

Programming statements give a user more control over a software package. In this example, we combine user-defined variables with Mathematica's programming functions to build a loop for simulating a stock's price path over time. The model we use for the change in price is

$$\Delta S = \mu \cdot S \cdot \Delta t + \sigma \cdot S \cdot \varepsilon \sqrt{\Delta t}$$

The variable ΔS is the change in the stock (S) price over a small period of time Δt, μ is the stock's expected return (per unit of time), and σ is its standard deviation. We assume that the expected return and the standard deviation are constant for the period. The last term, $\varepsilon\sqrt{\Delta t}$, represents the random volatility in the stock's price. We use ε as a random drawing from a Normal(0, 1) distribution, and this randomness of ε simulates the unforeseen events that affect a stock's price.

Although the model's notation may be confusing, it has an intuitive appeal. It says that the percentage change in a stock's price ($\Delta S/S$) is the sum of an underlying trend per unit of time, or expected return ($\mu\,\Delta t$), plus a random component ($\sigma\varepsilon\sqrt{\Delta t}$) over the same time period. The following example demonstrates an application of the model. The stock's expected return is 12 percent with a standard deviation of 19 percent (annual figures). We assume 250 trading days in the year, so we give the variable Δt a value of 1/250, or .004, so the daily expected return will be .00048 (.12 × .004) with a standard deviation of .01202 (19 × $\sqrt{.004}$). In statistical terms, $\Delta S/S$ follows a normal distribution with the parameters (.00048, .01202). We start with a stock price of $30 and run the simulation for 100 days.

To simulate random stock price changes, we use a built-in Mathematica function that generates a random number from a specified distribution. In this example we assign ε the normal distribution with a mean of zero and a standard deviation of one. This produces the following computation, which we first describe verbally. Our initial stock price is $30. We calculate each day's expected return (.00048) plus a random component, .01202 times a random number from the ε distribution. Because the random component can be positive or negative, the change in the stock price can be positive or negative. Figure 9–16 shows the simulation using Mathcad's programming language.

The example in Figure 9–16 uses a traditional programming language For loop. This design is not necessarily the most efficient way to develop a Mathematica program, but it has the advantage of being easy to understand. Although the input in line *In[83]* might seem intimidating at first, its structure will make more sense after we examine each line.

Line 1: stock = 30; mu = .12; sigma = .19; dt =.004;

This line declares the variables' initial values, which we calculated earlier. In this version of Mathematica, we cannot use Greek letters so we spell the names in their English equivalents (mu = μ, sigma = σ).

Line 2: (prices = { };

Mathematica allows the user to create an empty list—it exists in memory but it does not hold any elements. This line creates an empty list with the name "prices."

FIGURE 9–16

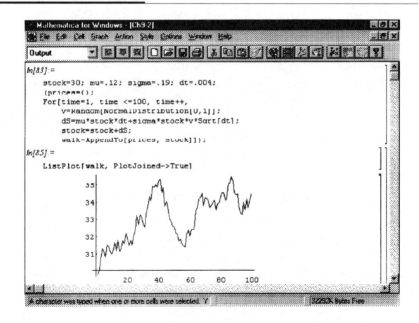

Line 3: For[time = 1, time <= 100, time++,

A benefit of programming is that it allows the user to automate the repetition of tasks. The For loop is a commonly used method to accomplish this, and If-then and While loops also are used frequently. The statement in line 1 tells the program to set the variable time's value equal to 1. It then tests to see if the value of time is less than or equal to the test value of 100. If it is, the program executes the statements that follow the loop, increases the value of the time variable to time = 2. It returns to the For statement, checks again to see if time is less than or equal to 100, and repeats the loop. It continues this loop until time equals 100, at which point the loop stops. The final effect in this example is that the program runs through the statements 100 times.

Line 4: The program's first step is to create a random variable from a normal distribution with mean 0 and standard deviation equal to 1 and assign that variable to v. Both the Random and NormalDistribution are built-in Mathematica functions. By pairing them this way, the program will generate a new random number from a Normal(0,1) distribution for each loop.

Line 5: We use the formula, $\Delta S = \mu \cdot S \cdot \Delta t + \sigma \cdot S \cdot \varepsilon \sqrt{\Delta t}$, to generate the random changes in the stock's price. The program takes the random variable v that was generated in line 4 and uses it in line 5 to represent ε in creating the variable dS.

Line 6: We create a new value for the stock variable by adding the dS value from line 5 to the value stored in the stock variable.

Line 7: We add the new stock price to the list prices created in line 2. The prices list expands with the stock price generated by each loop. We give the completed list a new name, "walk."

The program repeats these instructions 100 times, with each iteration adding a value to the prices list. The final instruction in line *In[85]* plots the stock values stored in the walk variable, with time on the x-axis and price on the y-axis. The overall trend is upward, as expected, but the simulation certainly generates price volatility around that trend.

Example: Simulating Portfolios

The previous example created its own price data by using random number generators. As we show in this example, Mathematica can also work with external data sources that provide historical prices. In this example, which uses the same problem illustrated in the Mathcad programming section, the goal is to create simulated portfolios by randomly selecting a specified number of individual stocks from the external data file that contains the stock prices. The file contains 60 months' returns for each stock, and the program must build the simulated portfolio, calculate its variance, repeat the simulation, and finally calculate the average variance for the simulated portfolios. We omit the original program's file loading and internal data manipulation code so we can focus on the analytical aspects. To assist the reader, we number the lines and discuss each line individually.

Mathematica Simulated Portfolio Variance Program (partial code)

1. <<Finance`Examples`
2. RandomPermutation[n_]:= Last/@Sort[Table[{Random[], i}, {i,n}]]
3. Mean[list_]:=N[Apply[Plus, list]/Length[list]]
4. k= 3;
5. (std = { };
6. For[index=1, index<=100, index++,
7. rp=RandomPermutation[n];
8. permutedReturns=Transpose[Transpose[returns] [[Take[rp,k]]]];
9. cov = CovarianceMatrix[permutedReturns];
10. weights = Table[1/k, {k}];
11. pvar=PortfolioVariance[weights, cov];
12. stds=AppendTo[std,pvar]]);
13. Mean[stds]

Line 1: Access the functions stored in the Examples file of Mathematica's Finance Pack, an add-on that we discuss in more detail shortly.

Line 2: A user-defined function that shuffles the individual stock returns in the data file to randomize the stocks' order in the file. It is analogous to shuffling a deck of playing cards.

Line 3: Another user-defined function that calculates the mean value of a list. This generic function can be used with any list whose name is supplied as the argument.

Line 4: k represents the number of securities to be included in the simulated portfolio. The user can change it as necessary. An alternative approach would be to add another loop to the program to cycle through predetermined values for k.

Line 5: Creates an empty list named "std."

Line 6: Sets up a For loop to run repeated iterations of lines 7 through 12. This example will run 100 iterations.

Line 7: Creates variable *rp,* calls the RandomPermutation function for *n* securities where *n* equals the number of securities in the data file, stores results in *rp.*

Line 8: Creates a new subset of returns (PermutedReturns) by taking the first *k* elements of the randomized securities. Using the playing cards analogy, this step is equivalent to taking the top *k* cards from the shuffled deck. Lines 7 and 8 ensure that the stocks in each simulated portfolio will be random.

Line 9: Calls on the Mathematica Finance Pack's CovarianceMatrix function to calculate the simulated portfolio's covariance matrix, which it stores in the variable cov.

Line 10: The program assigns equal weights to each security. If there are *k* securities, each is given a weight of $1/k$.

Line 11. Calls on the Finance Pack's PortfolioVariance function to calculate the portfolio's variance and stores it in the variable pvar. The function's arguments are the securities' weights (weights) and covariance matrix (cov).

Line 12: Takes the result (pvar) from line 11 and appends it to the list std. The expanding list is stored as the variable stds.

Line 13: After the For loop has completed its iterations, the Mean[stds] command calculates the average value of the results stored in stds. This calculation tells us the average variance for the simulated portfolios of size *k*.

The small size of this program might lead an observer to believe that it does not accomplish very much. Although the program does not have many lines, its utility increases considerably by including the Finance Pack's CovarianceMatrix and PortfolioVariance functions. This technique of calling on Mathematica's built-in or add-on functions extends the versatility of the user's programs and reduces programming time dramatically.

Mathematica Add-Ons

Finance Pack

We already mentioned the Finance Pack, an add-on collection of functions designed to extend Mathematica's financial analysis tools. These functions include

Calendar

Interest rate

Bonds

Cash flow

Options

Examples

In this section we examine several of the Finance Pack's analytical features and graphics capabilities.

Example: Bond Price Sensitivity

We developed an example in the previous section that used explicit formulas for calculating a bond's duration and convexity. The Finance Pack provides both calculations as functions to which the user supplies these arguments:

Duration[bond, settlement, ytm]: returns the Macaulay duration of the bond given the settlement date and yield to maturity (ytm).

Convexity[bond, settlement, ytm]: returns the convexity of the bond given the settlement date and yield to maturity (ytm).

We use these functions and several others in the following example. A brief explanation follows each input line.

In[1]:= Needs["Finance`Bonds`"]
This loads the Finance Pack's Bonds subpackage.

In[2]:= settle={6,15,1997}
We use a settlement date of June 15, 1997. The user can type the full date manually each time it is required, but it is more convenient to assign a variable name to the date.

In[3]:= mature1={9,15,2002}
The bond matures on September 15, 2002, and we assign this date to the mature1 variable.

In[4]:= bond1=Bond[{.065, mature1, 1000 USDollar, 2}]
The Bonds subpackage includes a function (Bond) that allows the user to create a bond object that contains information about the bond. The Bond function syntax is Bond[{coupon, maturity, par, frequency}]. In this example, the bond's coupon rate is 6.5 percent and the maturity date is mature1 (9/15/2002); the bond has a par value of $1,000, and it pays semi-annual interest.

In[5]:= Duration[bond1,settle,.075]
This function returns the Macaulay duration of the bond given the settlement date and appropriate yield to maturity. The function's syntax is

Duration[bond, settlement date, yield to maturity]. We assume a 7.5 percent yield to maturity in this example.

Out[5]: = 8.87912
The bond's duration stated in periods. To state the result in years, we divide by the bond's payment frequency.

In[6]: = %/2
Divides previous output by 2.

Out[6]: = 4.43956
The bond's duration stated in years.

In[7]: = Convexity[bond1,settle,.075]
The convexity function takes the same arguments as the duration function.

Out[7]: = 105.664
The bond's convexity in periods squared. To state it in years, we divide by periods squared.

In[8]: = %/2^2
Divides by periods squared.

Out[8]: = 26.4161
Convexity stated in years squared.

Example: Option Pricing
The Options subpackage contains tools to compute option values using the Black-Scholes method. The example in this section demonstrates the use of those tools and Mathematica's graphics capabilities.

In[1]: = Needs["Finance`Options`"]
Loads Options subpackage

In[2]: = xyzft = Option[{"Put", XYZ, 40, {12,20,1997}}]
Creates a put option on XYZ stock with a strike price of 40 dollars and an expiration date of December 20, 1997. Assigns these values to variable *xyzft*.

In[3]: = (Price[XYZ]^ = 40;
Volatility[XYZ]^ = .30;)
Specifies option price and volatility.

In[4]: = r =.07
Specifies risk-free rate and assigns it to variable r.

In[5]: = settlement = {8,20,1997}
Specifies settlement date for transaction and assigns it to variable settlement.

In[6]: = Value[xyzft, settlement, .07]
Calculates value of xyzft option using risk-free rate of 7 percent.

Out[6]: = 2.29456
Value of put according to Black-Scholes formula.

In the next two examples, we calculate a range of values for the hypothetical ABC option and plot the results in two dimensions (Figure 9–18) and three dimensions (Figure 9–19). Although Figure 9–19 is in black and white, the original version is in color.

In[7]: =
    abcft = Option[{"Call", ABC, 40, {12,20,1997}}]
    Volatility[ABC]=.30
Creates call option on ABC with strike price of 40 and expiration on December 20, 1997. Specifies stock's volatility as .30.

In[8]: = optionvalue[x_,t_]=Value[abcft, ToCalendar[ToJulian[settlement]+Floor[t]],r] /.
    Price[ABC]->x;
Plot[Evaluate[Table[optionvalue[x,t],
    {t,0,120,10}]],{x,25,45},
    PlotLabel->
    "   Call Option Value\nfor Different Maturities",
    FrameLabel->{"Stock Price", ""}]

Out[8]: = see Figure 9–17

In[9]: = Plot3D[optionvalue[x,t],{x,25,55}, {t,0,120},
    AxesLabel->{"Stock Price", "Time","Option Value"}]

Out[9]: = See Figure 9–18

MATLAB

MATLAB from The Math Works, Inc., is a command line, interactive system whose basic element is a matrix that does not require dimensioning. Figure 9–19 shows the basic MATLAB (version 4.2c.1) screen.

In Figure 9–19 the user's input follows the >> sign. In this example, we value a portfolio by creating a row vector of closing prices (close_prices =

F I G U R E   9–17

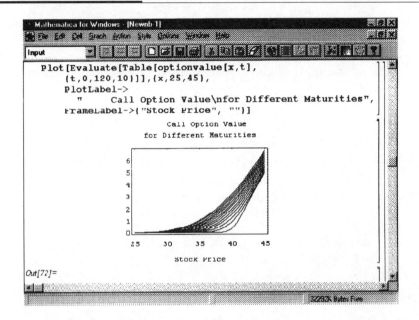

F I G U R E   9–18

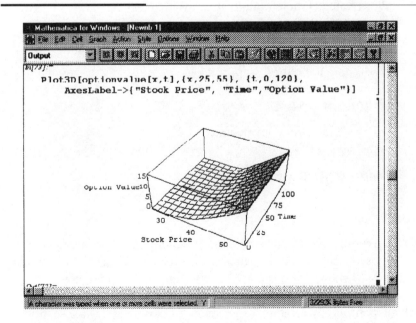

FIGURE 9–19

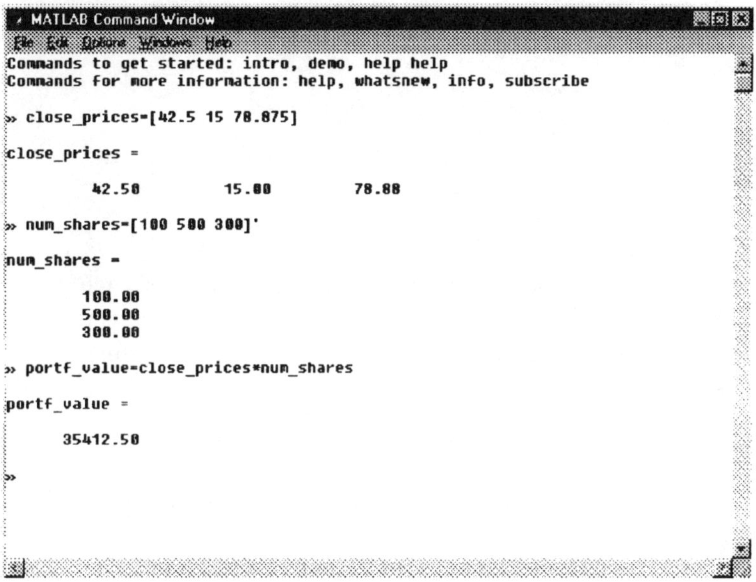

```
MATLAB Command Window                                      [X]

File  Edit  Options  Windows  Help
Commands to get started: intro, demo, help help
Commands for more information: help, whatsnew, info, subscribe

» close_prices=[42.5 15 78.875]

close_prices =

       42.50         15.00        78.88

» num_shares=[100 500 300]'

num_shares =

       100.00
       500.00
       300.00

» portf_value=close_prices*num_shares

portf_value =

       35412.50

»
```

[42.5   15.00   78.875]) and a column vector for the number of shares (num_shares = [100   500   300]'). The prime symbol after the values for num_shares transposes the data from a row vector to a column vector. The line's output shows the column form. Next we calculate the portfolio's value with portf_value = close_prices * num_shares and get the result 35412.50.

The matrix structure is widely used in financial calculations. (Figure 9–11 showed a simple application of matrices in portfolio problems.) A basic application is the solution of simultaneous linear equations, as this example from MATLAB's *Financial Toolbox* manual shows. You have two portfolios of mortgage-based instruments, Mort1 and Mort2. They have respective annual cash payments of $100 and $70 per unit, based on today's prime rate. If the prime rate moves down 100 basis points (1 percent), their payments would be $80 and $40. You hold 10 units of Mort1 and 20 units of Mort2, and your receipts from the holdings under both prime rate scenarios equal cash payments times number of units, or $R = C * U$. You could state the problem as

Prime flat: $100 * 10 units Mort1 + $70* 20 units Mort2 = $2400 receipts

Prime down: $80 * 10 units Mort1 + $40 *20 units Mort2 = $1600 receipts

You can easily translate this problem to matrix form, as the following screen dialogue shows (actual screen not shown):

```
» cash=  [100 70
      8040];
» units= [10 20]';
» receipts = cash * units
receipts =
      2400.00
      1600.00
```

Suppose you wanted to know how many units of each security to hold if you wanted to receive $7,000 if the prime is unchanged and $5,000 if it drops 1 percentage point. Once again you could structure this as a set of linear equations:

Prime flat: $100 * × units Mort1 + $70* y units Mort2 = $7000 receipts

Prime down: $80 * × units Mort1 + $40 * y units Mort2 = $5000 receipts

In matrix terms, you want to solve for U in the equation R = C * U. We set this up in MATLAB as follows:

```
» cash = [100  70
     80 40];
» receipts = [7000 5000]';
» units = cash \ receipts
units =
     43.75
     37.50
```

The result: You should hold 43.75 units of Mort1 and 37.50 units of Mort2 to achieve the desired cash flows.

Add-On: The Financial Toolbox

MATLAB offers a wide range of built-in functions, and the user can create customized functions and programs. Because the chapter's previous sections discussed user-defined functions and programs in detail, we do not review them again. We focus instead on MATLAB's financial add-on, the Financial Toolbox, which provides 95 specialized functions for the financial user. We present several sample problems from the toolbox and its manual, *Financial Toolbox User's Guide* by Christopher R. Garvin. The toolbox functions are classified into six task groups:

Handling and converting dates.

Formatting currency and charting financial data.

Analyzing and computing cash flows.

Price and computing yields for fixed-income securities.

Analyzing portfolios.

Pricing and analyzing equity derivatives.

Example 1: Bond Price Sensitivity

We examined duration and convexity for single bonds earlier in the chapter. In this example we look at the same measures for a bond portfolio. Since most investors hold bonds in a portfolio, this example is a useful extension of the measurements. Program comments sections are bracketed with the % sign, and program code is single spaced.

%%%

Filename FTSPEX1.M

Financial Toolbox Solving Problems Example:

Sensitivity of Bond Prices to Changes in Interest Rates

Step 1 Define a matrix, Bonds, that holds data for three bonds. Each row holds the information for a single bond: settlement date, maturity date, face value, coupon rate, number of coupons per year, and day-count basis. (Day count basis refers to the number of days used in a year. The default value of zero represents 365 days, while a value of 1 indicates 360 days.) The values for yields are determined from the prevailing yield curve.

```
%%%
Bonds = [today datenum('17-jun-2010') 100 0.07  2 0
         today datenum('09-jun-2015') 100 0.06  2 0
         today datenum('14-may-2025') 1000 0.045 2 0];
yields = [0.05 0.06 0.065];
format bank;

%%%
```

Step 2 Calculate the price, modified duration (in years) and convexity (in years) of each bond. Store these numbers in preallocated vectors.

```
%%%
temp = zeros(1,2);
prices = zeros(1,3);
durations = zeros(1,3);
convexities = zeros(1,3);

for i = 1:3
  [temp(1), temp(2)] = prbond(Bonds(i,1),
    Bonds(i,2),...
    Bonds(i,3), Bonds(i,4), yields(i),...
    Bonds(i,5), Bonds(i,6));
  prices(i) = temp(1) + temp(2);
  [temp(1), temp(2)] = bonddur(Bonds(i,1),
    Bonds(i,2),...
    Bonds(i,3), Bonds(i,4), yields(i),...
    Bonds(i,5), Bonds(i,6));
  durations(i) = temp(2);
  [temp(1), temp(2)] = bondconv(Bonds(i,1),
    Bonds(i,2),...
    Bonds(i,3), Bonds(i,4), yields(i),...
    Bonds(i,5), Bonds(i,6));
  convexities(i) = temp(2);
end
%%%
```

Step 3 Shift the yield curve by a chosen amount and store that value in dY. In this example, the curve shifts up by 20 basis points, or .002.

```
%%%
dY = 0.002;
portf_price = 100000;
portf_weights = ones(1,3)/3.0;
portf_amnts = portf_price * portf_weights ./ prices;

%%%
```

Step 4 Calculate the modified duration and convexity of the portfolio. Calculate the first- and second-order approximations of the percent price change as a function dY.

```
%%%
portf_duration = dot(portf_weights, durations)
portf_convexity = dot(portf_weights, convexities)
perc_approx1 = -portf_duration * dY * 100;
perc_approx2 = perc_approx1 + portf_convexity * dY^2 *
100/2.0;

%%%
```

Step 5 Estimate the new portfolio price using the two estimates for the percent price change.

```
%%%
price_approx1 = portf_price + perc_approx1 *
portf_price /100
price_approx2 = portf_price + perc_approx2 *
portf_price /100

%%%
```

Step 6 Calcluate the true new portfolio price.

```
%%%
new_prices = zeros(1,3);
for i = 1:3
  [temp(1), temp(2)] = prbond(Bonds(i,1),
    Bonds(i,2), ...
    Bonds(i,3), Bonds(i,4), yields(i)+dY,...
    Bonds(i,5), Bonds(i,6));
  new_prices(i) = temp(1) + temp(2);
end
new_price = dot(portf_amnts, new_prices)
%%%
```

End of FTSPEX1.M

```
%%%
```

Results of portfolio calculations (original portfolio value was $100,000):

```
portf_duration = 11.36
```

```
portf_convexity =192.09
price_approx1 =   97728.37
price_approx2 =  97766.79
new_price = 97766.27
```

Example 2: Hedging against Duration and Convexity

This example constructs a bond portfolio that hedges the portfolio developed in Example 1. It assumes a long position in the bonds of Example 1 and that three other bonds are available for hedging (short selling). The new portfolio's weights are chosen so that the duration and convexity of the new portfolio matches that of the original. By taking a short position in the new portfolio, the user can partially hedge against parallel shifts in the yield curve.

%%%

Filename FTSPEX2.M

Financial Toolbox Solving Problems Example 2:

Constructing a Bond Portfolio to Hedge Against Duration and Convexity

Step 1 Set up three bonds in a portfolio using the same approach as step 1 in Example 1.

```
%%%

Bonds = [today datenum('15-jun-2005')   500   0.07   2 0
         today datenum('2-oct-2010')   1000   0.066  2 0
         today datenum('1-mar-2025')    250   0.08   2 0];
yields = [0.06 0.07 0.075];
format bank;

%%%
```

Step 2 Compute and store price, modified duration, and convexity using same approach as step 2 in Example 1.

```
%%%

temp = zeros(1,2);
prices = zeros(1,3);
durations = zeros(1,3);
convexities = zeros(1,3);
```

```
for i = 1:3
  [temp(1), temp(2)] = prbond(Bonds(i,1), Bonds(i,2),...
     Bonds(i,3), Bonds(i,4), yields(i),...
     Bonds(i,5), Bonds(i,6));

  prices(i) = temp(1) + temp(2);

  [temp(1), temp(2)] = bonddur(Bonds(i,1), Bonds(i,2),...
     Bonds(i,3), Bonds(i,4), yields(i),...
     Bonds(i,5), Bonds(i,6));

  durations(i) = temp(2);

  [temp(1), temp(2)] = bondconv(Bonds(i,1), Bonds(i,2),...
     Bonds(i,3), Bonds(i,4), yields(i),...
     Bonds(i,5), Bonds(i,6));

  convexities(i) = temp(2);
end

%%%
```

Step 3 Set up and solve the system of linear equations whose solution is the weights of the new bonds in a portfolio whose duration and convexity match those in Example 1. Also scale the weights to equal one.

```
%%%

A = [durations
     convexities
     1 1 1];
b = [ 11.53
     200.27
        1];
weights = A\b;

%%%
```

Step 4 Check that the hedge portfolio's duration and convexity match those of Example 1.

```
%%%

portf_duration = dot(weights, durations)
portf_convexity = dot(weights, convexities)

%%%
```

Step 5 Scale the new portfolio to match the Example 1 portfolio.

```
%%%

portf_value = 100000;
hedge_amounts = weights' ./ prices * portf_value

%%%
```

End of FTSPEX2.M

```
%%%
```

Results of hedging calculation:

```
portf_duration = 11.53
portf_convexity = 200.27
hedge_amounts = -101.28          93.27          228.91
```

Example 3: The Efficient Frontier

As we discussed earlier, the efficient frontier is an important concept for investors concerned with a porfolio's risk-return trade-off. In this example, we use MATLAB to plot an efficient frontier and show the location of simulated portfolios in the risk-return space.

We start by creating a matrix of six securities' returns for 50 time periods. In this example we use MATLAB's random number generator to simulate the returns (details not shown) and assign them to a matrix, asset. Another possibility is to read in historical prices from a data file or on-line service. Next we calculate the securities' mean returns and assign the values to a vector, raret. Finally, we use the MATLAB function frontier to use that data and return 10 different points along that frontier.

```
%%%

[risk, ror] = frontier(asset,  raret,  10);
%%%
```

Next we find the global minimum variance portfolio (GMVP) and its rate of return.

```
%%%
minr = min(risk);
minror = max(ror(find(risk == minr)));

%%%
```

Using the GMVP as an "anchor" point, we plot the frontier as a line from the GMVP to the maximum return portfolio.

```
%%%
plot(risk, ror, 'k', 'linewidth',3, 'erase','none');
hold on;
minr = min(risk);
minror = max(ror(find(risk == minr)));
plot(minr, minror, 'k', 'linewidth',3,
'erasemode','normal');

%%%
```

We generate 1,000 random portfolios, plot each one's risk-return location with a + sign, add axis labels and a title, and show how the efficient frontier compares with the random portfolios. The graphical results are in Figure 9–20.

```
%%%
[randrisk, randror] = portrand(asset, raret, 1000);
plot(randrisk, randror, 'k+', 'linewidth',1);
xlabel('Risk')
ylabel('Aggregate ROR');
title('Efficient Frontier and Random Portfolios');

%%%
```

F I G U R E   9–20

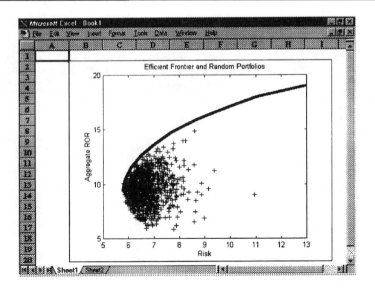

Example 4: The Yield Curve

The level of bond interest rates and the resulting shape of the yield curve probably receive more attention than any other factors in the financial markets. In this example we provide MATLAB with a set of Treasury bond prices and develop a program to fit a curve to those bonds' implied yields. As we show, the program ultimately produces four graphs to convey information about the yield curve.

Part 1 Calculate the implied yields for a hypothetical set of bonds whose maturities range from one month to 10 years. Next, use MATLAB's spline function to interpolate these yields and then plot the resulting market yield curves.

    Create a matrix of bond data. In the matrix each row represents an individual bond and each column represents a parameter: settlement date, maturity date, coupon rate, number of coupons per year, face value, price and day-count basis.

```
% settlement date      maturity date           rate   freq face price basis

bonds = [...
datenum('19-jun-95') datenum('19-jul-95')      0         1 100   99.654  2
datenum('19-jun-95') datenum('19-sep-95')      0         1 100   98.7589 2
datenum('19-jun-95') datenum('19-dec-95')      0         1 100   97.3901 2
datenum('19-jun-95') datenum('19-jun-96')      0         1 100   94.4555 2

datenum('19-jun-95') datenum('19-dec-96')      0.06      2 100   99.6191 3
datenum('19-jun-95') datenum('19-jun-97')      0.0625    2 100   99.2623 3
datenum('19-jun-95') datenum('19-dec-97')      0.063     2 100   98.5316 3

datenum('19-jun-95') datenum('19-jun-98')      0.0645    2 100   98.0083 3
datenum('19-jun-95') datenum('19-dec-98')      0.066     2 100   97.5723 3

datenum('19-jun-95') datenum('19-jun-99')      0.07      2 100   97.9634 3
datenum('19-jun-95') datenum('19-dec-99')      0.07125   2 100   97.4791 3

datenum('19-jun-95') datenum('19-jun-2000')    0.07      2 100   95.9446 3
datenum('19-jun-95') datenum('19-dec-2000')    0.069     2 100   94.5468 3

datenum('19-jun-95') datenum('19-jun-2001')    0.0725    2 100   95.1154 3
datenum('19-jun-95') datenum('19-dec-2001')    0.08      2 100   97.7843 3

datenum('19-jun-95') datenum('19-jun-2002')    0.0685    2 100   90.9377 3
datenum('19-jun-95') datenum('19-dec-2002')    0.0725    2 100   92.0299 3

datenum('19-jun-95') datenum('19-jun-2003')    0.075     2 100   92.3757 3
datenum('19-jun-95') datenum('19-dec-2003')    0.065     2 100   85.6314 3

datenum('19-jun-95') datenum('19-jun-2004')    0.08      2 100   93.6287 3
datenum('19-jun-95') datenum('19-dec-2004')    0.085     2 100   96.2377 3

datenum('19-jun-95') datenum('19-jun-2005')    0.08      2 100   92.2624 3];
num_bonds = size(bonds,1);
```

Part 2 The MATLAB program code for this example is rather lengthy so we do not include it here. To summarize the process, we recursively calculate spot rates for the bonds from the 1-month to 5-year maturities and find each successive spot rate by requiring that the bond of the previous maturity be priced correctly, given all the previous rates calculated. This process is known as the bootstrap method for calculating spot rates.

Next, we fit curves to the implied yields and bootstrapped spot rates, calculate the implied 6- and 12-month forward rates, and fit a curve to those rates. Figure 9–21 shows the results.

Excel Link

The next two examples demonstrate Excel Link, a software add-on that integrates Microsoft Excel and MATLAB. Excel Link positions Excel as a front end to MATLAB. This product is exciting for users of both programs because it links the popular Excel environment with MATLAB's computational power. We discussed Excel's macros and VBA language in Chapter 8. The following Excel Link examples demonstrate how those features can be used to expand a spreadsheet's capabilities.

Example: Regression and Curve Fitting

This example uses Excel worksheets to organize and display the data. Excel Link functions copy the data to MATLAB and execute MATLAB

FIGURE 9–21

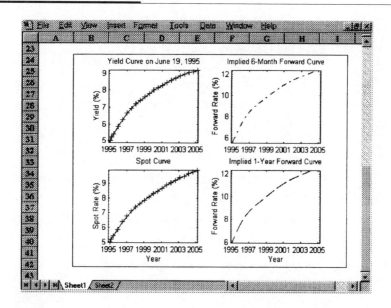

computational and graphic functions. Figure 9–22 shows the Excel worksheet layout with the computational steps listed under the heading, Excel
Link Functions. A brief description of the worksheet's activities follows.

Step 1 copies the data (three variables, 25 observations) to MAT-
LAB. Step 2 prepares the data for regressing the third column on the first
two, and step 3 calculates the regression coefficients. Steps 4 and 5 generate and measure the errors in fitting the regression line to the data. Step
6 fits a polynomial equation to the data and evaluates its goodness of fit.
The final step, step 7, plots the data and the fitted curves, as shown in
Figure 9–23.

The worksheet accomplishes its goals by using the commands that
begin in column E of Figure 9–22. Notice the syntax of the commands.
Each begins with ML, indicating that it is an Excel Link function. Until
the final graph is produced, though, the user does not have direct contact
with the MATLAB environment. Although it performs the computations,
MATLAB acts as a behind-the-scenes mathematical engine.

Example: Binomial Put Option Pricing

The binomial option pricing method is a widely used alternative to numerical implementations of the Black-Scholes and other option pricing formulas. The binomial method assumes that an asset price can move to only

FIGURE 9–22

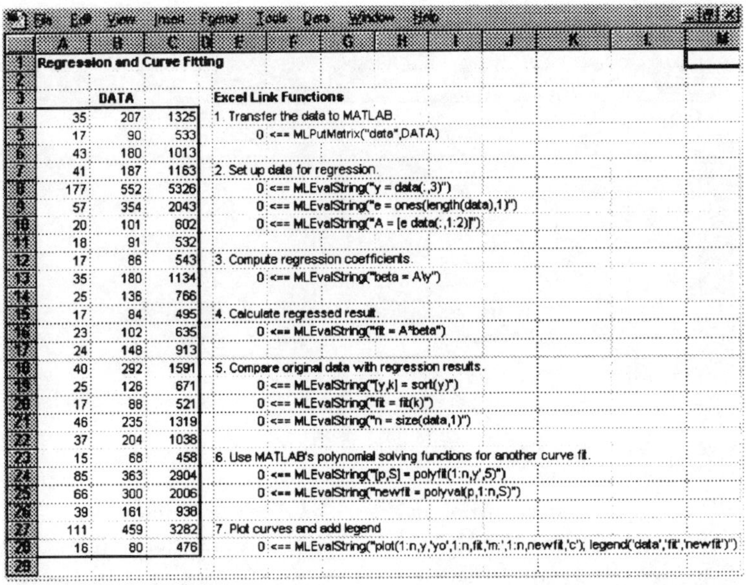

FIGURE 9–23

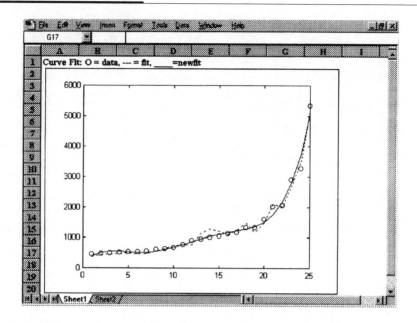

two values over a short period: It can move up or it can move down. By plotting each successive time period's values, we build a price "tree" that facilitates option pricing. In this example the key inputs are listed in the worksheet cells B4:B10 in Figure 9–24.

The program calculates option prices in three steps, as shown under Excel Link Functions in Figure 9–24. The first step is to transfer the B4:B10 data to MATLAB. Next the program calculates the asset pricing tree and resulting option prices and brings the results back to Excel, as shown in the ranges B15:G20 (asset prices) and B23:G28 (option prices) of Figure 9–25.

The advantage of using the spreadsheet for the binomial model becomes apparent, as the cells' values in Figure 9–25 provide a natural display of the tree (or lattice) approach. The key to interpreting the output is to look at the values when the option expires in Period 5 (Figure 9–25). Because this is a put, the option has a value at expiration only if the stock (asset) price is below the exercise price of $50. If the stock's price is above $50, the put expires worthless. If the stock's price is below $50, the put has a value of Exercise Price minus Stock Price (frequently written as E–S). You can see this relationship in the values shown in cells G15:G20 and G23:G28. In cell G15, for example, the stock's price is $92.628, and

F I G U R E   9–24

F I G U R E   9–25

Figure 9-25 contents:

Binomial Option Pricing

	bindata		**Excel Link Functions**				
Asset price, so	$ 52.00		1. Transfer data to MATLAB.				
Option exercise price, x	$ 50.00		0 <== MLPutMatrix("b", bindata)				
Risk-free interest rate, r	10%						
Time to maturity, t (yrs)	0.416667	=5/12	2. Execute MATLAB Financial Toolbox binomial option pricing function.				
Time increment, dt	0.083333	=1/12	0 <== MLEvalString("[p, o]=binprice(b(1), b(2), b(3), b(4), b(5), b(6), b(7))")				
Volatility, sig	0.4						
Call (1) or put (0), flag	0		3. Transfer output data to Excel.				
			0 <== MLGetMatrix("p", "asset_tree")				
			0 <== MLGetMatrix("o", "value_tree")				

	Start	Period 1	Period 2	Period 3	Period 4	Period 5
Asset price tree, p ($)	52.000	58.365	65.509	73.527	82.527	92.628
	0	46.329	52.000	58.365	65.509	73.527
	0	0	41.277	46.329	52.000	58.365
	0	0	0	36.776	41.277	46.329
	0	0	0	0	32.765	36.776
	0	0	0	0	0	29.192

Option value tree, o ($)	3.728	1.664	0.428	0	0	0
	0	5.918	2.964	0.876	0	0
	0	0	9.060	5.164	1.793	0
	0	0	0	13.224	8.723	3.671
	0	0	0	0	17.235	13.224
	0	0	0	0	0	20.808

Sheets: Sheet1 / Sheet2 / Module1 / Sheet3 / **Sheet4** / Sheet5

the corresponding put price in cell G23 is 0. In cell G18, though, the stock price is $46.239, which is less than $50, and the put's price is $3.671 (E–S, or $50–$46.329). The put prices before expiration are calculated using a discounted expected value method based on the asset price.

SOURCES AND SUGGESTED READING

Excel Link User's Guide. Natick, MA: The MathWorks, Inc., 1996.

Garvin, C. F. *Financial Toolbox User's Guide.* Natick, MA (1996).

Ingersoll, J. E. Jr. *Theory of Financial Decision Making.* Savage, MD: Rowman & Littlefield Publishers, Inc., 1987.

Mathcad 6.0/PLUS 6.0 User's Guide. Cambridge, MA: MathSoft, Inc., 1995.

MATLAB for Spreadsheet Finance: The Excel Link. Natick, MA: The MathWorks, Inc., 1996.

MATLAB User's Guide. Natick, MA: The MathWorks, Inc., 1992.

Sczaniecki, L. J. *Mathematica Finance Pack: Introduction and User's Guide.* Champaign, IL: Wolfram Research, 1994.

Siegel, J. K.; J. K. Shim; and S. W. Hartman. *The McGraw-Hill Pocket Guide to Business Finance.* New York: McGraw-Hill, 1992.

Taggart, Jr., R. A.*Quantitative Analysis for Investment Management.* Upper Saddle River, NJ: Prentice Hall, 1996.

Varian, H. R., ed. *Economic and Financial Modeling with Mathematica.* Santa Clara, CA: Telos, 1993.

Wolfram, S. *Mathematica: A System for Doing Mathematics by Computer.* 2nd ed. Redwood City, CA: Addison-Wesley, 1991.

SOFTWARE RESOURCES

Mathcad for Windows
MathSoft, Inc.
101 Main Street
Cambridge, MA 02142
Tel. 617-577-1017 or 800-628-4223
Fax 617-577-8829
E-mail: info@mathsoft.com
Web site: http://www.mathsoft.com
Suggested retail prices*
Mathcad 6.0 standard edition: $129.95
Mathcad PLUS 6.0: $349.95

Add-ons:
Mathcad Selections from Numerical Recipes Function Pack: $149.95
Personal Finance Electronic Book: $69.95
McGraw-Hill Financial Analyst: $69.95
*Academic discounts available

Mathematica for Windows
Wolfram Research, Inc.
100 Trade Center Drive
Champaign, IL 61820-7237
Tel. 217-398-0700
Fax 217-398-0747
E-mail: info@wolfram.com
Web: http://www.wolfram.com
Contact Wolfram Research for prices

MATLAB for Windows
The MathWorks, Inc.
24 Prime Park Way
Natick, MA 01760-1500
Tel. 508-647-7000
Fax 508-647-7101
E-mail: info@mathworks.com
Web: http://www.mathworks.com
Contact The MathWorks for prices

Chapter 1: Expert Systems

The following knowledge bases are supplied with the VP-Expert program. Comment lines start with a ! mark.

VP-Expert Example: Income Taxes

!This sample knowledge base was written in response to the article "Taxing the Expert System Shells" by Bill and Bev Thompson in the June 1987 issue of *AI Expert*. The Thompsons compared writing an application in four expert system shells. The example they used was the problem of determining exceptions to the tax laws based on specifics about the employee such as disability or relation to the employer.

! Federal income tax is represented by the variable tax[1].
! Social security tax is represented by the variable tax[2].
! Federal unemployment tax is represented by the variable tax[3].

```
RUNTIME;
ACTIONS
   COLOR = 14
   DISPLAY
"              Employer's Tax Guide
```

This sample expert system will help you determine if special tax considerations should be made for your employees.

```
Press any key to continue.~"
   COLOR = 0
   WOPEN 1,7,3,7,74,7
   ACTIVE 1
   FIND employee_type
```

! In finding employee_type elements of the dimensioned variable tax have
! been assigned the value "exempt" if the employee information satisfies
! the conditions for exception to the appropriate tax law.

```
x = 0
WHILEKNOWN tax[x]      ! This loop examines each value in the
x = (x + 1)            ! tax array.
FIND check             ! < This FIND fires Rule 9, which assigns
RESET check            ! the value "not exempt" to any elements
END                    ! of tax that have not been assigned the
                       ! value "exempt."


FIND display_tax_advice  ! Select the appropriate message based
DISPLAY "~";             ! upon the user's responses.
```

! Rules

! The following rules do two things: a) assign values to employee_type and b)
! assign "exempt" to the elements of the dimensioned variable tax.
! Since employee_type is a plural variable the inference engine will fire as
! many of these rules as it can to assign all possible values to employee_type.
! This reflects the ability of VP-Expert to consider all applicable cases.


```
RULE 0
IF        employee = other
THEN   employee_type = other
BECAUSE
"It is necessary to know the type of employee in order to ascertain
the need for special tax treatment.";


RULE 1
IF        employee = family_member
AND    relationship = husband
or        relationship = wife
THEN   employee_type = spouse
          tax[2] = exempt
          tax[3] = exempt
BECAUSE
"It is further necessary to describe the family relationship to
accurately assign tax exceptions";
```

RULE 2
IF   employee = family_member
AND   relationship = son
or   relationship = daughter
AND   age < 21
THEN employee_type = family
          tax[3] = exempt
BECAUSE
"Since the employee in question is a son or daughter, the age of
the employee is required";

RULE 3
IF   employee = family_member
AND   relationship = son
or   relationship = daughter
AND   age >= 21
THEN employee_type = family;

RULE 4
IF   employee = family_member
AND   relationship = other
THEN employee_type = relative;

RULE 5
IF   employee = deceased
AND   same_year = yes
THEN employee_type = deceased
          tax[1] = exempt
BECAUSE
"Tax exceptions are different for employees whose estates were paid
the same year that they died";

RULE 6
IF   employee = deceased
AND   same_year = no
THEN employee_type = deceased
          tax[1] = exempt
          tax[2] = exempt
          tax[3] = exempt;

RULE 7
IF   employee = disabled
AND   worked_during = yes
THEN employee_type = disabled
          tax[3] = exempt;

RULE 8
IF   employee = disabled
AND   worked_during = no
THEN employee_type = disabled
          tax[2] = exempt
          tax[3] = exempt;

! Other rules

RULE 9
IF   tax[x] = unknown
AND   x <= 3
THEN check = tax
          tax[x] = not_exempt
ELSE   check = exempt;

RULE 10
IF   employee_type<>other
THEN display_tax_advice = found
          WOPEN 2,16,5,6,70,3
          ACTIVE 2
          COLOR = 0
          DISPLAY
          " Income is {tax[1]} from federal income tax,
          is {tax[2]} from social security tax,
          and is {tax[3]} from federal unemployment tax.

          (Press any key to conclude this consultation)~"

ELSE   display_tax_advice = not_available
          WOPEN 3,18,8,5,64,1
          ACTIVE 3
          COLOR = 12
          DISPLAY
          "Special exemptions are not available for this employee type.

(Press any key to conclude this consultation)~";

! Plural Declarations, Questions, Menus

PLURAL: employee, employee_type;

ASK employee: "Which of the following best describes the employee?";
CHOICES employee: Family_member,Disabled,Deceased,Other;

ASK relationship: "What is the employee's relationship to the employer?";
CHOICES relationship: Husband,Wife,Daughter,Son,Other;

ASK same_year: "Was the estate paid in the same year the employee died?";
CHOICES same_year: Yes,No;

ASK age: "How old is the employee?";

ASK worked_during: "Did the employee work during disability?";
CHOICES worked_during: Yes,No;

VP-Expert Example: Insurance Underwriting

```
RUNTIME;
ENDOFF;
ACTIONS
COLOR=15
 DISPLAY "


                    WELCOME TO"
COLOR=9
 DISPLAY "
          THE AI SERVICES COMPANY's"
COLOR=15
DISPLAY "
      Demonstration Expert System For Underwriting Office Policies"
COLOR=14
DISPLAY "
          < Press any key to Continue >
~"
COLOR=14
CLS
```

```
FIND first_time
CLS
FIND Client_info
MENU Client_Name,ALL,Clients,Name
FIND Client_Name        ! < Check and/or update information on clients.
MRESET Client_Name
FIND info_client
CLS
FIND New_Name
FIND Policy_Type
FIND Eligible_three     ! < Determine client's initial eligibility.
FIND Building_props     ! < Go first to Rules Kickout1, Kickout2, and
                        ! Kickout3 to check eligibility. If these
                        ! rules do not fire, then user is asked to input
CLS                     ! information on the properties of the building.
MENU Location,ALL,CITY_DES,City
FIND Location
MRESET Location
FIND Building_AP
FIND Content_AP
FORMAT Content_AP,9.2
FORMAT Building_AP,9.2
FIND Finish     ! < Call to rule to display the annual premium
FIND Need_Extra_Coverage
WHILEKNOWN Extra     ! < Review client's need for extra coverage.
   RESET Extra
   POP Extra_Coverage,Extra
   CLS
   FIND   Var1
   RESET Var1
   FIND
Excesses
   RESET Excesses
   FIND Final
   RESET Final
   END
FIND Final_Content     ! < Sum annual premiums for building contents.
FIND Final_Building     ! < Sum annual premiums for building details.
FORMAT Final_Content,9.2
FORMAT Final_Building,9.2
```

```
    FIND  Show_premium      ! < Call to show total premium payment.
    DISPLAY "
```

This concludes this demonstration expert system.~";

! RULES SECTION

!Rules governing final calculations and display messages

```
RULE  Final_display
IF       Final_Content>0
THEN     CLS
         COLOR=15
         DISPLAY "
```

The Total Premium Payable for the Office Contents Policy is:
${Final_Content}


```
            Press any key.~"
    COLOR=0
    Show_premium=true;
```

```
RULE  Final_display2
IF       Final_Building>0
THEN  CLS
         COLOR=15
         DISPLAY "
```

The Total Premium Payable for the Office Building Policy is:
${Final_Building}


```
            Press any key.~"
    COLOR=14
    Show_premium=true;
```

!

RULE   Finish_one
IF   Content_AP>0.00
THEN   Final_cont1=(Content_AP+Glass_AP+Sign_AP)
       Final_cont2=(Final_cont1+Accounts_ap)
       Final_cont3=(Final_cont2+Papers_Ap)
       Final_Content=(Final_Cont3+Employee_DC)
ELSE   Final_Content=0;

RULE   Finish_two
IF   Building_AP>0.00
THEN   Final_Build1=(Building_AP+Glass_AP+Sign_AP)
       Final_Building=(Final_Build1+Employee_DC)
ELSE   Final_Building=0;

!Rules to check eligibility before going on
RULE Kickout1
IF   Eligible_one=Failed
THEN CLS
      COLOR=15
      DISPLAY "

The client failed the eligibility requirements because the combined
value of the building, contents, and 12 months of business interruption
exceeded the amounts allocated to building construction:
{building_const}"
      COLOR=14
      DISPLAY "
          < Press any key to Continue >

      ~"
      COLOR=14
      Quote1=known   ! In the case of non-eligibility, the
      Location=known   ! following variables are being assigned
      Building_AP=known   ! values so that further execution is
      building_props=known ! circumvented.
      Content_AP=known
      Finish=known

```
        excesses=known
        eligibility=failed
        Show_premium=known
        RESET extra;

RULE kickout2
IF    Eligible_one=passed AND
      Eligible_two=failed
THEN  CLS
      COLOR=15
      DISPLAY "
```

The client failed the eligibility requirements because too much of the building's space is allocated to non-office businesses or contains such businesses that are considered risks to other businesses located in the same building!"

```
      COLOR=14
      DISPLAY "
            < Press any key to Continue >

      ~"
      COLOR=14
      Quote1=Known
      Location=known
      Building_AP=known
      building_props=known
      Content_AP=known
      Finish=known
      excesses=known
      eligibility=failed
      Show_premium=known
      RESET extra;
RULE kickout3
IF    Eligible_one=passed AND
      Eligible_two=passed AND
      Eligible_three=Failed
THEN  CLS
      COLOR=15
      DISPLAY "
```

The client failed the eligibility requirement because his/her business
is considered to represent significant personal injury and/or contractual
liability exposure!"
    COLOR=14
    DISPLAY "
        < Press any key to Continue >

    ~"
    COLOR=14
    Quote1=Known
    Location=known
    Building_AP=known
    building_props=known
    Content_AP=known
    Finish=known
    excesses=known
    eligibility=failed
    Show_premium=known
    RESET extra
ELSE   eligibility=passed;

!Rules for checking client information
RULE Client_Info
IF   First_time=yes
THEN Client_info=known
    Client_Name=known
    Info_client=bypassed;

RULE 1a
IF   First_time=no
THEN GET Client_Name=Name,Clients,ALL ! < Load data from
client database.
    Policy_Type=(Policy)
    Building_const=(Const)
    Combined_Value=(Value)
    New_Name=known
    Info=known
    CLS;

RULE 1b   ! Rules 1b, 1c, and 1d permit the user
IF   Info=known AND   ! to examine the data from CLIENT.DBF

```
        Change_info1=No AND     ! and to update that information.
        New_PT<>unknown
THEN  Policy_Type=(New_PT)
        Info1=known
        CLS
ELSE  Info1=known
      CLS;


RULE 1c
IF    Info=known AND
      Change_info2=No AND
      New_BC<>unknown
THEN  Building_const=(New_BC)
        Info2=known
      CLS
ELSE  Info2=known
      CLS;


RULE 1d
IF    Info=known AND
      Change_info3=No AND
      New_CV<>unknown
THEN  Combined_Value=(New_CV)
        Info3=known
      CLS
ELSE  Info3=known
      CLS;


RULE 1e
IF    Info1=known AND
      Info2=known AND
      Info3=known
THEN  Policy=(Policy_Type)
        Const=(Building_const)
        Value=(Combined_Value)
      PUT clients                  ! < Update record of client in the
        Info_client=known;           ! database file CLIENTS.DBF

RULE 2
IF    Info_client=known OR
      Info_client=bypassed AND
```

Building_const<>unknown AND
Combined_Value<>unknown
THEN   building=known;

RULE 3
IF   Building=known AND
       Building_const=Frame AND
       Combined_Value<1600000
THEN   CLS
         Eligible_one=Passed;

RULE 3a
IF   Building=known AND
       Building_const=Masonry AND
       Combined_Value<2000000 OR
       Building_const=Non-Combustible AND
       Combined_Value<2000000
THEN   CLS
         Eligible_one=Passed;

RULE 3b
IF   Building=known AND
       Building_const=Non-Combustible AND
       Combined_Value<2000000
THEN   CLS
         Eligible_one=Passed
ELSE   CLS
         Eligible_one=Failed;

RULE 4
IF   Eligible_one=Passed AND
       Any_occupant=no AND
       occupancies_exceed=no AND
       ACV=no AND
       Restaurant=no
THEN   CLS
         Eligible_two=Passed
ELSE   CLS
         Eligible_two=Failed;

RULE 5
IF   Eligible_two=Passed AND
     Type_business=no
THEN CLS
     Eligible_three=Passed
ELSE   CLS
     Eligible_three=Failed;

!Rules for Checking Building Properties
RULE 5a
IF   Eligible_three=Passed AND ! < Check eligibility of new client
     Info_client=bypassed
THEN Name=(new_name)
     Policy=(Policy_Type)
     Const=(Building_const)
     Value=(Combined_Value)
     APPEND Clients   ! < Append record of new client
     Continue=true   ! data to the database file
     CLS
ELSE   Continue=true
     CLS;

RULE 6
IF   Policy_Type=Office_Building AND
     Continue=true
THEN COLOR=15
Display "

     We will now examine some properties of the office building.
"
     COLOR=14
DISPLAY "
       < Press any key to Continue >~"
     COLOR = 14
     CLS
     quote=seen;

RULE 6a
IF   Policy_Type=Office_Contents AND
     Continue=true

THEN   COLOR=15
DISPLAY "

We will now examine those facts relating to the Office Contents Policy.
"
COLOR=14
DISPLAY "
        < Press any key to Continue >~"
    COLOR = 14
    properties=known
    CLS;

RULE 7
IF   Quote=seen AND
      Sprinklered<>unknown AND
      Building_Age<>unknown
THEN   properties=known;

RULE 8
IF   Properties=known AND
      Sprinklered=Yes
THEN   Sprinkler_credit=.8
        Sprinkler=known
ELSE   Sprinkler_Credit=1
        Sprinkler=known;

RULE 9
IF   Properties=known AND
      Building_Age>35
THEN   CLS
        COLOR=14
        DISPLAY "

Any building older than 35 must be inspected by the company before
binding!"
        COLOR=15
        DISPLAY "
          < Press any key to Continue >~"
        COLOR = 14

          Age=known
ELSE   Age=known;

RULE 10
IF   Sprinkler=known AND
       Age=known
THEN   Building_props=known;

RULE 10a
IF   Location<>unknown AND
       Policy_Type=Office_Contents
THEN   Get Location=City,City_des,ALL   ! < Load location data from
       subgoal1=known;   ! CITY_DES.DBF.

RULE 11
IF   Location<>unknown AND
       Policy_Type=Office_building
THEN   GET Location=City,City_des,ALL   ! < Load location data from
       Subgoal1=known;   ! CITY_DES.DBF.

RULE 11a
IF   Subgoal1=known AND
       Pub_Prot>=1 AND
       Pub_Prot<=4
THEN   Protection=1-4
       GET Policy_Type=policy AND Building_const=Const AND
       Protection=Protect,Prop_Rate,ALL
       CLOSE Prop_rate
       GET Territory=Terr,Liab_Rate,ALL
       subgoal2=known
       CLS;

RULE 11b
IF   Subgoal1=known AND
       Pub_Prot>=5 AND
       Pub_Prot<=8
THEN   Protection=5-8
       GET Policy_Type=policy AND Building_const=Const AND
       Protection=Protect,Prop_Rate,ALL
       CLOSE Prop_Rate

```
        GET Territory=Terr,Liab_Rate,ALL
        subgoal2=known
        CLS;
```

RULE 11c
IF   Subgoal1=known AND
      Pub_Prot>=9 AND
      Pub_Prot<=10
THEN Protection=9-10
      GET Policy_Type=policy AND Building_const=Const AND
      Protection=Protect,Prop_Rate,Prate
      CLOSE Prop_Rate
      GET Territory=Terr,Liab_Rate,LRate
      subgoal2=known
      CLS;

RULE 12   ! This rule calculates the
IF   Policy_Type=Office_building AND   ! annual premiums for an
      Subgoal2=known AND   ! office building policy.
      deductible<>unknown AND
      Blimit_liability<>unknown
THEN ET deductible=deduct,Ded_fact,ALL
      Annual_Rate=(DFactor*PRATE)
      Building_LL=(Blimit_liability/100)
      Building_AP=(Building_LL*Annual_Rate) ! check this bug out
      Building_AP=(Building_AP*Sprinkler_credit)
      Content_AP=0;

RULE 13   ! This rule calculates the
IF   Policy_Type=Office_Contents AND   ! annual premiums for an
      Subgoal2=known AND   ! office contents policy.
      deductible<>unknown AND
      Climit_liability<>unknown
THEN GET deductible=deduct,Ded_fact,ALL
      Annual_Rate=(DFactor*LRATE)
      Content_LL=(Climit_liability/100)
      Content_AP=(Content_LL*Annual_Rate)
      Content_AP=(Content_AP*Sprinkler_Credit)
      Building_AP=0;
```
```

RULE 14
IF   Content_AP>0
THEN CLS
        DISPLAY "

      The Office Contents Policy Annual Premium is: ${Content_AP}
"
        COLOR=14
        DISPLAY "
            < Press any key to Continue >
~"
        COLOR = 14
        CLS
        Finish=known;

RULE 15
IF   Building_AP>0
THEN CLS
        DISPLAY "
        The Office Building Policy Annual Premium is: ${Building_AP}
"
        COLOR=14
        DISPLAY "
            < Press any key to Continue >
~"
        COLOR = 14
        CLS
        Finish=known;

!Rules for Handling Extra Coverage

RULE   Need_Extra_Coverage
IF   eligibility=passed
THEN   Need_Extra_Coverage=known
      FIND Extra_Coverage
ELSE   Need_Extra_Coverage=unnecessary;

RULE 16
IF   Extra=Glass AND

Linear_Feet<>unknown
THEN   Glass_rate=(Linear_Feet*2.60)
      excesses=known;

RULE 16a
IF   Extra=Glass AND
     Glass_rate<25
THEN   Glass_AP=25.00
      Final=known
ELSE   Glass_AP=(Glass_rate)
      Final=known;

RULE 17
IF   Extra=Exterior_Sign AND
     Sign_LL<>unknown
THEN   Sign_AP=((Sign_ll/100)*2.00)
      excesses=known;

RULE 18a
IF   Extra=Employee_Dishonesty AND
     Number_employees<>unknown
THEN   Employee_excess=(Number_Employees-5)
      Excess_charge=((Employee_excess*5)+72)
      var1=known;

RULE 18b
IF   Extra=Employee_Dishonesty AND
   Number_employees=unknown
THEN   Excess_charge=72
      var1=known;

RULE 18c
IF   Var1=known AND
     Dishonesty_charge<>Unknown
THEN   Additional_charge=(((Dishonesty_charge/5000)-1)*15)
      Employee_DC=(Excess_Charge+Additional_charge)
      Excesses=known;

RULE 18d
IF   Var1=known AND
     Dishonesty_charge=Unknown

THEN Employee_DC=(Excess_Charge)
        Execesses=known;

RULE 19
IF   Extra=Valuable_papers AND
       Papers_LL<>Unknown
THEN Papers_ap=(((Papers_LL-10000)*prate)*.7)
        Excesses=known;

RULE 19a
IF   Extra=Valuable_papers AND
       Papers_LL=Unknown
THEN Papers_ap=(prate*.7)
        Excesses=known;

RULE 20
IF   Extra=Accounts_receivable AND
       Accounts_LL<>unknown
THEN Accounts_AP=((.225*prate)*accounts_ll)
        Excesses=known;
!END of RULES SECTION

! DEFINE QUESTIONS AND ANSWERS

ASK First_time : " Is this the first time the client has been insured
through this company?";
CHOICES First_time : Yes, No;

ASK Policy_Type : " Indicate what the client wishes to insure:";
CHOICES Policy_Type : Office_Building, Office_Contents;

ASK Building_const : " Indicate the construction of the building:";
CHOICES Building_const : Frame, Masonry, Non-Combustible;

ASK Combined_Value : " Enter the combined value of building, contents and 12 months business interruption:";

ASK Any_occupant : " Is any occupant of the building other than
Office, Apartment or Mercantile?";
CHOICES Any_occupant : Yes, No;

ASK Occupancies_exceed : " Do Apartment/Mercantile occupancies exceed 25% of total floor Area?";
CHOICES Occupancies_exceed : Yes, No;

ASK ACV : " Is the Actual Cash Value of the building less than 75% of Replacement Cost?";
CHOICES ACV : Yes, No;

ASK Restaurant : " Is there a restaurant or cafeteria located in the building?";
CHOICES Restaurant : Yes, No;

ASK type_business : "

Advertising Agency	Bank/Investment Co./Financial Inst.
Better Business Bureau	Credit/Loan/Collection Agency
Detective,Guard,Patrol Service	Electronic Data Processing Center
Employment Agency	Manufacturer's Representative
Newspaper/Publisher	Non-Profit Organization
Professional (Engineer, etc.)	Real Estate Agency

Does a description of the client's business appear above?";
CHOICES type_business : Yes, No;

ASK Sprinklered : " Does the building have a sprinkler system?";
CHOICES Sprinklered : Yes, No;

ASK Building_Age : " How old is the building?";

ASK Client_Name : " Choose the appropriate client name:";

ASK Change_info1 : " We have the Policy Type for {Client_name} listed as: {Policy_Type}

Is this information still correct?";
CHOICES Change_info1 : Yes, No;

ASK Change_info2 : " We have the building construction for {Client_name} listed as: {building_Const}

Is this information still correct?";

CHOICES Change_info2 : Yes, No;

ASK Change_info3 : " We have the Combined value of building, contents and 12 months business
interruption for {Client_name} listed as: {Combined_Value}

Is this information still correct?";
CHOICES Change_info3 : Yes, No;

ASK New_PT : " Indicate the new Policy type:";
CHOICES New_PT : Office_Building, Office_Contents, Both;

ASK New_BC : " Indicate the new Building Construction:";
CHOICES New_BC : Frame, Masonry, Non-Combustible;

ASK New_CV : " Indicate the new amount of building, contents and 12 months business interruption:";

ASK Location : "Indicate what city the Office Building is located in:";

ASK New_Name : " Enter the Client's Last Name:";

ASK Deductible : " Choose the Deductible the Client wants:";
CHOICES Deductible : 100,250,500,1000;

ASK BLimit_liability : " What is the limit of liability the client wishes (The limit of liability is determined by the 100% insurable value for the building and related service equipment)?";

ASK Climit_liability : " What is the limit of liablility the client would like (The limit of liability is determined by 100% insurable value of the insured's stock, furniture and fixtures and improvements and betterments)?";

ASK Extra_Coverage : " Does the client need any of the following additional Coverages? (Move the cursor to choice press <Enter>, if applicable, make another choice in the same manner. When done press END. If the client does not want any of the additional coverages type: ? and press <Enter>)

";
CHOICES Extra_Coverage :
Glass,Exterior_Sign,Employee_Dishonesty,Valuable_Papers,Accounts_
Receivable;
PLURAL : Extra_Coverage;

ASK Linear_feet : " How much glass does the client have (In linear
Feet)?";

ASK Sign_LL : " What is the limit of liability the client wants on the
exterior signs?";

ASK Number_employees : " How many employees does your client
have (if 5 or less type: ?):";

ASK Dishonesty_charge : " The dishonesty coverage is default at
$5,000. If the client wishes to keep this coverage type: ?, else enter the
amount of coverage (in $5,000 increments) they would like:";

ASK Papers_LL : " What is the limit of liability the client wants on the
valuable papers?
    (If <= $10,000 type: ?, else enter the actual number)";

ASK Accounts_LL : " What limit of liability does the client want on the
Accounts Receivable?";

CHAPTER 3: SIMULATION

Goodness-of-Fit Measures

Palisade Corporation's BestFit program uses three goodness-of-fit tests
when it estimates a data set's distribution. In this section we include material from the BestFit manual that gives more details about the process.[1]

What Is Goodness-of-Fit?

Formally, goodness-of-fit is defined as "the probability of the data given
the parameters." In other words, the goodness-of-fit statistic tells you how
probable it is that a given distribution function produced your data set.
The goodness-of-fit statistic is usually used in a relative sense by comparing the values to the goodness-of-fit of other distribution functions.

---

1 Source: *BestFit User's Guide,* Newfield, NY: Palisade Corp. (1995), pp. 2–17 to 2–19.

BestFit offers three goodness-of-fit tests: chi-square, Kolmogorov-Smirnov and Anderson-Darling. The chi-square is the most common, but the others may supply more detailed information about your distribution.

Which Goodness-of-Fit Test Should You Use?
There is no specific goodness-of-fit test that will give you the "best" result. Each test has its strengths and weaknesses. You must decide which information is most important to you when considering which test to use.

Chi-Square Test
The chi-square test is the most common goodness-of-fit test. It can be used with any type of input data (sample, density, or cumulative) and any type of distribution function (continuous or discrete).

A weakness of the chi-square test is that there are no clear guidelines for selecting intervals. In some situations, you can reach different conclusions from the same data depending on how you specified the intervals (number of classes).

The chi-square statistic is defined as:

$$\chi^2 = \sum_{i=1}^{n} \frac{\left(P_i - p_i\right)^2}{p_i}$$

where

P_i = the observed probability value for a given histogram bar

p_i = the theoretical probability that a value will fall within the X range of the histogram bar

Kolmogorov-Smirnov Test
The Kolmogorov-Smirnov test does not depend on the number of intervals, which makes it more powerful than the chi-square test. This test can be used with any type of input data but cannot be used with discrete distribution functions. A weakness of the Kolmogorov-Smirnov test is that it does not detect tail discrepancies very well.

The Kolmogorov-Smirnov statistic is defined as:

$$D_n = \sup[\left|F_n(x) - \hat{F}(x)\right|]$$

where

n = total number of data points

$\hat{F}(x)$ = the hypothesized distribution

$$F_n(x) = \frac{N_x}{n}$$

N_x = the number of X_i's less than x

Anderson-Darling Test

The Anderson-Darling test is very similar to the Kolmogorov-Smirnov test, but it places more emphasis on tail values. It does not depend on the number of intervals. A weakness of the Anderson-Darling test is that it can only be used with sample input data.

The Anderson-Darling statistic is:

$$A_n^2 = n \int_{-\infty}^{+\infty} [F_n(x) - \hat{F}(x)]^2 \, \Psi(x) \hat{f}(x) dx$$

where

$$\Psi^2 = \frac{1}{\hat{F}(x)\left[1 - \hat{F}(x)\right]}$$

$\hat{f}(x)$ = the hypothesized density functions

$\hat{F}(x)$ = the hypothesized distribution function

$$F_n(x) = \frac{N_x}{n}$$

N_x = the number of X_i's less than x

Measures of Dispersion

A distribution's expected or mean value is an informative statistic. By itself, though, it provides only partial information about the data set's distribution. For example, assume that we have two data sets with five elements each: (16, 18, 20, 22, 24) and (0, 10, 20, 30, 40). Both sets have mean values of 20, but would you describe them as similar sets? Probably not, because in the first set the values are grouped "tightly" around the mean value. In the second set, though, the values are dispersed much more widely.

The @RISK simulation program includes three widely used dispersion measures in its simulation reports: variance, skewness, and kurtosis. Variance gives us a sense of how widely the data are dispersed about the mean. We calculate a sample's variance using the following formula:

$$\text{Variance} = \frac{n\sum x^2 - \left(\sum x\right)^2}{n(n-1)}$$

If two data sets have the same mean, the set with the smaller variance will have less dispersion around the mean.

The second measure, skewness, tells us about the distribution's symmetry. We are all familiar with the normal distribution's bell curve. That shape is an example of a symmetric distribution where the data are distributed evenly about the mean. Not all data sets have this property, though—some are asymmetric, meaning they have more points on one side of the mean. Distributions with a long tail to the right are called positively skewed, and those with tails to the left are negatively skewed. A normal distribution will have zero skewness. A formula for skewness is:

$$\text{Skewness} = \frac{n}{(n-1)(n-2)}\sum\left(\frac{x_1 - \bar{x}}{\sigma}\right),$$

where σ stands for the sample standard deviation.

The final dispersion measure we discuss is kurtosis, which compares the relative flatness or sharpness (at the peak) of a distribution compared to a normal distribution. A peaked distribution will have positive kurtosis (leptokurtic), while one with a flat top will have negative kurtosis (platykurtic). A normal distribution will have zero kurtosis. The formula for kurtosis is:

$$\text{Kurtosis} = \left[\frac{n(n+1)}{(n-1)(n-2)(n-3)}\sum\left(\frac{x_i - \bar{x}}{\sigma}\right)\right] - \frac{3(n-1)^2}{(n-2)(n-3)}$$

CHAPTER 5: FORECASTING

Linear Regression

Using a program for linear regression shields the user from the method's underlying mathematics. The mathematics isn't particularly difficult, though, and in this section we show how the regression's parameters are estimated using two explanatory variables, x_1 and x_2. We use the following notation:

y_t = observed value for the dependent variable.

x_{1t} = value of the first independent (explanatory) variable at time t.

x_{2t} = value of the second independent (explanatory) variable at time t.

β_1 = the first unknown parameter (a constant in this model).

β_2 = the second unknown parameter.

e_t = individual error term (discussed below).

E = total of squared error terms.

T = total number of observations.

As we discussed in the chapter, the goal of linear regression is to find estimates of the parameters (β_1, β_2) that minimize the total of the squared error terms, E. We calculate each individual squared error term by comparing the actual value with the model's value:

$$e_t = y_t - x_{t1} * \beta_1 - x_{t2} * \beta_2$$

We calculate each error, square it, and sum them to get the value

$$E = \Sigma(y_t - x_{t1} * \beta_1 - x_{t2} * \beta_2)^2$$

The intuition behind this approach is that good-fitting parameters will a produce a small value for E, while inaccurate parameter estimates will produce a poor-fitting model that will have a larger value for E.

It is helpful to visualize the data layout before we derive the parameter's estimates. If we arranged the multiple values for y, x, and e in columns, it would look like this:

$$\begin{bmatrix} y_1 \\ \vdots \\ y_T \end{bmatrix} = \begin{bmatrix} 1 \\ \vdots \\ 1 \end{bmatrix} * \beta_1 + \begin{bmatrix} x_{12} \\ \vdots \\ x_{T2} \end{bmatrix} * \beta_2 + \begin{bmatrix} e_1 \\ \vdots \\ e_2 \end{bmatrix}$$

We read across the columns, so in words, we say that result y_1 is the sum of β_1 (a constant) plus the x_{12} observation times β_2 plus some random error e_1. This result holds true for the y-values through the T observations.

Our next step is to find the values for β_1 and β_2 that minimize the value of E. This calculation is a classic minimization problem in calculus, and it requires us to take the partial derivative of E with respect to β_1 and β_2, set the partial derivatives to zero, and solve the remaining terms in the equations. We do this first for β_1:

$$E = \sum_t \left(y_t - x_{t1}\beta_1 - x_{t2}\beta_2\right)^2$$

$$\frac{\partial E}{\partial \beta_1} = -2\sum_t x_{t1}\left(y_t - x_{t1}\beta_1 - x_{t2}\beta_2\right) = 0$$

We divide each side by -2, leaving only the term enclosed in parentheses following the summation sign. We saw above that the values in the column vector of $[x_t...x_T]$ each have a value of one, so if we multiply the terms inside the parentheses by x_{t1}, they remain the same. Also, there are T entries of one in the $[x_{t1}...x_{T1}]$ vector. If we sum those entries, we will have a value of T. Using that change and moving the summation sign inside the parentheses gives us:

$$\left(\sum_t y_t - T\beta_1 - \sum_t x_{t2}\beta_2 \right) = 0$$

We can rewrite this equation as

$$T\beta_1 + \sum_t x_{t2}\beta_2 = \sum_t y_t$$

and we will use this new version shortly.

Next, we calculate the partial derivative of E with respect to β_2:

$$\frac{\partial E}{\partial \beta_2} = -2\sum_t x_{t2}(y_t - x_{t1}\beta_1 - x_{t2}\beta_2) = 0$$

You will notice one difference between this partial derivative and that for β_1: The $[x_{t2}...x_{T2}]$ column vector contains multiple values, not just ones. This vector holds the T observations for the independent variable x_2, so we cannot ignore its impact on the variables inside the parentheses. Instead, we must multiply it through the other variables. Doing this calculation and eliminating the -2 term gives us

$$\left(\sum_t x_{t2}y_t - \sum_t x_{t2}x_{t1}\beta_1 - \sum_t x_{t2}^2\beta_2 \right) = 0$$

The term x_{t1} in the middle term still has the same effect as multiplying by one, so we can rewrite the equation as

$$\sum_t x_{t2}\beta_1 + \sum_t x_{t2}^2\beta_2 = \sum_t x_{t2}y_t$$

The notation is messy, but using this approach leads to a neat solution. First, we work with the two intermediate solutions we have developed:

$$T\beta_1 + \sum_t x_{t2}\beta_2 = \sum_t y_t$$

$$\sum_t x_{t2}\beta_1 + \sum_t x_{t2}^2\beta_2 = \sum_t x_{t2}y_t$$

Our goal is to solve the values of β_1 and β_2, and we can rearrange the equations in matrix form to facilitate this:

$$\begin{bmatrix} T & \sum_t x_{t2} \\ \sum_t x_{t2} & \sum_t x_{t2}^2 \end{bmatrix} \begin{bmatrix} \beta_1 \\ \beta_2 \end{bmatrix} = \begin{bmatrix} \sum_t y_t \\ \sum_t x_{t2} y_t \end{bmatrix}$$

Once again we have an equation that looks far more difficult to solve than it really is. Look at the first matrix on the left side—each entry is a number that we can calculate directly from the data. The same is true for the vector on the right side. The point is that these are real numbers—we have moved from abstract partial derivatives to working with real numbers that we can calculate manually or in a spreadsheet.

The last step is to solve for the beta values by using standard techniques from linear algebra. We show the steps here:

$$\begin{bmatrix} \beta_1 \\ \beta_2 \end{bmatrix} = \begin{bmatrix} T & \sum_t x_{t2} \\ \sum_t x_{t2} & \sum_t x_{t2}^2 \end{bmatrix}^{-1} \begin{bmatrix} \sum_t y_t \\ \sum_t x_{t2} y_t \end{bmatrix}$$

$$\begin{bmatrix} \beta_1 \\ \beta_2 \end{bmatrix} = \frac{1}{T\left(\sum_t x_{t2}^2\right) - \left(\sum_t x_{t2}\right)^2} \begin{bmatrix} \sum_t x_{t2}^2 & -\sum_t x_{t2} \\ -\sum_t x_{t2} & T \end{bmatrix} \begin{bmatrix} \sum_t y_t \\ \sum_t x_{t2} y_t \end{bmatrix}$$

Working through the elements gives us the final equations for the beta vector:

$$\beta_1 = \frac{\left(\sum_t x_{t2}^2 \sum_t y_t\right) - \left(\sum_t x_{t2} \sum_t x_{t2} y_t\right)}{T\sum_t x_{t2}^2 - \left(\sum_t x_{t2}\right)^2}$$

$$\beta_2 = \frac{T\left(\sum_t x_{t2} y_t\right) - \left(\sum_t x_{t2}\right)\left(\sum_t y_t\right)}{T\sum_t x_{t2}^2 - \left(\sum_t x_{t2}\right)^2}$$

Depending on notation, the estimates of the beta values generated by these formulas will probably be denoted as (b_1, b_2) or (β_1, β_2).

Typical Regression Statistics

Each regression program presents slightly different analytical statistics, but a significant similarity appears among most programs' outputs. In this section we assume the user runs a simple regression with a constant (b_1) and one explanatory variable whose parameter we label b_2. This leads to the regression model:

Dependent variable $= b_1 + b_2$ * independent variable + error term

We use an example similar to one developed earlier in the text that relates square feet (independent variable) to housing prices (dependent variable). The table below lists the data.

Obs.	X Square Feet	Y Price ($)	X^2	Y^2	X*Y
1	1145	240	1311025	57600	274800
2	1334	273.6	1779556	74857	364982
3	1380	282	1904400	79524	389160
4	1657	342	2745649	116964	566694
5	1680	286.8	2822400	82254	481824
6	1700	275	2890000	75625	467500
7	1710	275	2924100	75625	470250
8	1740	320	3027600	102400	556800
9	1740	330	3027600	108900	574200
10	1780	360	3168400	129600	640800
11	1810	350	3276100	122500	633500
12	1830	351.6	3348900	123623	643428
13	1880	342	3534400	116964	642960
14	1950	438	3802500	191844	854100
15	2015	354	4060225	125316	713310
16	2028	348	4112784	121104	705744
17	2334	462	5447556	213444	1078308
18	2680	606	7182400	367236	1624080
19	2880	510	8294400	260100	1468800
20	3080	498	9486400	248004	1533840
Sum	38353	7244	78146395	2793484	14685080

In addition to the square feet (X) and price data, the table contains three other columns: the values for x-value squared (X^2), y-value squared (Y^2), and the product of each x–y combination (X * Y). The motivation for these calculations is found in the table's final row, which lists each column's sum. We denote these column sums by

$$\sum x_t, \sum y_t, \sum x_t^2, \sum y_t^2, \sum x_t y_t$$

and we will use these sums to demonstrate the origins of the most common regression statistics.

We start by calculating the value of b_1 with the formula we derived above:

$$b_1 = \frac{\left(\sum_t x_{t2}^2 \sum_t y_t\right) - \left(\sum_t x_{t2} \sum_t x_{t2} y_t\right)}{T \sum_t x_{t2}^2 - \left(\sum_t x_{t2}\right)^2}$$

(We can safely ignore the subscripts here since we have only one x column.) We substitute the values for the variables, which gives us:

$$b_1 = \frac{(78146395 * 7244) - (38353 * 1465080)}{20(78146395) - 38353^2}$$

or 31.2651. Next, we calculate b_2, with the formula:

$$b_2 = \frac{T\left(\sum x_{t2} y_t\right) - \left(\sum_t x_{t2}\right)\left(\sum_t y_t\right)}{T \sum_t x_{t2}^2 - \left(\sum_t x_{t2}\right)^2}$$

Using the same method of substituting our column sums where appropriate, we get:

$$b_2 = \frac{20(14685080) - (38353)(7244)}{20(78146395) - 38353^2}$$

which equals .1726. Therefore, our regression equation is:

Price = 31.2651 + .1726 * square feet

Now that we have estimated the b_1 and b_2 coefficients, we can use them to estimate prices (y_t) and the resulting error terms (e), which we do in the following table.

Obs.	Square Feet	Estimated Price	Actual Price	Error	Error^2 (ESS)	RSS	TSS
1	1145	228.9	240.0	−11.1	123.4	17771.0	14932.8
2	1334	261.5	273.6	−12.1	146.1	10137.8	7850.0
3	1380	269.5	282.0	−12.5	157.4	8602.0	6432.0
4	1657	317.3	342.0	−24.7	611.9	2019.3	408.0
5	1680	321.2	286.8	34.4	1185.6	1678.3	5685.2

6	1700	324.7	275.0	49.7	2468.6	1407.4	7603.8
7	1710	326.4	275.0	51.4	2643.1	1280.8	7603.8
8	1740	331.6	320.0	11.6	134.3	937.0	1780.8
9	1740	331.6	330.0	1.6	2.5	937.0	1036.8
10	1780	338.5	360.0	−21.5	462.5	562.0	4.8
11	1810	343.7	350.0	−6.3	40.1	343.3	148.8
12	1830	347.1	351.6	−4.5	20.0	227.3	112.4
13	1880	355.8	342.0	13.8	189.1	41.6	408.0
14	1950	367.8	438.0	−70.2	4923.1	31.8	5745.6
15	2015	379.1	354.0	25.1	627.7	284.1	67.2
16	2028	381.3	348.0	33.3	1108.8	364.7	201.6
17	2334	434.1	462.0	−27.9	777.7	5171.6	9960.0
18	2680	493.8	606.0	−112.2	12581.4	17327.3	59438.4
19	2880	528.4	510.0	18.4	336.8	27606.9	21844.8
20	3080	562.9	498.0	64.9	4208.5	40269.7	18441.6
Sum	38353	7245.0	7244.0	1.0298	32748.8	137000.7	169707.0
Mean		362.3	362.2				

The most important information in this table is in the last three columns and their sums, which show the error components of the predicted versus actual price. The ESS column is the squared difference between the predicted price and the actual, $(\hat{y}-y)^2$. RSS, or residual sum or squares, shows the squared difference between the predicted value for y and the actual prices' mean value of 362.2, $(\hat{y}-\bar{y})^2$. Finally, TSS (total sum of squares) is the squared difference between the actual value and the actual prices' average, $(y-\bar{y})^2$.

By using the sums of the appropriate columns from the preceding two tables, we can now calculate many of the statistics that a typical regression program generates. We show the output in two formats. The first has the formulas for the entries, and the second uses the numbers from the housing price regression. Because we interpreted the output in the text, we do not repeat that material here.

ANOVA (Analysis of Variance)

	Degrees of Freedom	Sum of Squares	Mean Square	F Statistic
Regression	1	total from RSS column	sum of squares / k	mean square (regression) / mean square (residual)
Residual	T − 2	total from ESS column	sum of squares / k	

Total	T – 1	combined total from ESS and RSS columns		
Regression	1	137000.7	137000.7	75.30
Residual	18	32748.8	1819.4	
Total	19			

Regression Statistics

	Coefficient	Standard Error	t-statistic
Intercept	calculated earlier	see formula (1) below	coefficient / standard error
Square feet	calculated earlier	see formula (2) below	coefficient / standard error

Formulas

(1)
$$\frac{\sqrt{\dfrac{ESS}{T-2}}}{\sum x_t^2 - \dfrac{\left(\sum x_1\right)^2}{T}}$$

(2)
$$\sqrt{\frac{ESS}{T-2}\left[\frac{\sum x_t^2}{T\left(\sum x_t^2 - \dfrac{\left(\sum x_t\right)^2}{T}\right)}\right]}$$

	Coefficient	Standard Error	t-statistic
Intercept	31.2651	39.317	.7952
Square feet	.1726	.0199	8.67

Other Statistics

Statistic	Formula	Value
R-square	1-ESS/TSS	.8070
Adjusted R-square	$1-\dfrac{ESS/(T-k)}{TSS/(T-1)}$	.7963
Standard error	$\sqrt{\dfrac{ESS}{T-2}}$	42.6542

Note: k equals 2, the total number of the independent variables (1) and the constant.

CHAPTER 7: OPTIMIZATION

Microsoft Solver Options

Microsoft Excel Solver offers several options that give the user more control over Solver's approach to solving a problem. These options are found by clicking on the Options button in the main Solver screen, which displays the Solver Options dialogue box. We briefly describe several of those options here.[2]

Max Time Limits the time taken by the solution process. While you can enter a value as high as 32,767, the default value of 100 (seconds) is adequate for most small problems.

Iterations Limits the time taken by the solution process by limiting the number of interim calculations. While you can enter a value as high as 32,767, the default value of 100 is adequate for most small problems.

Precision Controls the precision of solutions by using the number you enter to determine whether the value of a constraint cell meets a target or satisfies a lower or upper bound. Precision must be indicated by a fractional number between 0 and 1. Lower precision is indicated when the number you enter has fewer decimal places. The higher the precision, the more time it will take to reach a solution. Specifying a trial value that is close to the solution speeds up the solution process.

Tolerance Represents an allowable percentage of error in the optimal solution when the constraint used on the problem is an integer. A higher tolerance tends to speed up the solution process.

Assume Linear Model Speeds the solution process when all relationships in the model are linear and you are solving either a linear optimization problem or a linear approximation to a nonlinear problem.

Show Iteration Results Interrupts Solver to show the results of each iteration.

Use Automatic Scaling Turns on automatic scaling for use when inputs and outputs have large differences in magnitude. An example is maximizing the percentage of profit based on million-dollar investments.

---

2 Source: Microsoft Excel 7.0.

Estimates Specifies the approach used: Tangent or Quadratic to obtain initial estimates of the basic variables in each one-dimensional search.

Tangent Uses linear extrapolation from a tangent vector.

Quadratic Uses quadratic extrapolation, which can improve the results on highly nonlinear problems.

Derivatives Specifies the differencing used: Forward or Central to estimate partial derivatives of the objective and constraint functions.

Forward Use with functions whose graphical representations are smooth and continuous.

Central Use with functions whose graphical representations are not smooth and continuous. Although this option requires more calculations, using it might help when Solver returns a message that it could not improve the solution.

Search Specifies the algorithm used at each iteration ¾ Newton or Conjugate ¾ to determine the direction to search.

Newton Uses a quasi-Newton method that typically requires more memory but fewer iterations than the conjugate method.

Conjugate Requires less memory than the Newton method but typically requires more iterations to reach a particular level of accuracy. Try this option when you have a large problem and memory usage is a concern or when stepping through iterations reveals slow progress.

CHAPTER 8: SPREADSHEET TOOLS

Order Retrieval Macro

The following Excel macro is an extension of the macro presented in Chapter 8. You will need to create macro buttons and change my geographical and computer file references before using this macro.

'Financial Consultants Order Retrieval Macro

'Purpose: Retrieve state's data, create pivot table and sales graph, add close button.

```
Sub RetrieveMA()
   GetData getState:="MA"
   MakeChart
   AddDeleteButton
End Sub
Sub RetrieveCT()
   GetData getState:="CT"
   MakeChart
   AddDeleteButton
End Sub
Sub RetrieveNY()
   GetData getState:="NY"
   MakeChart
   AddDeleteButton
End Sub
Sub RetrieveNH()
   GetData getState:="NH"
   MakeChart
   AddDeleteButton
End Sub
Sub RetrieveME()
   GetData getState:="ME"
   MakeChart
   AddDeleteButton
End Sub
Sub Retrieve VT()
   GetData getState:="VT"
   MakeChart
   AddDeleteButton
End Sub
Sub RetrieveRI()
   GetData getState:="RI"
   MakeChart
   AddDeleteButton
End Sub

'GetData Macro
'
Sub GetData(getState)
   If getState = ""Then End
   ActiveSheet.PivotTableWizard SourceType:=xlExternal, SourceData:=_
```

```
    Array("DSN=Financial Consultant Sales;DBQ="file
name";FIL=dBase4;",_
    "SELECT orders.DATE, orders.STATE, orders.CATEGORY,
orders.SALES,orders.CHANNEL
FROM "file name" orders
WHERE (orders.STATE='" & getState &"')'_
    ), TableDestination:="",TableName:="PivotTable2",RowGrand:=_
    False, ColumnGrand:=False
  ActiveSheet.PivotTables("PivotTable2").AddFields RowFields:=Array(_
    "STATE", "CATEGORY"), ColumnFields:="DATE"
  ActiveSheet.PivotTables("PivotTable2").PivotFields("SALES").
Orientation_= xlDataField
  ActiveSheet.PivotTables("PivotTable2").PivotFields("STATE").
Subtotals_
    = Array(False, False, False, False, False, False, False, False, False,
    False,_
False, False)
End Sub
'
'DeleteSheet Macro
'Macro recorded 2/4/96 by EDM
'
Sub DeleteSheet()
    Application.DisplayAlerts = False
    ActiveWindow.SelectedSheets.Delete
End Sub
'
'AddDeleteButton Macro
'Macro recorded 2/4/96 by EDM
'
Sub AddDeleteButton()
    ActiveSheet.Buttons.Add(144, 0, 48, 12.75).Select
    Selection.OnAction = "DeleteSheet"
    Selection.Characters.Text = "Close"
    With Selection.Characters(Start:=1, Length:=5).Font
        .Name = "Arial"
        .FontStyle = "Bold"
        .Size = 10
        .Strikethrough = False
        .Superscript = False
```

```
    .Subscript = False
    .OutlineFont = False
    .Shadow = xlNone
    .ColorIndex = xlAutomatic
  End With
  Range("A1").Select
End Sub
'

'MakeChart Macro
'Macro recorded 2/4/96 by EDM
'

Sub MakeChart()
  Range("A1").Select
  Selection.CurrentRegion.Select
  Selection.Name = "ChartRegion"
  ActiveSheet.ChartObjects.Add(1.5, 127.5, 519, 115.5).Select
  Application.CutCopyMode = False
  ActiveChart.ChartWizard Source:=Range("ChartRegion"),
Gallery:=xlLine, _
    Format:=2, PlotBy:=xlRows, CategoryLabels:=1, SeriesLabels _
    :=2, HasLegend:=1
  Range("A1:AL9").Select
EndSub
```

CHAPTER 9: MODELING TOOLS

Portfolio Optimization

In the first part of Chapter 9 we used Mathcad to calculate optimal portfolio weights. We presented the optimization formulas from Professor Ingersoll's book used in that example in their finished form. In this section we review the method of Langrange multipliers for solving constrained optimization problems, and we show the derivations behind the formulas used in the portfolio problem.

Assume that we want to maximize a quantity V that is a function of two variables, x_1 and x_2, such that $V(x_1, x_2) = 3x_1x_2 + 2x_1$. If x_1 and x_2 were available in unlimited quantities, we could maximize V by setting x_1 and x_2 equal to positive infinity. In this example, though, we further assume that x_1 and x_2 are constrained: $x_1 + 3x_2 = 12$. Given this constraint, how do we select values for x_1 and x_2 that maximize V?

The Lagrange-multiplier method is a handy "trick" for solving constrained optimization problems like this one. To use it, we first combine the objective function V and the constraint into a single equation:

$$L = 3x_1x_2 + 2x_1 + \lambda(12 - x_1 - 3x_2)$$

(The technique also works with multiple constraints, although it can become unwieldy.) If you look at the equation inside the parentheses, you will notice that it equals zero by definition. Therefore, adding it to the objective function does not change the value of the objective function because adding zero does not change the result.

The next step is to take the partial derivatives of L with respect to x_1, x_2, and λ; set each partial derivative equal to zero; and solve the resulting system of equations. In this example, this action produces:

$$\frac{\partial L}{\partial x_1} = 3x_2 + 2 - \lambda = 0$$

$$\frac{\partial L}{\partial x_2} = 3x_1 - 3\lambda = 0$$

$$\frac{\partial L}{\partial \lambda} = 12 - x_1 - 3x_2 = 0$$

Solving these equations for $x1$, $x2$, and λ gives us optimizing values of $\{5/3, 7, 7\}$, respectively, which maximizes V at a value of 38.33.

The portfolio optimization formulas used in Chapter 9 are also an example of the Lagrange method. Before deriving the equations, though, we review the matrix notation used in Ingersoll (1987). (Note: This section draws extensively on unpublished lecture notes developed by Professor Carmelo Giaccotto at the University of Connecticut.) The expected return on a portfolio is $\bar{Z} = w'\bar{z}$, where $\bar{Z}$ refers to the portfolio's expected return, w' is the vector of asset weights, and $\bar{z}$ is the vector of the individual securities' expected returns. In other words, the portfolio's expected return is the sum of the assets' weighted returns.

We define portfolio variance in a similar manner: $\sigma^2 = w'\Sigma w$, where Σ is the variance-covariance matrix of the assets' returns. As discussed in the text, the investor's usual goal is to create a portfolio that minimizes risk for a specified expected return or that maximizes expected return for a given level of risk. If we denote the specified expected return as μ, we can state the problem as

$$\text{Minimize} \frac{1}{2} w'\Sigma w$$

subject to $1'w = 1$ and $\bar{z}w = \mu$. Stated in English, we want to minimize portfolio risk subject to the constraints that portfolio weights sum to one and the expected return equals μ. We can combine the objective function and the constraints to form a Lagrangian:

$$L = \frac{w'\sum w}{2} + \lambda(1 - 1'w) + \gamma(\mu - \bar{z}'w)$$

Using the same technique as the previous example, we take the partial derivatives of L with respect to w, λ, and γ:

$$\frac{\partial L}{\partial w} = \sum w - \lambda 1 - y\bar{z} = 0$$

$$\frac{\partial L}{\partial \lambda} = 1 - w'1 = 0$$

$$\frac{\partial L}{\partial y} = \mu - w'\bar{z} = 0$$

After solving the equations (not shown here), the final result is the vector of optimal portfolio weights w^* that we calculated in the text.

TRADEMARKS/CREDITS

VP-Expert is a registered trademark of Wordtech Systems, Inc.

XpertRule® is developed and marketed by Attar Software Limited, Newlands Road, Leigh, Lancashire WN7 4HN, UK; Telephone: 01942-60884; http://www.attar.com

DPL is a registered trademark of ADA Decision Systems.

Expert Choice is a registered trademark of Expert Choice, Inc.

Palisade, BestFit are registered trademarks of Palisade Corporation; RISK is a trademark of Parker Brothers, Division on Tonka Corporation, and is used under license.

Microsoft, Excel, Visual Basic, and Windows are registered trademarks of Microsoft Corporation. Screen shots reproduced with permission from Microsoft Corporation.

FuziWare and FuziCalc are registered trademarks of FuziWare, Inc.

Forecast Pro and Forecast Pro for Windows are registered trademarks of Business Forecast Systems, Inc.

BrainMaker and NetMaker are registered trademarks of California Scientific Software.

What'sBest! and LINDO are registered trademarks of LINDO Systems, Inc.

@analyst is a registered trademark of Tech Hackers Inc.

Mathcad is a registered trademark and *Electronic Book, QuickSheets,* and the MathSoft logo are trademarks of MathSoft, Inc.

Mathematica and MathLink are registered trademarks of Wolfram Research, Inc.

MATLAB is a registered trademark of The MathWorks, Inc.

INDEX